Singapore's Grand Strategy

Singapore's Grand Strategy

Ang Cheng Guan

NUS PRESS
SINGAPORE

© 2023 Ang Cheng Guan

Published by:
NUS Press
National University of Singapore
AS3-01-02, 3 Arts Link
Singapore 117569

Fax: (65) 6774-0652
E-mail: nusbooks@nus.edu.sg
Website: http://nuspress.nus.edu.sg

ISBN 978-981-325-223-3 (paper)
ePDF ISBN 978-981-325-224-0
ePub ISBN 978-981-325-225-7

All rights reserved. This book, or parts thereof, may not be reproduced in any form or by any means, electronic or mechanical, including photocopying, recording or any information storage and retrieval system now known or to be invented, without written permission from the Publisher.

National Library Board, Singapore Cataloguing in Publication Data
Name(s): Ang, Cheng Guan.
Title: Singapore's grand strategy / Ang Cheng Guan.
Description: Singapore : NUS Press, [2023]
Identifier(s): ISBN 978-981-325-223-3 (paperback) | ISBN 978-981-325-225-7 (ePub) | ISBN 978-981-325-224-0 (PDF)
Subject(s): LCSH: Singapore--Foreign relations. | Singapore--Strategic aspects. | Singapore--Military policy.
Classification: DDC 327.5957--dc23

Typeset by: Ogma Solutions Pvt Ltd
Printed by: Integrated Books International

Contents

Acknowledgements   vii

Introduction   1

Chapter 1   The Lee Kuan Yew Years (1965–90):
Singapore and Her Immediate Neighbours   16

Chapter 2   The Lee Kuan Yew Years (1965–90):
Singapore and the World   52

Chapter 3   The Lee Kuan Yew Years (1965–90):
Transforming/The Making of Singapore's Defence Strategy   76

Chapter 4   The Goh Chok Tong Years (1990–2004):
Singapore Enters the Post-Cold War Era   100

Chapter 5   The Lee Hsien Loong Years (since 2004):
Singapore and Globalisation   127

Conclusion   150

Bibliography   161
Index   183

Acknowledgements

I wish to express my thanks to Thierry Balzacq, Evelyn Goh, Yuen Foong Khong, Vikram Jayakumar, Chong Yee Ming, and Terence Chia who have assisted in this book project either directly or obliquely. At NUS Press, I wish to extend my deepest appreciation to Peter Schoppert and Lena Qua for their support. Finally, I wish to thank Elspeth Thomson for her insights, observations, and meticulous copyediting, which were invaluable in sharpening my ideas and prose. Any mistakes and shortcomings in this book are my own.

Introduction

I

Before Singapore's Grand Strategy is presented in detail, it is essential to unpack the debates and controversies surrounding the concept of "Grand Strategy" itself. The concept is not new. As Timothy Andrews Sayle reminds us, the term is "decades old" although "not used frequently in policy documents and its salience has ebbed and flowed in academic writing since as far as back as the 1920s".[1] While it is not new, it is unfortunately, as Hal Brands described it, a "slippery" and "widely abused" concept.[2] David Gethin Morgan-Owen, in a recent essay, noted that "the indiscriminate employment of the term compromises the sort of clear-sighted discussions of national security its advocates hope to foster".[3]

Since the 1990s, there has been a revival in the usage of the term. In the last thirty odd years, there has been much written about "Grand Strategy", although much of this has focused on the United States—whether the United States has had a grand strategy after the Cold War, whether it needs to have one, the grand strategies (or lack thereof) of the various administrations: Clinton, Obama, Trump.[4] In fact, in the past few decades, a number of teaching programmes and research centres with a focus on "Grand Strategy" have been established. Among

---

[1] Timothy Andrews Sayle, "Defining and Teaching Grand Strategy", *The Telegram*, Volume 4, 15 Jan. 2011, at https://www.fpri.org/article/2011/01/defining-and-teaching-grand-strategy/ (accessed 11 Jan. 2023).
[2] Hal Brands, *The Promise and Pitfalls of Grand Strategy* (Strategic Studies Institute, US Army War College, 2012), p. 1.
[3] David Gethin Morgan-Owen, "History and the Perils of Grand Strategy", *The Journal of Modern History* 92 (June 2020): 351.
[4] See, for example, James D. Boys, *Clinton's Grand Strategy: US Foreign Policy in a Post-Cold War World* (London: Bloomsbury, 2015); Colin Dueck, *The Obama Doctrine: American Grand Strategy Today* (Oxford: Oxford University Press, 2015); Benjamin Miller (with Ziv Rubinovitz), *Grand Strategy from Truman to Trump* (Chicago: The University of Chicago Press, 2020).

the best-known are the Yale Grand Strategy Seminar initiated by John Lewis Gaddis and Paul Kennedy, both internationally renowned scholars, and the Centre for Grand Strategy at King's College, London helmed by another internationally renowned scholar, John Bew.[5]

There are those who believe that "Grand Strategy" is a useful concept worthy of both research and application. As Andrew Ehrhardt and Maeve Ryan assert: "Grand Strategy is no silver bullet, but is indispensable".[6] Conversely, there are also those who argue that its value is limited: "to debate grand strategy is to indulge in navel-gazing while the world burns. So it is time to operate without one".[7] Bilahari Kausikan, the former permanent secretary, Singapore Ministry of Foreign Affairs, wrote that he had "never understood the obsession of some academics with the so-called 'grand strategy'; [it is] a meaningless term. One must set goals. But having done so, all one can do is to keep a distant star in sight even as one tacks hither and thither to avoid treacherous reefs and shoals to scoop up

---

[5] The Brady-Johnson Program in Grand Strategy (Yale University); for the King's programme, see https://www.kcl.ac.uk/research/kcl-centre-for-grand-strategy (accessed 29 Nov. 2022). Timothy Andrews Sayle in his article (see footnote 1), listed Grand Strategy programmes at several US universities: Columbia University, Duke University, Temple University, the University of Wisconsin-Madison, the University of Georgia and MIT. There is a 'Making Grand Strategy' course offered by the Strategic and Defence Studies Centre at the Australian National University (Acton, ACT), at https://programsandcourses.anu.edu.au/2019/course/stst8055 (accessed 6 Jan. 2021).

[6] See for example, Andrew Ehrhardt and Maeve Ryan, "Grand Strategy is No Silver Bullet, But it is Indispensable", in *War on the Rocks*, 19 May 2020, at https://warontherocks.com/2020/05/grand-strategy-is-no-silver-bullet-but-it-is-indispensable/#:~:text=Grand%20Strategy%20Is%20No%20Silver,National%20security (accessed 10 Jan. 2021) and Thierry Balzacq, Peter Dombrowski and Simon Reich, "Is Grand Strategy a Research Program? A Review Essay", *Security Studies* 28, no. 1 (2019): 58–86.

[7] Daniel W. Drezner, Ronald R. Krebs and Randall Schweller, "The End of Grand Strategy: America Must Think Small", *Foreign Affairs* 99, no. 3 (May/June 2020): 107–17; Thomas Meany and Stephen Wertheim, "Grand Flattery: The Yale Grand Strategy Seminar", *The Nation*, 28 May 2012, at https://www.thenation.com/article/archive/grand-flattery-yale-grand-strategy-seminar/ (accessed 20 Dec. 2022). See also Edwin Moise's view of why a grand strategy is not useful in a "very complex and messy" world, in his response to Rosemary A. Kelanic's review of William C. Martel's *Grand Strategy in Theory and Practice: The Need for an Effective American Foreign Policy* (2015), at https://networks.h-net.org/node/28443/reviews/79718/kelanic-martel-grand-strategy-theory-and-practice-need-effective (accessed 8 Jan. 2021).

opportunities that might drift within reach".[8] Lawrence Freedman highlighted the difference between having a strategy (meaning having a plan) and acting strategically (meaning exercising flexibility and responding to events). He further pointed out that good/successful crisis management required good strategy, that is, clarity about core interests.[9]

I do not intend to go much further here into the arguments for and against or to recount the genealogy of the concept. Readers who are interested can refer to the references and pursue their investigations further.[10] I propose instead to highlight the key issues pertinent to the objective of this book.

There are two: One, the view that "Grand Strategy" is the preserve of "great states" or big powers (such as the United States, arguably the focus of much GS theory); small and most medium-sized states do not have the wherewithal to craft a grand strategy.[11] I do not find this argument persuasive. Indeed, as Rebecca Friedman Lissner observed, "the grand-strategy literature suffers needlessly from American parochialism…grand-strategy debates are likely to proliferate and amplify as power continues to diffuse over the coming decades".[12] And as Balzacq, Dombrowski and Reich—who published the first systematic/comparative study on the grand strategies of "great" and "small" states—argued, "if you begin with

---

[8] Bilahari Kausikan, "Pragmatic Adaptation, Not Grand Strategy, Shaped Singapore's Foreign Policy", in *Perspectives on the Security of Singapore: The First Fifty Years*, ed. Barry Desker and Ang Cheng Guan (Singapore: World Scientific and Imperial College Press, 2016), p. 295. See also Eliot A. Cohen, "The Return of Statecraft: Back to Basics in the Post-American World", *Foreign Affairs* 101, no. 3 (May/June 2022): 117–29, in which he argues for substituting statecraft for grand strategy.

[9] Lawrence Freedman, *Ukraine and the Art of Strategy* (Oxford: Oxford University Press, 2019), pp. 12–13, 15.

[10] Three books which are particularly useful for the understanding of the concept of Grand Strategy are: William C. Martel, *Grand Strategy in Theory and Practice: The Need for an Effective American Foreign Policy* (Cambridge: Cambridge University Press, 2015); Lukas Milevski, *The Evolution of Modern Grand Strategy* (Oxford: Oxford University Press, 2016) and Thierry Balzacq and Ronald R. Krebs, eds., *The Oxford Handbook of Grand Strategy* (Oxford: Oxford University Press, 2021). See also discussion in *H-Diplo Roundtable* 7, no. 2, 17 Oct. 2014, of Hal Brands, *What Good is Grand Strategy?: Power and Purpose in American Statecraft from Harry S. Truman to George W. Bush* (Ithaca, NY: Cornell University Press, 2014); Alexander Kirss, "Review: Does Grand Strategy Matter?", *Strategic Studies Quarterly* 12, no. 4 (Winter 2018): 116–32.

[11] Martel, *Grand Strategy in Theory and Practice: The Need for an Effective American Foreign Policy*, p. 11; Thierry Balzacq, Peter Dombrowski and Simon Reich, eds., *Comparative Grand Strategy: A Framework and Cases* (Oxford: Oxford University Press, 2019), p. 5.

[12] Rebecca Friedman Lissner, "What is Grand Strategy? Sweeping a Conceptual Minefield", *Texas National Security Review* 2, no. 1 (Nov. 2018): 70–1, at https://tnsr.org/2018/11/what-is-grand-strategy-sweeping-a-conceptual-minefield/ (accessed 29 Nov. 2022).

the assumption that the purpose of grand strategy primarily involves moulding the global system, rather than responding to its exigencies, then the belief that few states can do so is self-affirming, perhaps even tautological". Small states also engage in "long-term strategic planning".[13] This leads to my second, more pivotal (and challenging) point in defining "Grand Strategy", which is also the subject of this book.

Lukas Milevski, who has probably done the most to elucidate the evolution and usage of the concept, noted that "the modern literature on grand strategy, *emanating from multiple disciplines*, does not adhere to a single overarching understanding of the term, which is frequently invoked without any definition at all". Milevski counted six different interpretations of the term. He concluded that "Grand Strategy" remains a "standardless, incoherent concept" which requires "rehabilitation"[14] (emphasis added). For someone embarking to write on Singapore's Grand Strategy, this can be quite discouraging but at the same time, I believe, also challenging. William Martel, on the other hand, highlighted four different approaches to the study of American Grand Strategy—through the lenses of history, theory, practice and the military; these would correspond to the overlapping but discrete domains of the historian, the social scientist, the practitioner or policymaker, and the military strategist.[15]

It seems to me that we are in a situation not unlike the six blind men describing an elephant in the Indian parable.[16] Six blind men set out to determine what an elephant was like by feeling different parts of the elephant's body. One felt the leg and concluded that the elephant is like a pillar, the one who felt the tail concluded that the elephant is like a rope; the third who touched the trunk said

---

[13] Balzacq, Dombrowski and Reich, eds., *Comparative Grand Strategy: A Framework and Cases* (2019), pp. 5, 284. See also William I. Hitchcock, Melvyn P. Leffler and Jeffrey W. Legro, eds., *Shaper Nations: Strategies for a Changing World* (Cambridge, MA: Harvard University Press, 2016) which prefers the term "National Strategy". The main difference between the two books is that the latter does not insist on a "specific comparative framework". The 2019 book covered ten countries plus the European Union whereas the 2016 book covered eight countries. Both books included the US, China, India, Russia, Brazil and Israel. See also Peter Dombrowski's review of Miller (with Rubinovitz), *Grand Strategy from Truman to Trump*, in *H-Diplo, ISSF Roundtable 13-11*, 27 May 2022, where he reiterated that "studying grand strategy, including changes, must move beyond analysis of great powers including the United States".

[14] Lukas Milevski, *The Evolution of Modern Grand Strategy* (Oxford: Oxford University Press, 2016), pp. 1, 141, 153–4.

[15] Martel, *Grand Strategy in Theory and Practice: The Need for an Effective American Foreign Policy*, pp. 7–8. See Chapter 2.

[16] See, as recounted by US author James Baldwin, "The Blind Men and the Elephant", at https://americanliterature.com/author/james-baldwin/short-story/the-blind-men-and-the-elephant (accessed 11 Jan. 2021).

that the elephant is like a tree trunk, the fourth who touched the ear believed that the elephant is like a hand fan, the fifth who felt the belly thought the elephant is like a wall and finally the one who felt the tusk concluded that the elephant is like a pipe. They thus ended in complete disagreement and never got to know what a real elephant is like. We all know that the elephant is the sum of its parts, and every feature is as important as the other.

In coming up with a working definition of "Grand Strategy" for this project, I have distilled what I have believed to be the most useful elements and components of "Grand Strategy" presented by other key scholars who have given much thought to the subject, while keeping Milevski and Martel in mind.

Although phrased differently, there is in fact much in common and a broad consensus on the definition of "Grand Strategy". According to William Martel, "a coherent grand strategy that plays a fundamental role in guiding the state's foreign and domestic policies is key in both times of peace and war because it provides the broad sense of direction, clarity and vision that policy makers operating at the highest levels of government need as they make difficult and consequential decisions. Fundamentally, grand strategy describes a broad consensus on the state's goals and the means by which to put them into practice".[17] John Lewis Gaddis defined grand strategy as "the alignment of potentially unlimited aspirations with necessarily limited capabilities…because ends can be infinite and means can never be. Whatever balance you strike, there'll be a link between what's real and what's imagined: between your current location and your intended destination. You wouldn't have a strategy until you've connected these dots… It is 'grand' because of 'what's at stake'".[18]

Barry Posen has defined grand strategy, quite simply and concisely, as "a state's theory of security".[19] In a parallel vein, Jeffrey W. Taliaferro, Norrin M. Ripsman and Steven E. Lobell described grand strategy as "the organizing principle or conceptual blueprint that animates all of the state's relations with the outside world, for the purpose of securing itself and maximizing its interests".[20] Athanassios G. Platias and Constantinos Koliopoulos in their study of Thucydides described grand strategy as essentially "a state's theory about how it can 'cause' security for itself, namely preservation of its sovereignty, territorial integrity, and

---

[17] Martel, *Grand Strategy in Theory and Practice: The Need for an Effective American Foreign Policy*, p. 339.
[18] John Lewis Gaddis, *On Grand Strategy* (New York: Penguin Books, 2018), p. 21.
[19] Posen quoted in Rebecca Lissner, *Wars of Revelation: The Transformative Effects of Military Intervention on Grand Strategy* (Oxford: Oxford University Press, 2022), p. 8.
[20] Qtd. in Balzacq, Dombrowski and Reich, eds., *Comparative Grand Strategy: A Framework and Cases*, p. 7.

relative power position".[21] And Hal Brands defined it as "the theory, or logic, that binds a country's highest interests to its daily interactions with the world... dedicated grand strategists should have a clear understanding of their country's most essential interest, the primary threats to those interests, and the extent and limits of the resources available to ward off these threats and advance core interests".[22] And—one last for the road—the Centre for Grand Strategy (King's College, London) describes the core emphasis of grand strategy to be "to secure the long-term security, peace and prosperity of a nation".[23]

It is true that in the 19th century, the term "Grand Strategy" focused on "the actual fighting of wars", principally "the deployment of forces".[24] But by the first third of the 20th century, with the advent of "Total War",[25] the concept has broadened substantially. As the Centre for Grand Strategy at King's reminds us, quoting from the British military historian Basil Liddell Hart, the role of Grand Strategy is "to coordinate and direct all the resources of a nation, towards the attainment of the political objective...the goal defined by fundamental policy".[26] The objective and context were however still largely war-related, towards the achievement of war aims, although Liddell Hart also thought of grand strategy as "a way of thinking...beyond the war to the subsequent peace".[27] The concept evolved further during the Cold War. Thomas Christensen defined grand strategy as "the full package of domestic and international policies designed to increase

---

[21] Athanassios G. Platias and Constantinos Koliopolis, *Thucydides on Strategy* (Oxford: Oxford University Press, 2017), p. 14.
[22] Brands, *The Promise and Pitfalls of Grand Strategy*, pp. 3–4.
[23] Centre for Grand Strategy (King's College, London), at https://www.kcl.ac.uk/research/kcl-centre-for-grand-strategy (accessed 8 Jan. 2021).
[24] Alasdair Roberts, "Grand Strategy Isn't Grand Enough", *Foreign Policy*, 20 Feb. 2018, at https://foreignpolicy.com/2018/02/20/grand–strategy-isnt-grand-enough/ (accessed 11 Jan. 2021).
[25] A term originating mainly in the context of the First World War (e.g. Georges Clemenceau's 1917 speech on being sworn in as French Prime Minister, in which he used the term "guerre intégrale" ['integral' or 'total war'] and General Erich Ludendorff's *Der totale Krieg* [Total War], 1935).
[26] Centre for Grand Strategy (King's College, London). According to Liddell Hart, "all resources of a nation" would include "'civilian', 'economic' and 'moral' and not just 'military'".
[27] Ehrhardt and Ryan, "Grand Strategy is no Silver Bullet, but it is Indispensable"; Andrew Ehrhardt, "War and Adjustment: Military Campaigns and Grand Strategy", in *War on the Rocks*, 2 May 2022, at https://warontherocks.com/2022/05/war-and-adjustment-military-campaigns-and-national-strategy/ (accessed 9 Feb. 2023). See also Platias and Koliopolis, *Thucydides on Strategy*, pp. 5–6.

power and national security" in both peace and war time.[28] Indeed, the eminent military historian Michael Howard spoke of grand strategy as more than about "war fighting", as it extended to "war avoidance" as well.[29] In a 2020 article, David Gethin Morgan-Owen showed that grand strategy in fact "emerged from peacetime debates among policy makers" rather than being "conceived in response to changes in the character of warfare" as is often thought.[30]

We can draw two conclusions from the above. The first is that grand strategy must, in James Boys's view, be "specific enough to identify a series of criteria, yet fluid enough to adapt to changing circumstances as well as interpretation".[31] This opinion is shared by Andrew Monaghan who described strategy as "a dialogue with a changing context and of constant adaptation to evolving conditions and circumstances in a world in which chance, uncertainty and ambiguity dominate, not least in respect of the actions, intentions and purposes of other actors".[32] Secondly, although grand strategy "usually remains fixed on matters of national security and foreign policy", there is the domestic dimension which we also need to take into consideration.[33] This view is shared by a group of scholars who point out that "domestic factors have been neglected as determinants of grand strategy, and that ideas, institutions, or interdependence play important roles in shaping national policy".[34] Indeed, James Boys noted that "today's approach to grand strategy…has evolved from a narrow focus on military methodology and now seeks to chart the manner in which the full resources of a nation (economic, diplomatic, social, political, military, even cultural) may be operationalized to advance the national interest".[35] Boys's observation is not an isolated one. Writing in a 2013 article on Russian grand strategy, Andrew Monaghan noted that "over the last ten

---

[28] Thomas Christensen quoted in Alasdair Roberts, "Grand Strategy Isn't Grand Enough". See Thomas Christensen, *Useful Adversaries: Grand Strategy, Domestic Mobilisation, and Sino-American Conflict, 1947–1958* (Princeton: Princeton University Press, 1996), p. 7.
[29] Ehrhardt and Ryan, "Grand Strategy is no Silver Bullet, But it is Indispensable".
[30] Morgan-Owen, "History and the Perils of Grand Strategy", p. 353.
[31] James D. Boys, *Clinton's Grand Strategy: US Foreign Policy in a Post-Cold War World* (London: Bloomsbury, 2015), p. 8.
[32] Andrew Monaghan, "Putin's Russia: Shaping a 'Grand Strategy'?", *International Affairs* 89, no. 5 (2013): 1227.
[33] Alasdair Roberts noted that the academic community tends to bifurcate domestic and foreign policy, and this "bears no relation to the way leaders actually think". In his essay, he argued for a comprehensive approach rather than compartmentalisation of domestic or foreign components. See Alasdair Roberts, "Grand Strategy Isn't Grand Enough".
[34] Richard Rosecrance and Arthur A. Stein, *The Domestic Bases of Grand Strategy* (Ithaca, NY: Cornell University Press, 1993), p.12. See also Kevin Narizny, *The Political Economy of Grand Strategy* (Ithaca, NY: Cornell University Press, 2007).
[35] Boys, *Clinton's Grand Strategy: US Foreign Policy in a Post-Cold War World*, p. 8.

to fifteen years the meaning has expanded to cover a wider range of issues, including not just military, but also economic and political matters".[36] Julian Lindley-French (Eisenhower Professor of Defence Strategy, Netherlands Defence Academy), noted that grand strategy was "informed by history, identity, and the credibility of the national narrative both domestically and internationally".[37] Balzacq, Dombrowski and Reich proposed going beyond "the common rationalist approach adopted by Liberals and Realists" by "emphasising the significance of perpetual factors, such as historical memory and resulting national pathologies" and strategic culture.[38] Thierry Balzacq further highlighted that for a nation to be able to develop and execute a grand strategy, the society "needs to understand and accept as legitimate the goals, ways, and means selected by the state". Thus, "grand strategy intersects with social cohesion".[39]

Besides the above, in writing this book, I am also guided by the views of three other scholars in particular. The first, Nina Silove, noted in a 2017 essay that the concept of grand strategy "has evolved to have three distinct meanings": (a) "a deliberate plan devised by individuals", (b) "an organizing principle that is consciously held and used by individuals to guide their decisions" and (c) a "pattern of state behaviour". Without privileging any of the three, she argues that all meanings "provide a distinct and valuable addition to the corpus of conceptual tools in security studies, and that differentiating them will facilitate investigation into the most fundamental and important questions about grand strategy". Such questions include whether grand strategy exists, whether it is intentional, changing, or constant, or whether all states can or do have a grand strategy.[40] The second scholar is Rebecca Friedman Lissner who identified three "component research agendas within the grand strategy literature", which she describes as (a) a variable agenda: "a prism" through which to study "the origins of state behaviour, with particular attention to the perennial question of how agency and structure

---

[36] Monaghan, "Putin's Russia: Shaping a 'Grand Strategy'?", p. 1224.
[37] Julian Lindley-French, "Who Does UK Grand Strategy?", Written Evidence to the UK [House of] Commons Select Committee on Public Administration, Sept. 2010, at https://publications.parliament.uk/pa/cm201011/cmselect/cmpubadm/memo/grandstrat/gs12.htm (accessed 11 Jan. 2021).
[38] Balzacq, Dombrowski and Reich, eds., *Comparative Grand Strategy: A Framework and Cases*, p. 1.
[39] SciencesPo, Interview with Thierry Balzacq, 19 Feb. 2019, at https://www.sciencespo.fr/ceri/en/content/interview-thierry-balzacq-professor (accessed 27 April 2021).
[40] Nina Silove, "Beyond the Buzzword: The Three Meanings of 'Grand Strategy'", *Security Studies* 27, no. 1 (2018): 27–57, at https://www.tandfonline.com/doi/pdf/10.1080/09636412.2017.1360073 (accessed 13 Jan. 2021). For the online version published on 28 Aug. 2017, see pp. 3–4, 30.

interact to produce grand-strategic outcomes", (b) a process agenda—essentially decision-making, for example "government strategic planning process" and (c) a blueprint agenda—which "proffers broad visions in hopes of influencing future governmental behaviour". Like Nina Silove, Lissner also does not privilege any of the three but argues that "identifying these component research agendas and placing them in dialogue" would be useful for understanding the concept of grand strategy. Lissner also highlighted the need to engage with policymakers/practitioners "who provide insight into real-world processes of grand strategy development and implementation".[41]

Third—last but not least—is David Gethin Morgan-Owen who has reminded us of the importance of reintegrating history into the discussion of grand strategy because the concept is always rooted "in a specific context" and "a particular set of assumptions". Therefore, "only by recreating a broader picture of such other contexts can we move to a fuller understanding of the practice of strategy at the national level throughout history, and therefore of the place of grand strategy today".[42] This point was also highlighted by Lukas Milevski.

As can be seen from the above, while there are differences in emphasis, focus and nomenclature, there are also considerable overlaps and a fair amount of consensus amongst the scholars who study "Grand Strategy".

This book on "Singapore's Grand Strategy" will adopt an expansive definition of the concept and will not privilege any school of thought or discipline. It will adopt all four lenses—history, theory, practice and the military—as described by William Martel mentioned above. It will also adopt Peter Feaver's definition of grand strategy which he describes as "a term of art from academia" which "refers to the collection of plans and policies that comprise the state's deliberate effort to harness political, military, diplomatic, and economic tools together to advance that state's national interest. Grand Strategy is the art of reconciling ends and means. It involves purposive action" which is "constrained by factors leaders explicitly recognize…and by those they might only implicitly feel".[43] This

---

[41] See Lissner, "What is Grand Strategy? Sweeping a Conceptual Minefield", pp. 70–1.
[42] Morgan-Owen, "History and the Perils of Grand Strategy", p. 354. See also Graham Allison, "The Key to Henry Kissinger's Success", *The Atlantic*, 27 Nov. 2015.
[43] Peter Feaver, "What is Grand Strategy and Why do we Need it?", *Foreign Policy*, 8 April 2009, at https://foreignpolicy.com/2009/04/08/what-is-grand-strategy-and-why-do-we-need-it/ (accessed 11 Jan. 2023). My understanding of and approach to the study of Singapore's Grand Strategy are also very much in line with Avery Goldstein's definition of the term. See Avery Goldstein, "China's Grand Strategy under Xi Jinping", *International Security* 45, no. 1 (Summer 2020): 164–201; he defines grand strategy as "the combination of political-diplomatic, economic, and military means that a state embraces to ensure its vital interests and pursue its goals - at minimum, its survival - in a potentially dangerous world" (pp. 166–7).

study will also directly or indirectly (through writings and memoirs) engage with practitioners. Finally, yet importantly, it will consider both the international and domestic contexts which underpin the development and evolution of Singapore's grand strategy.

II

Having delineated the concept of "Grand Strategy" for the purpose of this book, I will now move on to discuss it in relation to Singapore. As Hal Brands has noted, the term should be "formally enunciated and defined to qualify as such".[44] Yet, as far as I know, the term has never been used in the context of Singapore. It is more common to talk or read about Singapore's foreign policy or defence policy, or occasionally, Singapore's National Strategy or National Security Strategy. Essentially, they refer to the same set of concerns. In his speech at the first session of the Singapore Parliament on 8 December 1965, the Yang Di-Pertuan Negara (aka President) Inche Yusof bin Ishak said, "as an independent Republic, we have assumed two new responsibilities—Defence and Foreign Affairs—subjects closely related to our survival... Foreign Affairs and Defence are closely-related subjects. The policies we pursue in foreign affairs inevitably decide our defence commitments and our defence commitments in turn limit the range of options of our foreign policy".[45]

It is very challenging to write about Singapore's Grand Strategy (aka Foreign and Defence policies/strategies) because archival records of the Foreign and Defence ministries in Singapore remain hermetically sealed and are exempt from mandatory declassification. As the Senior Minister of State for Communications and Information, Sim Ann, said in the Singapore Parliament in September 2019, "Not all Government records can be released for open access, especially those that relate to our national defence, foreign relations and internal security".[46] There are several oral history interviews in the inventory of the National Archives of Singapore but most of the relevant ones have severely restrictive access conditions, even if they are not embargoed for many more years. Even if permitted to listen

---

[44] Brands, *The Promise and Pitfalls of Grand Strategy*, p. 6.
[45] Yang di Pertuan Negara's Speech, *Singapore, Parliamentary Debates: Official Report*, First Session of the First Parliament Part 1 of First Session, Volume 24, 8 Dec. 1965, p. 11. On 22 Dec. 1965, the Constitution was amended to change this title to President (of the Republic of Singapore) with retrospective effect from 9 August 1965, the date of independence.
[46] Tee Zhuo, "Parliament: Only 8% of 2 Million Public Government Records Searchable on National Archives Online Portal", *The Straits Times*, 4 Sept. 2019, at https://www.straitstimes.com/politics/parliament-only-160000-of-two-million-public-government-records-have-metadata-on-nas-web (accessed 11 Jan. 2023).

to them, historians will find it extremely difficult to cite or make any reference to them. Thus, because of the long-standing secrecy, we are very much dependent on information that the government has chosen to release publicly. Given the obscurity of the decision-making process, this study will out of necessity focus principally on strategic planning and implementation "within formal institutions" and will mention "informal politics and networks" when possible.[47] In short, this book is very much focused on "declaratory" grand strategy, and uses speeches, comments, recollections and official publications to describe and analyse Singapore's Grand Strategy. But whenever possible, particularly for the years before the end of the Cold War—the first half the book—the missing pieces or gaps can be filled by archival information from other countries, particularly American, Australian and British sources, which I have collected. As Joey Long opined, "for the historian... archival restrictions need not result in narrative or analytical paralysis. As air travel shrinks the globe, sources can be obtained from multiple archives".[48] For the post-Cold War period, one will inevitably have to depend on open sources.

In recent years, there has been a proliferation of recollections, mostly short essays or book chapters, penned by Singaporeans who played a direct part in, if not shaped, the events of their time. A few relate to foreign affairs. Even fewer deal with defence and security matters. The best-known are of course the memoirs of the founding (and longest serving) prime minister of Singapore, Lee Kuan Yew, who opened the floodgates, so to speak, for others to the same.

Given the above constraints[49] and because diplomatic and military history has been out of fashion for some time (and does not attract budding historians), the writings on issues related to Singapore's foreign and defence policies are composed mostly by political scientists who are less reliant on archival sources. The next section will introduce/describe some of the key publications, most of which are dated and indeed ripe for revisiting.

To date, there is only a handful of writings on the diplomatic and military history of Singapore, almost all of which deal with the subject of World War II and the Japanese Occupation of Singapore, events prior to Singapore's independence.

---

[47] See Monaghan, "Putin's Russia: Shaping a 'Grand Strategy'?". There are hardly any 'leaks' in Singapore (pertaining to security matters) and those few policymakers who publish their memoirs/recollections are extremely coy in describing the decision-making process.
[48] S.R. Joey Long quoted in Loh Kah Seng and Liew Kai Khiun, eds., *The Makers & Keepers of Singapore History* (Singapore: Ethos Books, 2010), p. 156. See also Chapters 11 (by Joey Long) and 13 (by Ang Cheng Guan).
[49] Albert Lau noted that writing on contemporary Singapore history remains heavily dependent on foreign archives. See Albert Lau, "Nation-Building and the Singapore Story: Some Issues in the Study of Contemporary Singapore History", *Nation Building: Five Southeast Asian Histories*, ed. Wang Gungwu (Singapore: ISEAS, 2005), pp. 239–41.

The standard texts on Singapore's history by Mary Turnbull[50] and Edwin Lee contain little on Singapore's foreign relations. Lee has a brief chapter on National Service and its relationship with nation-building, the unifying theme of his book.[51] Michael Barr, in the most recent attempt at writing a history of Singapore, also hardly discusses diplomacy and defence.[52]

Turning to the writings by political scientists, the most notable are the following.

The first substantial study of Singapore's foreign policy since its independence is that by Kawin Wilairat. This is essentially a descriptive piece detailing foreign policy decisions and activities between the years 1965 and 1975 based on published sources, although the author also briefly covers the pre-1965 period (divided into 1959–63 and 1963–65). Published by the Institute of Southeast Asian Studies (ISEAS) as part of its Field Report series entitled "Singapore's Foreign Policy: The First Decade", this was distilled from Wilairat's 1975 PhD thesis entitled "Singapore's Foreign Policy: A Study of the Foreign Policy System of a City-State". The thesis contains a useful chapter, based on interviews with Foreign Ministry officials and others, on the formation and structure of the Foreign Service, as well as the decision-making process Although it was written almost forty years ago and covers only the first ten years of Singapore's foreign policy, the unpublished thesis is the most comprehensive account written of the period.[53]

In 1988, Bilveer Singh published *Singapore: Foreign Policy Imperatives of a Small State* as a Centre for Advanced Studies Occasional Paper, which, ten years later, he expanded into a book-length study entitled *The Vulnerability of Small States Revisited: A Study of Singapore's Post-Cold War Foreign Policy*. As the title suggests, the book's emphasis is on Singapore's "smallness" and vulnerability; it describes how Singapore "tried to increase its political, economic and strategic space...in a largely 'borderless world' that is fast 'shrinking'". Singh argues that

---

[50] Mary Turnbull, *A History of Singapore 1819–1975* (Kuala Lumpur: Oxford University Press, 1977). A revised edition, published in 1989, brought Turnbull's narrative up to 1988. The most recent edition, published posthumously, brought the account up to 2005. See C.M. Turnbull, *A History of Modern Singapore, 1891–2005* (Singapore: NUS Press, 2009). Mary Turnbull passed away in 2008.

[51] Edwin Lee, *Singapore: The Unexpected Nation* (Singapore: ISEAS, 2008). Lee's book is among the case studies of the project on nation-building in Southeast Asia launched by the Institute of Southeast Asian Studies.

[52] Michael D. Barr, *Singapore: A Modern History* (London: I.B. Tauris, 2019) is touted as a revisionist or "counter-narrative" to the standard account represented by Turnbull and Lee.

[53] Kawin Wilairat, *Singapore's Foreign Policy: The First Decade*, Field Report Series No. 10 (Singapore: ISEAS, 1975). See also Wilairat, *Singapore's Foreign Policy: A Study of the Foreign Policy System of a City-State*, unpublished PhD dissertation, Georgetown University, 1975.

while "there is definitely something new and novel in Singapore's post-Cold War foreign policy...as far as principles and precepts are concerned, there is more continuity than change".[54]

Perhaps the best-known book on Singapore's foreign policy is Michael Leifer's *Singapore's Foreign Policy: Coping with Vulnerability*. The late-Professor Leifer has been described as "the ultimate insider with whom many of Southeast Asia's political and policy elites were happy to share their strategic perspectives as well as pour out their delights and frustrations over an informal meal".[55] Published in 2000, the book "assesses the profound influence on Singapore's foreign policy of its government's perception of the island-state's innate vulnerability". According to Leifer, "Singapore inspires admiration and respect primarily because of its economic and social accomplishments but its diplomatic role has not been the subject of the same attention".[56]

Another significant study is that by N. Ganesan who, like Bilveer Singh, has paid considerable attention to issues pertaining to Singapore's foreign policy. In his book, published in 2005, *Realism and Interdependence in Singapore's Foreign Policy*, Ganesan argues that while "Singapore's preoccupation with vulnerability is an enduring feature of policy output...cooperation and prosperity are better obtained through liberal arrangements". The latter, in his view, has not received sufficient attention, particularly in economic diplomacy as most writers tend to focus on "the vulnerabilities deriving from Singapore's size, geographical location and related constraints".[57] Michael Leifer, cited above, made more or less the same point when he argued that while Singapore's foreign policy is based on underlying vulnerability, its future is dependent on its ability to project Singapore's economy beyond the region and to push for multilateralism.[58]

---

[54] Bilveer Singh, *Singapore: Foreign Policy Imperatives of a Small State*, CAS Occasional Paper, Centre for Advanced Studies, National University of Singapore (Singapore: Heinemann Asia, 1988) and *The Vulnerability of Small States Revisited: A Study of Singapore's Post-Cold War Foreign Policy* (Yogyakarta: Gadjah Mada University Press, 1999), pp. xvi–xvii. See also two earlier articles: Chan Heng Chee, "Singapore's Foreign Policy, 1965–1968", *Journal of Southeast Asian History* X [10], no. 1 (March 1969): 177–91 and Lee Boon Hiok, "Constraints on Singapore's Foreign Policy", *Asian Survey* XXII [22], no. 6 (June 1982): 524–35 which also use the vulnerability and survival tropes.

[55] Yuen Foong Khong, "The Elusiveness of Regional Order: Leifer, the English School and Southeast Asia", *The Pacific Review* 18, no 1 (2005): 23–41.

[56] Michael Leifer, *Singapore's Foreign Policy: Coping with Vulnerability* (London: Routledge, 2000), p. xiii. This was Leifer's last book as he passed away in 2001.

[57] N. Ganesan, *Realism and Interdependence in Singapore's Foreign Policy* (London: Routledge, 2005), p. 2. See also N. Ganesan, "Singapore's Foreign Policy Terrain", *Asian Affairs: An American Review* 19, no. 2 (Summer 1992): 67–79.

[58] Leifer, *Singapore's Foreign Policy: Coping with Vulnerability*, pp. 161–2.

Finally, Amitav Acharya in 2008 published a collection of his essays written between 1992 and 2005. Acharya is an international relations scholar who is noted for his study of Southeast Asia through a constructivist lens. Thus, the essays in this volume "highlight the need for moving beyond the traditional realist perspective on Singapore's foreign policy". He is of the view that the realist approach "neglects the strong underpinnings of Singapore's economic and security policy in liberal market economics", "overstate[s] the balance of power approach to regional order", and "understates" both "the impact of ASEAN in realizing Singapore's vital foreign policy and security interests" and "the significance of Singapore's role in global multilateral forums". He proposed that Singapore's foreign policy is better understood through the concepts of liberal institutionalism and social constructivism.[59]

As for the writings on Singapore's defence and military-related matters, they are extremely limited. There are three recent books (one single-authored and two edited). Ho Shu Huang and Graham Ong-Webb's *National Service in Singapore* (2019) is a compilation of essays on various aspects of National Service. It was published to mark the 50th anniversary of the introduction of National Service in Singapore in 1967.[60] The other edited volume is broadly on the security of Singapore, of which the military is one dimension. The book was published to commemorate the 50th anniversary of Singapore's independence and contains essays on traditional and non-traditional security issues, as well as foreign policy.[61] The third book, Samuel Ling Wei Chan's *Aristocracy of Armed Talent: The Military Elite in Singapore*, was developed from his PhD thesis. Chan attempts to follow in the footsteps of American sociologist Morris Janowitz's *Professional Soldier: A Social and Political Portrait*. In his case, however, he is "focused on

---

[59] Amitav Acharya, *Singapore's Foreign Policy: The Search for Regional Order* (Singapore: World Scientific, 2008), pp. 1, 4–7. See also Alan Chong, "Singapore's Foreign Policy Beliefs as 'Abridged Realism': Pragmatic and Liberal Prefixes in the Foreign Policy Thought of Rajaratnam, Lee, Koh, and Mahbubani", *International Relations of the Asia-Pacific* 6, no. 2 (2006): 269–306. Chong describes Singapore's foreign policy as an abridged form of Realism. See also a concise account on Singapore's Diplomacy published to commemorate the 50th anniversary of Singapore's independence in 2015 by a political scientist and a historian: Goh and Chua, *Singapore Chronicles: Diplomacy*.

[60] Ho Shu Huang and Graham Ong-Webb, eds., *National Service in Singapore* (Singapore: World Scientific, 2019). See also a concise account on Singapore's Defence published in a series to commemorate the 50th anniversary of Singapore's independence in 2015: Ho Shu Huang and Samuel Chan, *Singapore Chronicles: Defence* (Singapore: Straits Times Press, 2015).

[61] Desker and Ang, eds., *Perspectives on the Security of Singapore: The First Fifty Years*.

Singapore's military establishment".[62] Chan noted that a Freedom of Information Act or its equivalent does not exist in Singapore, and that one can research "anything you wish to research in Singapore with the exception of two topics", of which the military is one.[63]

Although published more than two decades ago (in 2000), the book that remains essential reading for anyone interested in the military dimension of Singapore's security is Tim Huxley's *Defending the Lion City: The Armed Forces of Singapore*. The "first-ever", it remains, as touted then, the "major study of the Singapore Armed Forces (SAF)" and "provides a comprehensive...assessment of Singapore's impressive military capability and the strategic outlook and policies which have shaped it".[64]

It is true that Singapore has not fought a war since 1965. But, as Pascal Vennesson has pointed out, "from the perspective of grand strategy, the linkage between strategy and tactics is not central. What matters instead is the link between military capabilities (land, naval, air, cyber) and economic and geographical effects, not necessarily or primarily mediated by the actual use of force".[65]

There are of course other journal articles and book chapters which examine specific aspects of Singapore's security policy, foreign relations and related issues, but the above form by far the main bulk of the scholarship. The studies, though still useful, are mostly compartmentalised and dated. The scholarship is generally ensconced within a realist framework although, as noted above, there have been some efforts to move beyond the realm of *Realpolitik*,[66] particularly in the writings after 1990 (post-Cold War). This book is therefore an attempt to bring together the separate pieces into an up-to-date and holistic discussion of Singapore's Grand Strategy, while constantly bearing in mind the on-going discourse surrounding the concept itself.

---

[62] Samuel Ling Wei Chan, *Aristocracy of Armed Talent: The Military Elite in Singapore* (Singapore: NUS Press, 2019). See also "Five Minutes with Samuel Ling Wei Chan" (an interview largely about the book), at https://nuspress.nus.edu.sg/blogs/news/five-minutes-with-samuel-ling-wei-chan (accessed 29 Nov. 2022).
[63] Chan, *Aristocracy of Armed Talent: The Military Elite in Singapore*, pp. 26–7.
[64] Tim Huxley, *Defending the Lion City: The Armed Forces of Singapore* (Sydney: Allen & Unwin, 2000).
[65] I wish to thank Pascal Vennesson for sharing with me his book chapter "Grand Strategy and Military Power", prior to publication in Balzacq and Krebs, eds., *The Oxford Handbook of Grand Strategy* (2021).
[66] Cp. for example John Bew, *Realpolitik: A History* (Oxford: Oxford University Press, 2015).

CHAPTER 1

The Lee Kuan Yew Years (1965–90): Singapore and Her Immediate Neighbours

I

The aim of this opening chapter, covering the years 1965 to 1970, is to describe the policies taken and their rationale to ensure Singapore's necessary territorial security as an independent country, even as the government rushed to satisfy the basic needs of the population: "to clothe them, feed them, to give them housing, to have good transportation".[1] The first and foremost policy involved Singapore's relations with its immediate neighbours, Malaysia and Indonesia.

The opening session of the first Parliament of Singapore, which became an independent country on 9 August 1965, is an appropriate point to begin our exploration of Singapore's grand strategy. The formation of Malaysia ("Merger") and the subsequent events leading to the independence of Singapore ("Separation") are well-known. Both countries have their own interpretation of the causes of the separation, and both agree to disagree. Thus, what is laid out here are the undisputed essentials that would put the first parliamentary session, which took place in December 1965, four months after Singapore seceded or separated from Malaysia, and the elucidation of Singapore's grand strategy into context.

---

[1] Liu Thai Ker, often described as "the architect of modern Singapore", qtd. in Faris Mokhtar, "The Man Who Helped Create Singapore's Housing Boom is Getting Worried", *The Business Times*, 23 June 2022, at https://www.businesstimes.com.sg/real-estate/the-man-who-helped-create-singapores-housing-boom-is-getting-worried (accessed 1 July 2022).

We now know that contrary to the official/dominant narrative crafted since 1965, Singapore was not "kicked" or "thrown" out of Malaysia. It was a secretly negotiated secession involving a very small group within the leadership on both sides of the causeway from July to early August 1965 (although Tunku Abdul Rahman had intimated to Goh Keng Swee[2] in December 1964 his intention to separate Singapore from the mainland). When the news was announced, it caught everyone, including most of the political leadership on both sides, by surprise. The Prime Minister of Malaysia, Abdul Rahman, thought that there would be bloodshed if Singapore remained in Malaysia given the irreconcilable vision of the political system of Malaysia espoused by Lee Kuan Yew, on the one hand, and the Malay political leadership, on the other.

On 8 August 1965, the new country had an area of 581.5 square kilometres and a population of just under 1.9 million. It was a trading port without a hinterland and unable to defend itself. It is important to note first that the separation averted violence and bloodshed, but it did not resolve the bad blood between the countries going forward, particularly the hostility towards Lee Kuan Yew. Second, overnight, an independent Singapore became unviable. Hence, thoughts about Singapore being part of Malaysia as an existential necessity (this had been the main argument proffered in the late 1950s and early 1960s in support of a merger to form Malaysia in 1963) had to be abruptly revised. Any hope that Singapore would become the "New York" of Malaysia also evaporated.[3] But, as Lee Kuan Yew said, "before

---

[2] Goh Keng Swee in 1965 was Minister for the Interior and Defence. He was also one of the founding members of the People's Action Party (PAP) which is the ruling party

[3] The fact that independence was not foisted on Singapore was no longer a secret by the late-1990s. See Melanie Chew, *Leaders of Singapore* (Singapore: Resource Press, 1996). The above summary is distilled from the interviews with Devan Nair, Lim Kim San, Toh Chin Chye, Goh Keng Swee and S. Rajaratnam in Chew's book. See also Lee Kuan Yew, *The Singapore Story: Memoirs of Lee Kuan Yew* (Singapore: Singapore Press Holdings, 1998), Chapters 42 and 43, which corroborate the interviews. However, the narrative of Singapore being ousted remained in the history books used in schools. It was only in 2015 when Singapore commemorated its 50th anniversary of independence that the revised narrative became more pervasive (although the old narrative continues to live on). See Susan Sim, "Drafting 'A Bloodless Coup'", *The Straits Times*, 4 Dec. 2016, which was extracted from Susan Sim, *E.W. Barker: The People's Minister* (Singapore: Straits Times Press, 2016); Edmund Lim, "Secret Documents Reveal Extent of Negotiations for Separation", *The Straits Times*, 22 Dec. 2015. Lim summarised three documents from the "Albatross File" which Goh Keng Swee alluded to in his interview with Melanie Chew. Some of the top-secret Cabinet papers in the "Albatross File" were declassified in 2015.

a new working relationship is established, we must first dispel the illusion that because we wanted merger with Malaysia,....we were vulnerable without merger".[4]

Third, Singapore's relationships with its immediate neighbours, which were many times the size of the island in both area and population, were poor, if not hostile. As mentioned above, Singapore–Malaysia relations remained acrimonious after separation. Meanwhile, Jakarta (under the pro-communist Sukarno) was still in a state of war, commonly referred to as 'Confrontation' (*Konfrontasi*) with Kuala Lumpur because of the merger of Singapore (as well as Sabah and Sarawak) to form relations with Malaysia in 1963, which the Indonesians viewed as a neo-imperial/colonialist plot. Singapore and Indonesia eventually established formal diplomatic relations in September 1967, two years after Singapore's independence.

The Yang Di-Pertuan Negara Yusof Ishak's opening speech at the first session of the first Parliament of independent Singapore on 8 December 1965 alluded to the above issues and problems when he said that "our [Singapore's] survival as a people, distinct and separate from our neighbours in South-East Asia, depends upon our patience and resolution in dealing with physically bigger and hence difficult neighbours and upon our perseverance in seeking long-term solutions to the problems of finding a new balance of forces in this part of the world".[5] He went on to state that "the best guarantee of our future as a distinct and separate people" in the region "is the creation of a tolerant multi-racial society" and warned against both "Communalists" and "Communists". The Communists were assessed to be the "more potent of the two groups as they were supported by external sponsors and "play on communal heart strings, if only more skilfully and cynically". Implied in his speech was the concern about the intentions of Indonesia and Malaysia, given that Confrontation hostilities ceased only on 11 August 1966 with the signing of the Bangkok Accords; Singapore and Malaysia had separated just a few months earlier due to differences related to race/ethnicity. Thus, the Yang Di-Pertuan Negara counselled that Singapore "must anticipate and prepare for all contingencies". This triangular relationship is discussed further later.

Finally, the Yang Di-Pertuan Negara spoke of the "two new responsibilities" Singapore now had to shoulder as an independent republic—Defence and Foreign Affairs. These were "two closely inter-related subjects" essential for the country's

---

[4] "Speech by the Prime Minister, Mr. Lee Kuan Yew, when he moved the motion of thanks to the Yang Di-Pertuan Negara, for his policy speech on the opening of Parliament on 14 December 1965". All quotes henceforth by the Yang Di-Pertuan Negara, Defence and Foreign Ministers as well as Prime Minister are from *Parliamentary Debates of Singapore Official Report, Volume 24*. All quotations/citations from the Singapore Parliament Reports (Hansard) in this paper can be accessed from https://www.parliament.gov.sg.

[5] From *Parliamentary Debates of Singapore Official Report, Volume 24*.

survival. Foreign policy choices determine defence commitments which in turn have limited the range of options of Singapore's foreign policy. Singapore's security depended upon having the minimum number of unfriendly countries and the maximum number of friendly ones "for no other reason than that we wish to be as independent of foreign defence assistance as possible".

In his speech at the first Parliament, the Minister of Foreign Affairs, S. Rajaratnam, also addressed the issue of the security of Singapore.[6] About Foreign Affairs, he said that "the primary task…will always be to safeguard our [Singapore's] independence from external threats". Rajaratnam gave the following guidance to ensure Singapore's security:

(a) "In the hard world of international realities, there are bound to be degrees of friendship between countries" and "those closest to us will naturally be those whose foreign policy principles and deeds coincide with our national interests and our basic aspirations". From time to time, there may be differences and disagreements on specific issues, but so long as the fundamentals of their foreign policy and their deeds coincide with Singapore's, then they should remain close friends and allies. Singapore should not allow "temporary irritations and minor disagreements" to affect its foreign relations.

(b) In international politics, it is not wise to formulate policies on the basis of permanent enemies.

(c) It is necessary for Singapore to adhere to a policy of non-alignment "because to be aligned to any big country would eventually have meant the loss of our freedom of action even in domestic fields, because foreign policies are in fact an extension of domestic policies into the international field". Non-alignment, however, did not mean indifference "to the real issues of peace and war" or "even feigning blindness as to what is right and wrong". On the contrary, a non-alignment policy gives Singapore greater freedom of manoeuvrability on specific international issues based on its national interests. An aligned position, on the other hand, would automatically oblige Singapore to adopt the stance of the major ally.

(d) The pursuit of national interests is not absolute, as national independence needs to "be balanced against the reality of interdependence between nations…. There will arise occasions when we may have to make some sacrifice of our national interests for the long-term interests of the nation".

---

[6] Speech by the Minister of Foreign Affairs (Mr. S. Rajaratnam), 16 Dec. 1965 and the Yang Di-Pertuan Negara's Speech: Debate on the Address, 17 Dec. 1965, Singapore Parliament Reports (Hansard). Rajaratnam's speech can be found online at the Singapore Hansard site, https://sprs.parl.gov.sg/search/#/report?sittingdate=16-12-1965 and https://sprs.parl.gov.sg/search/#/report?sittingdate=17-12-1965 (accessed 2 Jan. 2023).

As for Defence, before independence, the external security of Singapore was in the hands of the British, and then from 1963 it came under the purview of Kuala Lumpur.[7] Lim Kim San, who succeeded Goh Keng Swee as Minister for the Interior and Defence in 1967, recalled that when the country became independent, the top two priorities were defence and water (which comes from the Malaysian state of Johor).[8] As Lee Kuan Yew said, "We must survive. We have a right to survive. And, to survive, we must be sure we cannot be just over-run... invaded by armies or knocked out by rockets...".[9]

While the aim, as the Yang Di-Pertuan Negara said, was to "to be as independent of foreign defence assistance as possible", in 1965, Singapore had to "accept British bases for some time to come" because it was at that time unable to defend itself. Thus, the creation of a "hard well-trained if small regular army supported by a large people's volunteer force" would be an immediate priority and form a significant item in Singapore's annual budget.

Goh Keng Swee, Singapore's first Minister of Defence, recalled in a 1995 interview with Melanie Chew that at independence, Singapore had "two battalions, three quarters of them were Malaysians and British. You have to get rid of these people".[10] Goh elaborated during the second reading of the Singapore Army Bill on 23 December 1965 that the army was meant to defend Singapore and its people against external aggression but "today we are unable to do this task by ourselves" and "there is no use pretending that without the British military forces in Singapore today, the island cannot be easily overrun within a matter of hours by any neighbouring country within a radius of 1,000 miles, if any of these countries care to do so". But Singapore cannot always depend on Britain. As early as December 1965, Goh was already laying plans for an eventual British withdrawal. In his words, "British military protection today had made quite a number of our citizens complacent about the need to conduct our own defence preparations. These people assume that this protection will be permanent. I regard it as the height of folly to plan our future on this assumption. And if there is any

---

[7] Lee Kuan Yew, in his capacity as Prime Minister from 1959 when Singapore gained self-government in all matters except foreign affairs and defence (which remained within the purview of the British), was involved in foreign affairs in a limited way. He thus had experience in foreign affairs matters, but not in defence matters. Lee admitted as much when he said in a 9 Aug. 1965 interview, "I'm not a military man". He left/delegated "defence" matters to Goh Keng Swee who had been a corporal in the British-led Singapore Volunteer Corps until Singapore fell to the Japanese in February 1942.

[8] Melanie Chew, *Leaders of Singapore* (Singapore: Resource Press, 1996), p. 167.

[9] Transcript of a press conference given by the Prime Minister of Singapore, Mr. Lee Kuan Yew, at Broadcasting House, Singapore, 9 Aug. 1965.

[10] Chew, *Leaders of Singapore*, p. 147.

basis on which we, as an independent country, can plan our future, it will be on the opposite assumption, that is, the removal of the British military presence at some time in the future. Nobody—neither we nor the British—can say when this will be. It may be 5, 10 or 15 years—maybe longer, maybe shorter. Whatever the time maybe, it will be useless then to think of building up our defence forces. The time to do so is now...".[11]

In his speech, the Minister of Foreign Affairs, S. Rajaratnam, also addressed the issue of the security of Singapore and the matter of the British bases. He reiterated that the bases were "not for any aggressive or imperialistic purposes but for the defence of Singapore and Singapore's national interests" as the new nation's capacity to defend itself against external threats was limited. Singapore would of course build its own defence forces "to the fullest extent" it was capable of but what "we are interested in is the defence of Singapore in the context of a major conflict in regard to major and more powerful neighbours. We are in no position to build or finance an army capable of defending Singapore in a conflict of this kind. Even big powers with far greater resources of money, men and material plan their defence on the basis of friends and allies".[12]

In summary, how to overcome Singapore's vulnerability and ensure its survival as an independent country has been from the beginning in 1965 the goal of Singapore's grand strategy.[13]

II

It is now perhaps the right time to pause and turn our attention to the makers and shapers of Singapore's grand strategy before continuing to recount how the strategy as the leadership spelt it out above was implemented. According to S. Rajaratnam, the first and longest serving foreign minister of Singapore, Singapore's foreign policy was shaped principally by him and Lee Kuan Yew, with inputs from Goh Keng Swee when there were economic implications.[14] Kishore Mahbubani described the three men as "Singapore's three exceptional geopolitical masters".[15]

---

[11] Speech by the Minister of Defence (Dr. Goh Keng Swee), Singapore Army Bill, 23 Dec. 1965, Singapore Parliament Reports (Hansard).
[12] Speech by the Minister of Foreign Affairs (Mr. S. Rajaratnam), 16 Dec. 1965 and Yang Di-Pertuan Negara's Speech: Debate on the Address, 17 Dec. 1965, Singapore Parliament Reports (Hansard).
[13] It is thus not surprising that most of the writings on Singapore's foreign and defence focus on the themes of "vulnerability" and "survival". See Introduction.
[14] Chan Heng Chee and Obaid ul Haq, eds., *The Prophetic and the Political: Selected Speeches and Writings of S. Rajaratnam* (Singapore: Graham Brash, 1987), pp. 485–6.
[15] Kishore Mahbubani, *Has China Won?* (New York: Public Affairs, 2020), p. 3.

Indeed, historians who have perused the archival documents, both in Singapore and abroad, may well agree that it is not possible at all to reconstruct Singapore's foreign policy without reference to Lee Kuan Yew. In a 2000 book, Michael Leifer noted that by the time Rajaratnam stepped down as Foreign Minister in 1980, the pattern of Singapore's foreign policy had been well established, and subsequent foreign ministers "had little to do by way of radical innovation although foreign policy had become more proactive". His successors have had, in the main, continued to implement "Lee Kuan Yew's and Rajaratnam's design".[16] Indeed, one cannot miss the echoes of Lee's thinking in every single foreign policy speech and interview given by the second, third and even fourth generation Singapore leadership. Amongst his other portfolios, Goh Keng Swee was twice the Minister of Defence.

Readers will find Lee (1923–2015), Rajaratnam (1915–2006) and Goh (1918–2010) frequently mentioned throughout this book, especially Lee who remained influential up to his death (and some may say even after his death).[17] An understanding of their beliefs and premises is imperative for anyone interested in understanding and analysing Singapore's grand strategy because they serve as "a prism" which shapes their "perceptions and diagnoses" of international politics as well as "[providing] norms, standards and guidelines" that influence Singapore's choice of "strategy and tactics, structuring and weighing of alternative courses of action".[18]

Rajaratnam and Goh retired from political office in 1986 and 1988, respectively. They gradually faded out in the 1990s due to poor health. After Lee stepped down as Prime Minister in 1990, he assumed the title of Senior Minister from 1990 till 2004,[19] and then Minister Mentor from 2004 to 2011. He remained a member of Parliament till his death in 2015. Thus unlike his other two colleagues, Lee was a key maker and shaper of Singapore's grand strategy during the Cold War as well as the post-Cold War periods.

---

[16] Michael Leifer, *Singapore's Foreign Policy: Coping with Vulnerability* (London: Routledge, 2000), p. 7. See also Ang Cheng Guan, *Lee Kuan Yew's Strategic Thought* (London: Routledge, 2013), Introduction.

[17] See Kawin Wilairat, *Singapore's Foreign Policy: A Study of the Foreign Policy System of a City-State*, unpublished PhD dissertation, Georgetown University, 1975, Chapter 4.

[18] Alexander L. George, "The 'Operational Code': A Neglected Approach to the Study of Political Leaders and Decision-Making", *International Studies Quarterly* 13, no. 2 (June 1969): 190–222.

[19] S. Rajaratnam was Senior Minister from 1985 to 1988, the first time the title was introduced.

III

It is one thing to propound a strategy or a policy, but, as the saying goes, "the devil is in the details". Many things had to be done concurrently, and rather quickly, to entrench Singapore's independence. The first concerned Singapore's relations with its two nearest neighbours—Malaysia and Indonesia.

In his December 1965 foreign policy speech, S. Rajaratnam said that he found it "difficult to keep a straight face in talking about a foreign policy towards Malaysia" and that "there was something unreal and odd about lumping relations with Malaysia under foreign relations". But given that the separation had taken place, the relationship between the two countries by default "comes under the category of foreign relations". The Minister went on to say that "Constitutional forms are one thing and the hard facts of history, geography, economics and demography are another". Thus "we should try to make the best" of the situation and "we should be more than usually careful to devise rational and intelligent policies in regard to Malaysia". It must be a foreign policy "of a special kind, a foreign policy towards a country, which though constitutionally foreign, is essentially one with us and which, when logic and sanity reassert themselves, must once more become one". The "survival and well-being" of both Singapore and Malaysia depended on each other, regardless of survival of the governments and political parties on both sides.[20] Lee Kuan Yew, in a series of interviews during the first week of Singapore's independence, between 9 and 14 August 1965, made essentially the same points. For example, according to Lee, the separation was an "artificial" one: "it goes against geography. It goes against history. It goes against economics. It goes against demography. There are blood ties, kinship which cannot be cut off just by legislation...Singapore will not go back without cast iron guarantees. But I think it will come back. There is no choice".[21]

Fresh from the separation, the first few years of Singapore–Malaysia relations were, not unexpectedly, difficult and prickly. Just a cursory reading of the newspapers, particularly in the early years, reveals the torrent of polemic, insults, vitriolic name-calling and brinkmanship on both sides of the causeway. According

---

[20] Speech by the Minister of Foreign Affairs (Mr. S. Rajaratnam), 17 December 1965, Singapore Parliament Reports (Hansard).
[21] Transcript of an interview with the Prime Minister, Mr. Lee Kuan Yew, recorded at TV Singapura Studios on 13 August 1965. See also Abdul Rahman Yaacob, "Singapore's Threat Perception: The Barter Trade Crisis and Malaysia's Decision to Use Military Force against Singapore, October–December 1965", *Australian Journal of Politics and History* 68, no. 1 (2022): 72–89, at https://onlinelibrary.wiley.com/doi/abs/10.1111/ajph.12719 (accessed 1 July 2022).

to a recent study by Abdul Rahman Yaacob, for a brief period between October and December, the relationship was on a knife's edge.[22]

The Singapore government, believing that Malaysia intended to "strangle Singapore to death", accused Kuala Lumpur of "hypocrisy" in pledging economic cooperation with Singapore "while attempting to strangle Singapore's economic life".[23] Lee Kuan Yew recalled Ghazali bin Shafie (Permanent Secretary, Malaysia's Ministry of External Affairs) who had stated soon after the separation that after "a few years on the limb, Singapore would be in severe straits and would come crawling back—this time on Malaysia's terms".[24] Mahathir Mohamad (then a Malaysian MP, and who would later become Malaysia's Prime Minister, not once but twice) said that before there could be reunification, Singapore "must conform, not only with the policies of Malaysia, but also with the pattern of this region of Asia...Singapore can be a part of Malaysia as a state with the same rights and privileges as all the other states". He described Singapore as a "racial island of Chinese in a sea of Malays". Although he claimed that he was speaking in his own personal capacity, he added that his "opinion exists in UMNO and the Alliance".[25]

As mentioned above, upon independence, one of Singapore's top two priorities was water, which comes from the Malaysian state of Johor. In his 9 August 1965 interview, Lee Kuan Yew said that despite what was, in his view, the "largely ideological differences between us and the former Central Government, between us and the Alliance Government, we want to cooperate with them, on the most fair and equal basis. The emphasis is cooperate. We need them to survive". He went on to highlight the fact that Singapore's "water supply comes from Johore...".[26] Indeed, the Tunku had told British officials that Kuala Lumpur could exercise control over policies made by Singapore which the Malaysians did

---

[22] Yaacob, "Singapore's Threat Perception".

[23] From the American Consul, Singapore to the US Department of State, 22 Nov. 1965, RG 59, Box 2651, POL 2-1/Singapore 10/16/65; from the American Consul, Singapore to the Department of State, 30 October 1965, RG 59, Box 2651, POL 2-1/Singapore 10/16/65.

[24] Lee Kuan Yew, *The Singapore Story* (Singapore Press Holdings, 1998), p. 663.

[25] Qtd. in a memo from the American Consul, Singapore to the Department of State, 19 June 1966, RG 59, Box 2651, POL 1/Singapore 5/1/66. Mahathir was Prime Minister of Malaysia from 1981 to 2003 and from 2018 to 2020. UMNO (the United Malays National Organisation) is the oldest nationalist party in Malaysia. The Alliance refers to the coalition of UMNO, the Malaysian Chinese Association (MCA) and the Malaysian Indian Congress (MIC). Together they formed the ruling party of Malaysia in that period.

[26] "Transcript of a Press Conference given by the Prime Minister of Singapore, Mr. Lee Kuan Yew, at Broadcasting House, Singapore, at 1200 hours on Monday, 9 August 1965", at https://www.nas.gov.sg/archivesonline/speeches/record-details/740acc3c-115d-11e3-83d5-0050568939ad (accessed 2 Dec. 2022)

not like through controlling Singapore's water supply.[27] Lee Kuan Yew recalled in his memoir that "the Tunku and Razak thought they could station troops in Singapore, squat on us and if necessary close the causeway and cut off our water supply".[28] In a 13 August 1965 interview, Lee explained the importance of Singapore's relations with Malaysia: "But more important: I have two pipelines carrying water to Singapore. Every time we open the tap, three-quarters of water comes from two rivers in Johore, two reservoirs in Johore and only one quarter comes from the reservoirs in Singapore. So if Malaysia were to fall into the hands of a regime or group which is hostile to Singapore, then I think Singapore will be a very difficult place to live in [but] I am not saying we are finished: people fight to the end and we intend to fight to the end". Both sides had signed a water agreement: "we have a firm guarantee of water. And the guarantee of water depends upon a government which, at least is not hostile to Singapore... I do not want anybody to blackmail us on this".[29] In an interview the following day, Lee said that "every time a phrase is put in the form of a threat"—he was referring to the Tunku objecting to Singapore having any relationship with Indonesia while Confrontation was still on-going—"my position becomes more difficult. I do not want to jeopardise Malaysia's security because my water supply comes from Johore".[30] In 1994, former Malaysian Chief of Defence Force General Tan Sri Hashim Mohammed Ali recounted that Lee Kuan Yew had told him that if the Islamic Party of Malaysia (PAS) came to power and "tried to meddle with the water in Johore Bahru", he would move his troops in and not wait for the Security Council.[31]

In March 1966, the two prime ministers met in Singapore when the Tunku came to Singapore to attend the horse races. Describing it as a "business-cum-pleasure visit" as well as describing the differences between the two governments as "teething problems", he invited Lee and his ministers for a series of golf games in

---

[27] "UK Official's Reaction to Singapore Separation", Incoming Telegram, US Department of State, 9 August 1965, RG 59, Box 2652, POL 16 Singapore.
[28] Lee Kuan Yew, *The Singapore Story* (Singapore Press Holdings, 1998), p. 663.
[29] "Transcript of an Interview with the Prime Minister, Mr. Lee Kuan Yew, Recorded at TV Singapura Studios", 13 Aug. 1965.
[30] "Transcript of an Interview Given by the Prime Minister, Mr. Lee Kuan Yew, to Four Foreign Correspondents on 14 August 1965, at the Studios of Television Singapura". The Tunku was asked whether Malaysia would cut off the water pipeline if Singapore "did anything with Indonesia which would endanger Malaysia", such as trading with Indonesia which was seen to be a "hostile act". The Tunku said he would not. Asked what he would do, he laughed and said, "well, we must keep some things secret, but we could do things".
[31] Qtd. in Bilahari Kausikan, *Dealing with an Ambiguous World* (Singapore: World Scientific Publishing, 2017), p. 155; Bilahari Kausikan, *Singapore is Not an Island: Views on Singapore Foreign Policy* (Singapore: Straits Times Press, 2017), p. 176.

Kuala Lumpur to keep up a "constant contact". American Embassy officials were of the view that while informal meetings and golf games might help reduce the tension between the two sides, "the problem of Malaysia–Singapore relations does not stem from a clash of personalities but from deep-seated communal, political and economic differences which cannot be papered over".[32]

George Bogaars (Permanent Secretary, Singapore's Ministry of the Interior and Defence) in several conversations with American Embassy officials in January 1968 revealed the thinking of the Singapore leadership on Malaysia. According to Bogaars, after Indonesia, Malaysia was "the other potential military threat" but "not primarily from the present political leadership there". One scenario was a "take-over by Malay extremists".[33] American Embassy officials believed that Singapore had prepared an assessment which included the possibility that there would be "a security threat from its neighbour to the North [Malaysia] or the one to the South [Indonesia] within five to ten years".[34]

In its 1969 prediction of developments in Malaysia and Singapore up to 1975, the Australian government was of the view that "action by Malaysia or by elements beyond the control of the Malaysian Government to interfere with Singapore's water supply could result in Singapore's forces endeavouring to take over a limited area of Johore to assure control of the supply". Although the study concluded that "the possibility of such a development" up to 1975 "appears remote",[35] it was not an impossibility beyond that time frame. Indeed, a June 1968 analysis noted that "Singapore has less fear of Malaysia, where it considers essentially moderate men to be in charge, restrained, moreover, from too violent a hostility to Singapore by the risk of trouble among the large Malaysian Chinese population. There is anxiety, however, lest after the Tunku goes, power should move to Malays with deep communal antagonisms towards Singapore...".[36] In his 1972 book, David

---

[32] From the American Consul, Singapore to the US Department of State, 27 March 1966, RG 59, Box 2651, POL 2-1/Singapore 1/1/66. See also Lau Teik Soon, "Malaysia-Singapore Relations: Crisis of Adjustment, 1965–68", *Journal of Southeast Asian History* X [10], no. 1 (1969):155–76.
[33] "Singapore's Security Problem", Memorandum of Conversation, 12 Jan. 1968, RG 59, Box 1622, POL 7- Singapore-US.
[34] "GOS [Government of Singapore] Interest in US Military Policy towards Singapore", Memorandum of Conversation, 8 Jan. 1968, RG 59, Box 1622, POL 7- Singapore-US.
[35] "The Implications for Australia of Likely Developments in Malaysia and Singapore Up to the End of 1975", A1209, 1969/9036 Part 7, National Archives of Australia.
[36] "Aspects of Singapore's Foreign Relations", June 1968, A/1838/318, Item 3024/12, Part 1, National Archives of Australia. The Tunku would remain as Prime Minister of Malaysia till September 1970. He was succeeded by his deputy Tun Razak Hussein who held the post from September 1970 until his untimely death in January 1976.

Hawkins noted that Singapore's decision to procure tanks was seen by Malaysia as an unfriendly act. In his words: "Where could Singapore deploy tanks except across the Causeway in Malaysia?"[37]

It was not until Tun Abdul Razak succeeded Tunku Abdul Rahman as Malaysian Prime Minister in 1970 that both sides experienced a "relatively trouble-free" relationship for a few years.[38] Lee Kuan Yew eventually made his first official visit to Malaysia in March 1972 and Tun Razak reciprocated the following year.

IV

As for Indonesia, George Bogaars called it a potential threat to Singapore.

The Indonesians opposed the formation of Malaysia as a neo-imperialist plot. In January 1963, Jakarta announced a policy of Confrontation, which has been described[39] as a "low-intensity" type of warfare, against Malaya and which escalated into a "Crush Malaysia" campaign in September. Singapore had no alternative but to condemn Indonesian policy. According to Kawin Wilairat, the period of Singapore–Indonesia entente (1959–63) ended with Sukarno's official declaration of Confrontation in January 1963.[40] On 10 March 1965, two Indonesian saboteurs carried out the bombing of MacDonald House in Singapore, killing three and injuring thirty-three others. The bombing was described as "the darkest episode in the three years of confrontation which saw 37 attacks on Singapore, mostly on soft targets that included public parks, cinemas and telephone booths".[41]

Singapore however separated from Malaysia in August 1965 while Confrontation was still on-going. Asked on 9 August 1965 how Singapore planned to conduct relations with Indonesia, Lee replied that Singapore–Indonesia relations were a "delicate matter". Singapore always wanted "to be

---

[37] David Hawkins, *The Defence of Malaysia and Singapore: From AMDA to ANZUK* (London: RUSI, 1972), p. 53.
[38] "A Close but Difficult Relationship", *Today*, 23 March 2015.
[39] E.g. by Daniel Wei Boon Chua, "Konfrontasi: Why it Still Matters to Singapore", Nanyang Technological University, Singapore: RSIS Commentaries, No. 054 (2015); an overview is available at the History SG website: https://eresources.nlb.gov.sg/history/events/126b6b07-f796-4b4c-b658-938001e3213e and https://eresources.nlb.gov.sg/history/events/f950e04d-44d7-47ad-a10c-16dfb0cc9ce3.
[40] Wilairat, *Singapore's Foreign Policy: A Study of the Foreign Policy System of a City-State*, pp. 348, 368–9. The Indonesians had for a long time been unhappy with Singapore which they saw as a "sanctuary and supply base" for rebels in Sumatra and also for turning a blind eye to the "flourishing smuggling trade between Singapore and the nearby Indonesian islands".
[41] "Konfrontasi a Key Episode for Ex-soldier and S'pore", *The Straits Times*, 5 Oct. 2017.

friends with Indonesia". But "we must survive. We have a right to survive. And, to survive, we must be sure we cannot just be over-run". The first step was for Indonesia to recognise Singapore as "an independent, sovereign nation". Any rapprochement between the two countries must also take into consideration "the security and future of Malaysia". Thus, it could be possible only based on a concurrent settlement between Indonesia and Singapore, and between Indonesia and Malaysia. There was also the concern about the kinship or blood ties between Indonesia and Malaysia; as Lee put it, "we cannot foolishly get into a position where we are confronted, or being confronted, by both sides".[42] In his 14 August 1965 interview, Lee reiterated this when he said: "We are not going to jeopardise our long-term survival. And our long-term survival demands that there is no government in Malaysia which would go with the Indonesians and then between Malaysia and Indonesia and Singapore in between [*sic*], life will be very difficult...".[43] Lastly, there was the concern about the Leftist (Communist Party of Indonesia [PKI]) influence prevalent in the Indonesian leadership at this time.

The complexity of Singapore's entangled relations with its two immediate neighbours can be discerned from Lee's responses during separate interviews around the same time.

On 11 August 1965, Lee mentioned the issue of water again in an interview in the context of Singapore–Indonesia relations. When asked how this relationship would affect Malaysia given that Indonesia and Malaysia were still in a state of Confrontation whereas, according to Indonesian Foreign Minister Subandrio, there was no confrontation with Singapore, Lee explained, "If Singapore [were] a big country and [had] sufficient water, sufficient men without any relationship with Malaysia, I think the confrontation would not affect us at all. But... should someone put poison in our pipeline, if Malaya is under a country which is our enemy, wouldn't we suffer? or if they are not that mean, and do not poison but just blow up the pipeline and then say this was done by communist guerrillas, wouldn't we be in trouble...? So, in spite of everything, we must uphold Singapore's interests and part of that interest is its water in Johore...".[44]

In another interview, Lee said that "we want to be friends with Malaysia, but that does not mean that we have to be unfriendly with all the people who

---

[42] "Transcript of a Press Conference Given by the Prime Minister of Singapore, Mr. Lee Kuan Yew, at Broadcasting House, Singapore, on 9 Aug. 1965".
[43] "Transcript of an Interview Given by the Prime Minister, Mr. Lee Kuan Yew, to Four Foreign Correspondents", Studios of Television Singapura, 14 Aug. 1965.
[44] "Press Conference of the Singapore Prime Minister, Mr. Lee Kuan Yew, with Malay Journalists at the Studio of TV Singapura", 11 Aug. 1965. at https://www.nas.gov.sg/archivesonline/speeches/record-details/783597f1-115d-11e3-83d5-0050568939ad (accessed 3 Dec. 2022).

are unfriendly to Malaysia. Their friends may be our friends... But Malaysia's enemies need not be our enemies... Singapore wanted rapport with Malaysia, regardless of our position with Indonesia; and we want rapport with Indonesia regardless of our position with Malaysia". Having said that, he added that it was unwise, short-sighted and opportunistic for Singapore to improve relations with Indonesia at the expense of Malaysia.[45] In short, while recognising that Singapore's and Malaysia's interests were inter-dependent, Singapore also wanted to "assert its right to determine where those interests lie".[46]

The demise of the PKI, the removal of Sukarno and the ascendancy of Suharto—a consequence of the tragic events of the abortive coup that took place in Indonesia on 30 September/1 October 1965—finally brought Confrontation to an end on 11 August 1966 with the signing of the Bangkok Accords in Jakarta. By August, American assessment was that the objective to prevent Indonesia from turning communist had been achieved "for the time being".[47] Even after the coup in 1965, Jakarta continued to "perceive Singapore as a third China" and a centre for "smuggling and other illegal commercial activities, and a sanctuary for anti-nationalist elements despite the assurances given by Singapore".[48] Indonesia eventually recognised Singapore as a sovereign country in June 1966. Kuala Lumpur kicked up quite a ruckus over what Singapore's Acting Prime Minister Toh Chin Chye had earlier described as a "unilateral act...which did not mean the establishment of diplomatic relations".[49] A liaison office was set up in Jakarta in December 1966. Both countries established formal diplomatic relations on 7 September 1967, after Indonesia and Malaysia had renewed their diplomatic ties which had been broken off by Confrontation.

According to American officials based in Singapore, the resumption of diplomatic relations between Indonesia and Malaysia aroused some concerns in

---

[45] "Transcript of a Press Conference the Prime Minister, Mr. Lee Kuan Yew, Gave to a Group of Foreign Correspondents at the Television Singapura Studio", 11 Dec. 1965.
[46] From the American Consulate, Singapore to the US Department of State, 17 Dec. 1965, RG 59, Box 2651, POL 2-1/Singapore 10/16/65.
[47] See Ang Cheng Guan, "United States-Indonesia Relations: The 1965 Coup and After", *War & Society* 21, no. 1 (2003): 135.
[48] Ernest C.T. Chew and Edwin Lee, eds., *A History of Singapore* (Oxford: Oxford University Press, 1991), p. 374.
[49] For the Malaysian response, see the memo from the American Embassy, Kuala Lumpur to the US Department of State, 25 April 1966, RG 59, Box 2652, POL 16 – "Independence & Recognition/Singapore"; From the American Embassy, Singapore to Department of State, 20 April 1966, RG 59, Box 2652, POL 16 – "Independence & Recognition/Singapore"; From the American Embassy, Singapore to Department of State, 17, 24 April, 1 May 1966, RG 59, Box 2651, POL 2-1/Singapore 1/1/66.

Singapore. Privately, several Singapore officials expressed concern over the "one race, one religion" atmosphere in Kuala Lumpur (referring to the "surprise" arrival of an Indonesian military goodwill mission to Kuala Lumpur) which Singapore officials "fear[-ed] may presage a revival of Maphilindo or some form of pan-Malayanism".[50] (This was exactly what Lee Kuan Yew referred to in his 14 August 1965 interview recounted above.) According to the Americans,[51] the Singaporean side saw two possible threats: (a) given the numbers, the Malays might no longer regard it a necessity to come to terms with the non-Malay communities in Malaysia, "thus virtually ruling out any hope of re-merger and greatly reducing the chances of reaching any Singapore–Malaysia agreement on economic cooperation"; (b) Singapore, a predominantly "Chinese" states could easily find itself isolated and its survival placed in jeopardy by a Muslim, pan-Malayan and anti-Chinese alliance which would probably receive Western [i.e., US] support as a "bulwark against Communist China". The American report further noted the "frustration" felt by the Singapore side regarding its "impotence to control or influence to any substantial degree the developments leading to the end of confrontation... Singapore has now seen how quickly and easily the Malaysian government was able to push Singapore to one side and reach its own bilateral understanding with Indonesia". Singapore was not informed in advance of the Indonesian military goodwill mission. One Singapore official commented, "You can imagine what would have happened if we had pulled anything like that".

According to George Bogaars in a 1968 conversation, Singapore's "first concern was with [a] potential threat from Indonesia". The threat was "not immediate" as the Singapore government was "quite happy with the present Indonesian leadership" and was doing what it could to support it. Bogaars described the Singapore-Indonesian relationship as "excellent" but Singapore could not be complacent about the future. Singapore was worried about the consequences if the Suharto regime failed, which could lead to another "foreign adventure à la Sukarno to divert public discontent or...it might be replaced by another regime with an adventurism outlook". The concern about the potential Indonesian threat was apparently shared in some quarters in Malaysia (notably by Malaysian Chinese, British and Australian expatriates, security officials, but not Malays, and particularly not the "higher political levels") who agreed that "the

---

[50] The Confederation of Malaya [Ma-], the Philippines [-Phil-] and Indonesia [-Indo] founded in July 1963. See Joseph Scalice, "A Region in Dispute: Racialized Anticommunism and Manila's Role in the Origins of Konfrontasi 1961–63", *Modern Asian Studies* 57, no. 3 (2023): 1004–26 for a discussion of racial politics.

[51] From the American Embassy, Singapore to the US Department of State, 5 June 1966, RG 59, Box 2651, POL 1/Singapore 5/1/66.

threat was a real contingency" and that it required "a joint Singapore/Malaysia response".[52] According to Australian officials, there was "little doubt" that the Singapore air force and navy were being built up with Indonesia in mind.[53]

One episode in the early years of the bilateral relations is worth highlighting for the purposes of this study. The 10 March 1965 bombing of MacDonald House in Singapore by two Indonesian saboteurs was described earlier. In October 1968, the two Indonesian marine commandos were hung after court appeals against the death penalty were unsuccessful and despite Indonesian appeals, both at the diplomatic and personal levels, for clemency. This briefly affected Singapore–Indonesian relations. S.R. Nathan (Principal Assistant Secretary) told American Embassy officials that the decision to proceed with the executions had been "debated in-depth in cabinet" and a unanimous decision was reached to abide by the decree of the Privy Council. The "primary issue", according to Nathan, was "whether Singapore should knuckle down under to a larger neighbour or should uphold the law, as determined by fair trial and subsequent appeal procedures". The conclusion reached was that it was better for the Singapore government "to stand up" to Indonesia now, while the British were still in Singapore and the US was still in the region. He also stressed that Singaporean public opinion overwhelmingly favoured execution in view of the damage and lives lost. He expected some tensions as well as a "certain amount of economic retaliation on the part of Djakarta" over the next few months but believed that it would eventually blow over. George Bogaars shared the same view in his conversation with the Americans. In its explanatory statement, Singapore also highlighted the fact that it had, on compassionate grounds, released many Indonesians detained for various Confrontation offences where no loss of lives ensued.[54] Cooler heads eventually prevailed, and Lee Kuan Yew paid his first official visit to Indonesia in May 1973.[55]

It is perhaps appropriate to end this discussion of Singapore's relations with Malaysia and Indonesia by recalling what Goh Keng Swee said in a 1970 speech. He mentioned that businessmen (who "often compete in their

---

[52] "Singapore's Security Problem", Memorandum of Conversation, 12 Jan. 1968, RG 59, Box 1622, POL 7- Singapore-US.
[53] From the Australian High Commission in Singapore to the Department of External Affairs, Canberra, "ANZUS: Five Power Defence Arrangements – Singapore Attitudes", 6 Aug. 1969, A1838, Item 3024/11/161 Part 2, Singapore—Relations with United States of America.
[54] From the American Embassy, Singapore to the US Department of State, 18 Oct. 1968, RG 59, Box 2479, POL 7 Singapore.
[55] See Barry Desker (Singapore's ambassador to Indonesia, 1986–93), "Lee Kuan Yew and Suharto: Friends Till the End", *The Straits Times*, 8 April 2015. For Lee's visit, see Lee Khoon Choy, *Diplomacy of a Tiny State* (Singapore: World Scientific, 1993), Chapter 13. Lee Khoon Choy was Singapore's ambassador to Indonesia from 1970 to 1974.

supplications" for favours) had never hesitated to give him "free advice" on how to conduct foreign relations "during the periodic rows we have had with our neighbours". "Unfortunately", Goh continued, "they do not understand—and I am afraid cannot understand—that in the nature of things, relations between independent sovereign states cannot be conducted on the basis of supplicant and overlord. The methods they found so successful in business are not available to us as a government".[56]

V

Closely tied to the above issues is that of Defence, the other top priority of newly independent Singapore. It was mentioned above that the defence of Singapore was highlighted by the Yang di-Pertuan Negara as well as by the Defence and Foreign Ministers during the first Parliament session. Kawin Wilairat noted that "in contrast to foreign policy or internal security, defence was a completely new area of responsibility that the Singapore Government had to handle... From the time of her founding, Singapore's defence had been the responsibility of a larger power—Britain's until 1963, and Malaysia's from 1963 to 1965".[57] Goh Keng Swee, in his opening remarks on the second reading of the National Service (Amendment) Bill in the Singapore Parliament on 13 March 1967, said that "one of the difficulties confronting" him as Minister of Defence was "the novelty of the responsibility. There are no precedents to fall back on".[58]

Singapore, in 1965, could neither secure nor protect its water supply without a military force of its own, not to mention protecting itself from a hostile Indonesia. As Lee described the situation, Singapore was "like a suburban villa just placed in a tenement area with a very flimsy fence, and outside are a lot of hungry people and angry people who are being worked up by all kinds of oratory...And all that I have got is two battalions and the Indonesians have got 400,000 armed men".[59]

---

[56] Text of a Speech by the Minister for Defence, Dr. Goh Keng Swee, at the Adult Education Board Forum on "Qualities Required in the Seventies" at the University of Singapore, 22 Nov. 1970.
[57] Wilairat, *Singapore's Foreign Policy: A Study of the Foreign Policy System of a City-State*, p. 198.
[58] Speech by the Minister of Defence, Dr. Goh Keng Swee, in Moving the Second Reading of the National Service (Amendment) Bill in the Singapore Parliament, 13 March 1967.
[59] "Transcript of an Interview Given by the Prime Minister, Mr. Lee Kuan Yew, to Mr. Neville Peterson of the Australian Broadcasting Commission on 12 August 1965 and Recorded on the Same Day at the Studios of Television Singapore".

Winston Choo, Singapore first and longest-serving Chief of the Singapore Armed Forces (1974–92), recalled the day he heard about the separation. He was then a career soldier in the 1st Battalion, Singapore Infantry Regiment (1 SIR) commanded by a Malaysian; the Singaporeans in the battalion were all "more subdued" compared to the cheering British officers. In his words, "we had two army battalions then. In 1 SIR, three-quarters were Singaporeans, one-quarter Malaysians. The ratio in 2 SIR was almost 50–50. We realised we would only have one and one quarter of a battalion after the Malaysians left. And even after independence, the presence of the Malaysian Armed Forces in Singapore was still overwhelming. Any thinking Singaporean, especially those involved in the military, would realise how naked we were as a small country".[60]

As Goh Keng Swee said, Singapore needed to "get rid" of the foreign military still based in the country. Circumstances however required that the British remain for some time as Singapore could not build a defence force overnight. In an interview on 11 August, referring to Indonesia, Lee Kuan Yew said, if "we get rid of the bases...it is not necessary to send 400,000 (troops), it is sufficient to send 40,000—Singapore would be finished...remember how the Japanese came in?"[61] A few days later, when asked if he was truly keen on having the bases and whether or not the bases would affect Singapore's professed non-alignment posture, Lee reiterated "I cannot survive without the bases. So I am keen about the bases as I am keen about the survival of my fellow countrymen".[62] Some of the Afro-Asian countries "might be a little unhappy about the bases" but "I cannot make a concession there because this is my survival".[63]

During their simultaneous goodwill tours to the Afro-Asian countries, deputy Prime Minister Toh Chin Chye and Foreign Minister S. Rajaratnam explained the paradox of a foreign base in a newly-independent Singapore: Singapore needed to retain the base at present for both security and economic reasons. Rajaratnam explained that "Singapore wished to retain [the] existing British base in Singapore unless and until alternative water-tight arrangements could be made by the United Nations or some other grouping to guarantee Singapore, with its army of 5,000, against its powerful neighbour which had an

---

[60] "From Scepticism to Accepted Way of Life", *The Straits Times*, 24 Aug. 2013; Loke Hoe Yeong, ed., *Speaking Truth to Power: Singapore's Pioneer Public Servants*, Vol. 1 (Singapore: World Scientific, 2020), p. 271.
[61] "Press Conference of the Singapore Prime Minister, Mr. Lee Kuan Yew, with Malay Journalists at the Studio of TV Singapura", 11 Aug. 1965.
[62] "Transcript of an Interview with the Prime Minister, Mr. Lee Kuan Yew, recorded at TV Singapura Studios", 13 Aug. 1965.
[63] "Transcript of an Interview Given by the Prime Minister, Mr. Lee Kuan Yew, to Four Foreign Correspondents", 14 Aug. 1965, Television Singapura Studios.

army of 250,000 and the avowed intention of destroying Singapore".[64] During his visit to Ceylon in November 1965, Rajaratnam said that as the interests of Singapore and Britain coincided, Singapore believed that it would be better for her to be defended by three British battleships which were in the region than to have her own battleships. Asked what the consequences would be if Britain decided to abandon Singapore, he said that such a "desperate situation" would lead Singapore to take "desperate action".[65] Toh Chin Chye said that Singapore would be negotiating a new defence treaty with Britain and would not allow the base "to be used for aggression". Singapore's policy was that the base should be run down when Singapore could absorb the 50,000 workers employed there.[66]

The first step was therefore to build an indigenous military as soon as possible while the British were still in Singapore. As Minister for Defence Goh Keng Swee told Lee Kuan Yew, "...you are a Prime Minister, but you don't have any army!"[67] It is known now—in fact, it was one of the worst kept secrets—that Israel helped Singapore develop its armed forces. The Israeli advisers came disguised as Mexicans.[68] As Peter Ho recalled, "the defence ties between Singapore and Israel are almost as old as independent Singapore". But, he added, "for many years, it was shrouded in secrecy"[69] to "avoid riling up sensitivities" and "offending our Muslim neighbours".[70] Singapore did not learn just from the Israelis, though they played the major role in the early years (until around 1973).[71] As Winston

---

[64] From the Australian Mission to the United Nations, New York to the Department of External Affairs, Canberra, 24 Sept. 1965, A1838, Item 3024/7/1 Part 2, Singapore – Political – Foreign policy.

[65] "Singapore Keen on More Trade – Not Aid", *Ceylon Daily News*, 17 Nov. 1965.

[66] From the Australian High Commission to the Department of External Affairs, Canberra, "Singapore: Views of the British Base", 27 Oct. 1965, A1838, Item 3024/7/1 Part 2, Singapore – Political – Foreign policy.

[67] Chew, *Leaders of Singapore*, p.148.

[68] Loke, ed., *Speaking Truth to Power: Singapore's Pioneer Public Servants*, Vol.1, p. 273; Winston Choo (with Chua Siew San and Judith D'Silva), *A Soldier at Heart: A Memoir* (Singapore: Landmark Books, 2021), pp. 81, 90–8, 108, 142–5, 149.

[69] Mattia Tomba, ed., *Beating the Odds Together: 50 Years of Singapore-Israel Ties* (Singapore: World Scientific, 2020), p. 35. Peter Ho further noted that "to this day, little has been written about the Singapore-Israel defence relationship despite its significance". See also Amnon Barzilai, "A Deep, Dark, Secret Love Affair", *Haaretz*, 16 July 2004, at https://www.haaretz.com/1.4758973 (accessed 25 Feb. 2021).

[70] Winston Choo and George Yeo (former Singapore Foreign Minister) qtd. in Tomba, ed., *Beating the Odds Together: 50 Years of Singapore-Israel Ties* , pp. 12, 28.

[71] Choo (with Chua and D'Silva), *A Soldier at Heart: A Memoir*, p. 144.

Choo recalled, Goh "had always favoured opening ourselves to advice from people who had relevant experience and could show us what to do".[72]

Goh Keng Swee recalled that the first mission Israel sent to Singapore was headed by Jack Ellazari who told the Singapore leadership that Singapore "must have a National Service force" and that it would take time to build up.[73] It was decided that creating "a citizen's army of conscripts built around the nucleus of regulars serving in the two SIRs" was "the most cost- and manpower effective solution to build a credible SAF".[74] It took one and half years to prepare all the military infrastructure for National Service (such as setting up the Singapore Armed Forces Training Institute, establishing a Central Manpower Base and developing a training programme).[75] The first batch of 9,000 young men were enlisted for compulsory National Service in 1967.

The Minister of Defence's speech on 13 March 1967 at the reading of the National Service (Amendment) Bill deserves mentioning here.[76] Goh began by making the point that in thinking of the elements that should be taken into consideration in framing a meaningful defence policy for Singapore, one needed to begin from first principles, that is, "why bother about defending Singapore at all?" He was not facetious in asking this question because there was the view held by "laymen as well as experts" that Singapore was "quite indefensible" and that if there were to be a sustained major attack on the island-state, the likelihood was that Singapore could not hold out without external assistance. As such, the view ran, it would be useless to expend resources on defence that could be better spent somewhere else.

Goh thought otherwise. In his words, "the conclusion drawn from their premise must be that Singapore should revert to a colony or a satellite of whoever wishes to afford it protection. If you are in a completely vulnerable position, anyone disposed to do so can hold you to ransom and life for you will then become very tiresome". He argued that while Singapore could not achieve "complete invulnerability", the fact was that even the larger countries, other than the two

---

[72] Ibid., p. 146. There was also a German adviser. Soon after the end of the Vietnam War, Dr. Goh approached the US Department of Defence for a briefing on US military experience in Vietnam. See Choo (Chua and D'Silva), *A Soldier at Heart: A Memoir*, Chapter XVII [17].
[73] Chew, *Leaders of Singapore*, p. 148.
[74] Ho Shu Huang and Graham Ong-Webb, eds., *National Service in Singapore* (Singapore: World Scientific, 2019), p. 7.
[75] Ibid.
[76] Singapore Government Press Statement, "Speech by the Minister of Defence, Dr. Goh Keng Swee, in Moving the Second Reading of the National Service (Amendment) Bill in the Singapore Parliament of Monday, 13th March, 1967", at https://www.nas.gov.sg/archivesonline/data/pdfdoc/PressR19670313b.pdf (accessed 4 Jan. 2023).

nuclear superpowers, were indefensible from a nuclear attack. But that did not stop them from spending enormous sums of money in defence. Small states, if poorly managed, are likely "to be a great source of trouble in the world". They could lead to civil war and disorder, which in turn could tempt larger states to intervene as in the case of South Vietnam. This scenario is especially relevant for a small state strategically situated like Singapore, thus the need to maintain "adequate defence forces".

Goh then went on to make the point that "the real security which we want can be found, not by our unaided efforts alone, but in an alliance with others". Thus, he proposed that Singapore should work towards an establishment of a regional defence arrangement of some form, possibly within a larger international framework.

Lee Kuan Yew put this somewhat more colourfully when he said, "I am going to defend myself to the best of my ability. And since the best of my ability is not equal to the best of other chaps' abilities, I am going to get whatever help from whoever I can get it, to make it as good as their abilities and better. And if it is better than the abilities of those who intend to involve me in such a military entanglement, then I will have peace".[77]

There is another dimension to Singapore's defence effort: its role in "nation-building", which harks back to the Yang Di-Pertuan Negara's remarks at the opening of Parliament regarding "communalists" and "the creation of tolerant multi-racial society" mentioned above. According to Goh in his 13 March 1967 Parliament speech, "nothing creates loyalty and national consciousness more speedily and more thoroughly than participation in defence and membership of the armed forces...The nation-building aspect of defence will be more significant if the participation is spread over all strata of society".[78] In short, the aims of National Service were (and remain so today) as much sociological as military. Goh noted that Singapore was "not yet a closely-knit community". There existed in Singapore "the values of a rootless parvenu society" and he hoped that military training could lead to a stronger national consciousness.[79]

---

[77] Lee Kuan Yew, Transcript of a Press Conference at Hyderabad House, New Delhi, 3 Sept. 1966, at https://www.nas.gov.sg/archivesonline/speeches/record-details/7403d383-115d-11e3-83d5-0050568939ad (accessed 5 Dec. 2022).
[78] Speech by the Minister of Defence (Dr. Goh Keng Swee), National Service (Amendment) Bill, 13 March 1967, Singapore Parliament Reports (Hansard).
[79] Goh qtd. in a memo from the American Embassy to the US Department of State, 2 Dec. 1966, RG 59, Box 2451, POL 6 – Singapore 1/1/65. In his 13 March 1967 speech, Goh mentioned that "social discipline and moral values" had not been "instilled in [the] education system" and that National Servicemen would receive "instruction in moral values".

VI

As soon as Singapore became independent, Goh Keng Swee was already anticipating the eventual withdrawal of the British, as he made clear in his 23 December 1965 Parliament speech mentioned earlier in this chapter.[80] The plan was to quickly establish a reasonable, credible defence force before the British left, which, he anticipated, could be between 5 and 15 years ahead.[81] Lee had publicly stated that he wanted the British to stay until "I can be sure I'll be secure when they go. I can think of quite a number of bigger countries that might see Singapore as [a] useful province".[82]

But no sooner had National Service been introduced, on 18 July 1967, that London announced that the British would withdraw their troops from Singapore by the mid-1970s. Six months later, the timeline was shortened to 1971. It was subsequently moved from March 1971 to end 1971 after much intense negotiation between Singapore and Britain. The last British soldier left Singapore in March 1976. As Lee Kuan Yew told British Prime Minister Harold Wilson, the British decision to withdraw was "a matter of life and death to Singapore". Lee was concerned not about the economic effect of the British withdrawal but about the security implications as Singapore's prosperity could only continue "if its security could be assured". Lee was particularly fearful of a possible attack from Indonesia which he described as being "in a mess".[83]

Between 1968 and 1973, in order to maintain business confidence in Singapore, about a third of Singapore's annual expenditure was allocated to defence whereas a ceiling was imposed for other needs such as health and education.[84] Alec Douglas-Home, British Foreign Secretary 1970–74, summed it up well when he said that "Lee wants us to stay there not in any great strength but

---

[80] Speech by the Minister of Defence (Dr. Goh Keng Swee), Singapore Army Bill, 23 December 1965, Singapore Parliament Reports (Hansard).
[81] Ibid. and see Wilairat, *Singapore's Foreign Policy: A Study of the Foreign Policy System of a City-State*, p. 202.
[82] From the American Embassy in London to the US Department of State, 27 April 1966, RG 59, Box 2651, POL 7 - Visits & Meetings/Singapore 1/165.
[83] Document 109: "Visit of the Prime Minister of Singapore to London: Record of a Meeting between Mr. Wilson and Mr. Lee Kuan Yew on the Implications for Singapore of Britain's Defence Cuts", 14 Jan. 1968, PREM 13/2081, SMV (68)1, rpt. in *British Documents on the End of Empire, Series A, vol. 5, East of Suez and the Commonwealth, 1964–1971*, ed. S.R. Ashton and Wm Roger Louis (London: TSO, 2004), pp. 373–4.
[84] Wilairat, *Singapore's Foreign Policy: A Study of the Foreign Policy System of a City-State*, p. 203; See also Chin Kin Wah, "Singapore: Threat Perception and Defence Spending in a City-State", in *Defence Spending in Southeast Asia*, ed. Chin Kin Wah (Singapore: ISEAS, 1987), pp. 205–12.

on a scale which would provide a visible token of commitment and be the core around which a five-power arrangement in which he would have confidence could be built up".[85] In his memoir, Lee Kuan Yew wrote that the residual presence of the British gave Singapore "time to sort out our relations with Indonesia without making precipitate moves we might later regret".[86]

The unexpected early withdrawal of British forces from Singapore is relevant for our understanding of Singapore's grand strategy in two areas: its security vis-à-vis its immediate neighbours seen from the lens of the formation of the Five Power Defence Arrangements (FPDA), and its relationship beyond the region, particularly with the United States (discussed in the next chapter).

Much has been written about the British withdrawal "east of Suez" and the Five Power Defence Arrangements (FPDA) which replaced the Anglo-Malayan Defence Agreement (AMDA) established in 1957, the objective of which was to defend Malaya (in particular) and all British territories in the Far East against external attack. Writing in 1972, David Hawkins noted that "AMDA was devised to help newly independent Malaya through a difficult transition period; it was never intended to be permanent and few people in 1957 would have anticipated its survival more than twenty years later".[87]

Our focus here is on the Singapore dimension.[88] Although Singapore had begun a crash programme to develop its armed forces, the government was "under no illusion that Singapore is capable in defending itself...the deterrence of other than minor local threats will require at least the possibility of outside support and assistance". In addition to the fact that there was no obvious alternative regional defence arrangement, this made the FPDA of strategic importance to Singapore.[89]

The establishment of the FPDA on 1 November 1971 attests to the indivisibility of the defence of both Malaysia and Singapore, now separate independent countries which were, however, not on the best of terms. Indeed, Zaiton (Secretary-General, Malaysian Ministry of Foreign Affairs) and Samad Noor

---

[85] Qtd. in Geoffrey Till, "A Little Ray of Sunshine; Britain, and the Origins of the FPDA - A Retrospective on Objectives, Problems and Solutions", in *Five Power Defence Arrangements at Forty*, ed. Ian Storey, Ralf Emmers and Daljit Singh (Singapore: ISEAS, 2011), p. 18.
[86] Lee Kuan Yew quoted in Ibid.
[87] David Hawkins, *The Defence of Malaysia and Singapore: From AMDA to ANZUK* (London: RUSI, 1972), p. 28.
[88] The section below on the FPDA negotiations is extracted from Ang Cheng Guan, "Malaysia, Singapore, and the Road to the Five Power Defence Arrangements (FPDA), July 1970–November 1971", *War & Society* 30, 3 (2011): 207–25.
[89] From the Australian High Commission in Singapore to the Department of External Affairs, Canberra, "ANZUS: Five Power Defence Arrangements – Singapore Attitudes", 6 Aug. 1969, A1838, Item 3024/11/161 Part 2, Singapore –Relations with United States of America.

(Secretary-General, Malaysian Ministry of Defence) told the Australians during the FPDA negotiations that, while they could accept the word "indivisibility" of Malaysia and Singapore's defence, they did not wish to have any reference to the need for "cooperation" between the two countries in the document.

Singapore's views on and attitude towards the FPDA can be distilled from the records of conversations Lee Kuan Yew and Goh Keng Swee had with the British, Australians and New Zealanders respectively between July 1970 and November 1971. Whereas the Malaysian attitude was to stress that the political commitment of Britain would influence their decision whether or not to have British forces in Malaysia, Singapore's approach was not to rely too heavily on the British presence "but yet to make it easy to maintain" British forces in Singapore.[90] In actual fact, Lee accepted an ANZUK brigade in Singapore with some reluctance, preferring "sophisticated naval and air units than ground forces".[91] In the end, he reasoned that a small British force based in Singapore would provide "added security for another 3½ to 4½ years" to allow the government to "readjust our plans and have thorough training for our air and naval forces, and go on to more sophisticated weapons".[92]

Lee Kuan Yew was of the view that some British troops should be stationed in Malaysia. He apparently advised Lord Carrington (British Defence Secretary, 1970–74, in Edward Heath's Conservative government) to probe the Malaysians on this question. Lord Carrington informed Lee that he had done so "to the point of rudeness" but had received no clearer response than that they were short of accommodation for their own army and would find it hard to find space for British forces, unless the British really wanted this. Lee said that he was quite content to leave that matter there. Lee told Carrington that he did not fully understand Razak's "public insistence upon an independent defence and foreign policy", though he conjectured that Razak "was probably rationalising an unsatisfactory situation and putting on a show". On his willingness to discuss with the Russians the use of Singapore to bunker and provision their ships, Lee assured a worried Carrington that he knew what he was doing and could keep the situation under control. Lee told Carrington that "he knew which side Singapore's bread was

---

[90] From Kuala Lumpur to the Department of External Affairs, Canberra, "Renewal of British Presence", 27 July 1970 (Secret), A4359, Item 221/4/31/4 PART 1.

[91] Lee qtd. in "Singapore: Annual Review for 1970 and Some Personal First Impressions", 1 January 1977 (Confidential), FCO 24/1193, National Archives of Singapore, Microfilm Number NAB 1909.

[92] Andrea Benvenuti and Moreen Dee, "The Five Power Defence Arrangements and the Reappraisal of the British and Australian Policy Interests in Southeast Asia, 1970–1975", *Journal of Southeast Asian Studies* 41, no. 1 (2010): 108.

buttered, however a little Russian jam in peace time would be acceptable, and he was very well aware that he was 'supping with a long spoon'". Turning to the prospects for a continuing British military presence in Southeast Asia beyond 1975, Lee predicted that the Liberal Party would lose the next Australian general elections (1972) and the chances of Gough Whitlam[93] keeping Australian forces in Southeast Asia would depend significantly on whether British forces also remained. He shared the common pessimism about Britain's economy. For the British to stay in the region, Lee believed it was vital for the Conservative Government's policy on Southeast Asia "to become bi-partisan" and equally vital to cut the cost of the British military presence "right down to the bone". To help cut costs, Lee suggested the maximum use of Singapore's civilian facilities, such as hospitals and schools. (Apparently, Lee repeated this offer to the British High Commissioner on several occasions after this. When asked by the British what they thought of the idea, the Australians thought it was a good idea in principle but would require a detailed feasibility study.[94]) Lee also informed Carrington that he would raise his support for a bi-partisan policy when he met opposition Labour leaders. Lord Carrington hoped that Singapore would grant the Australian and New Zealand forces real estate "on terms no less favourable than those for the British forces". Lee "dismissed the thought with references to nickel and the equivocal attitude of the Australians to Southeast Asian defence".[95]

The report of a meeting between Singapore Defence Minister Dr Goh Keng Swee and the New Zealand High Commissioner Tim Francis on 10 November 1970 sheds considerable light on Singapore–Malaysia relations during this period as well as Goh's view about the FPDA.[96] According to the report, Goh "showed every sign of being absolutely worried about the deterioration of relations between Singapore and Malaysia". He hoped that the High Commissioner would report the conversation back to the New Zealand Government and "if things got any worse", Singapore might consider asking Wellington to persuade Kuala Lumpur "to take a more reasonable attitude". Goh highlighted several issues: Malaysia was accusing Singapore of "stealing" good men from the Malaysian Armed Forces for the Singapore Armed Services.

---

[93] Australian Labor Party, PM (1972–75).
[94] Department of External Affairs, Canberra, Record of Conversation: Post–AMDA Arrangements, 27 Aug. 1970 (Confidential), A4359, Item 221/4/31/4 PART 1.
[95] "Record of Discussion between the Secretary of State for Defence and Mr. Lee Kuan Yew on Monday, 5 October 1970", MO 25/8 (Confidential), FCO 24/654, National Archives of Singapore, Microfilm Number NAB 1636.
[96] From Singapore to Wellington, 10 November 1970 (Confidential), FCO 24/655, National Archives of Singapore, Microfilm Number NAB 1636.

Goh conceded that Singapore had not been too careful as it might have accepted some who claimed Singapore citizenship who had opted out of the Malaysian Armed Services. He was tightening up procedures and was trying to work out some understanding with Kuala Lumpur but "they [would] not listen"; Malaysia refused to allow the Singapore Naval Training Ship to call at Port Swettenham (now Port Klang) and would not give any reason for this; Malaysia wanted to restrict Singaporean use of the Jungle Warfare Centre; Malaysia was determined not to let Singapore use China Rock[97] for aerial bombing practice; there were problems related to the splitting up of Malaysia–Singapore Airlines (MSA). The "most serious issue" was that of water supply. Singapore was anxious to proceed with its plans for expanding its reservoirs but its approach for a loan from the Asia Development Bank (ADB) was "being jeopardised by the Malaysian refusal to give its consent".[98] There was, according to Goh, a "whole range of minor matters over which the Malaysians were being more than usually sticky".

With regards to the FPDA, Goh was of the view that the arrangements were "essential particularly as a means of bringing Singapore and Malaysia together". The Malaysians, according to Goh, needed the FPDA too. Kuala Lumpur needed British, Australian and New Zealand forces in the area as an ultimate assurance that they could call for help "if things go sour". All these cries for closer relations with China and the emphasis on neutrality (re: ZOPFAN[99]) were "window dressing". "The Malaysians knew", Goh said, "if they could not rely on Britain, Australia and New Zealand, they would have to turn to the Indonesians and Razak knew the Indonesians would gobble him up".[100]

Given the poor state of Singapore–Malaysia relations, Lee Kuan Yew was concerned about training facilities for the Singapore Armed Forces. During a meeting with the British High Commissioner to Singapore, Sam Falle, on 9 December 1970, he informed Falle that he was already in touch with Canberra about allowing Singaporean troops to exercise on Australian soil. This, according to Lee, was not solely related to the jungle warfare training. Lee also enquired about the possibility of using Brunei (in lieu of China Rock) for air defence training.

---

[97] The author has not been able to locate China Rock on a map.
[98] For Goh's recounting of the Water Supplies issue to New Zealand Deputy High Commissioner John Hickman, a copy of the report of which meeting was sent to the FCO, see From Singapore to [UK] Foreign and Commonwealth Office, Telegram Number 893, 20 November 1970 (Confidential), FCO 24/894, National Archives of Singapore, Microfilm Number NAB 1260.
[99] The Zone of Peace, Freedom and Neutrality (ZOPFAN), a declaration signed in 1971 by the Foreign Ministers of the then-five ASEAN states (Indonesia, Malaysia, the Philippines, Singapore and Thailand).
[100] From Singapore to Wellington, 10 Nov. 1970 (Confidential), FCO 24/655, National Archives of Singapore, Microfilm Number NAB 1636.

Lee further requested that Britain station some British troops in Malaysia: "one company of the British battalion should be stationed in Johore leaving their families in Singapore, so that they would not be in danger from race riots". His ostensible reason was that "the Malaysians were so insecure in themselves that they would welcome even a very small British presence". Lee believed that Kuala Lumpur's insecurity was driving the Malaysians closer to Indonesia.[101] The Australians noted that one of the chief attractions of having British forces stationed in Malaysia was their "effect on confidence" which Tun Dr Ismail (Second Deputy Prime Minister, Malaysia) understood but others did not.[102]

Goh Keng Swee had approached the British about the possibility of Australia providing training space for Singapore's tank and armoured personnel carriers. What Goh had in mind was the possibility of stationing several tanks and vehicles in Australia and rotating about a company of trainees each time. The approach arose from the problems created for Singapore by "the Malaysian reluctance to provide access by Singapore to the Commonwealth Jungle Warfare Centre (CJWC) and to training areas in Malaysia".[103] Goh also met Falle on 17 December 1970 regarding Singapore air defence training in Brunei. According to Goh, "this was in addition to facilities they still hope to obtain at China Rock, not merely instead of China Rock if the Malaysians should not make this available". Apparently, Goh had told the Australians that Singapore also hoped to conduct Jungle Warfare Training in Brunei although neither Lee nor Goh mentioned this in their meetings with Falle.[104]

The British position was that they should discourage Singapore from thinking of training in Brunei at this stage. (In fact, the British were reluctant to seek training facilities in Brunei even for themselves until their on-going negotiations with the Sultan were completed.) Rather, they would do their utmost to persuade Kuala Lumpur to accede to Singapore's needs. Should the Malaysians be persuaded to make China Rock available to Singapore, the British wanted to find out whether Singapore would be agreeable for it, "subject to satisfactory assurances", to be under Malaysian and not Singapore control (which was proposed by the Air Force Working Group). The British also hoped that air defence facilities

---

[101] From Singapore to the [UK] Foreign and Commonwealth Office, Telegram Number 968, 9 Dec. 1970 (Confidential), FCO 24/656, National Archives of Singapore, Microfilm Number NAB 1260.
[102] From Kuala Lumpur to the Department of External Affairs, Canberra, Renewal of British Presence, 27 July 1970 (Secret), A4359, Item 221/4/31/4 PART 1.
[103] "Training by Singapore Armed Forces in Australia", 14 Dec. 1970 (Confidential), FCO 24/656, National Archives of Singapore, Microfilm Number NAB 1260.
[104] From Singapore to the [UK] Foreign and Commonwealth Office [FCO], 17 Dec. 1970 (Confidential), FCO 24/657, National Archives of Singapore, Microfilm Number NAB 1260.

required by Singapore in addition to China Rock could also be found in Malaysia. If the Malaysians persisted in their refusal, "this would create [a] new situation". The Australians concurred with the British position that "it would be unwise to pursue the question of facilities outside Malaysia until Malaysian position [sic] had been thoroughly explored in January" when the Five Powers Officials' meeting was scheduled to be held in Singapore.[105]

The British stance was conveyed to Goh when British High Commissioner Falle met him on 23 December. Goh thought that the Malaysians would be prepared to make China Rock available in exchange for facilities at Khatib in northern Singapore. He also fully accepted the point that it was necessary to have a thorough discussion with the Malaysians during the January 1971 meeting before looking for alternatives. Goh further said that Samad Noor (Secretary-General, Malaysian Ministry of Defence) was "easy to deal with" but unfortunately, he did not have the final say: "some of the people behind him are the difficulty".[106] Goh did not "react much" to the suggestion that China Rock should be under Malaysian control. His general approach, according to Falle, was "practical, pragmatic and unemotional". Falle found this "mildly encouraging" and "almost too good to be true". However, he did not know how far Goh reflected "his master's voice" (referring to Lee Kuan Yew).[107]

The negotiations over the issue of rent and training facilities in Singapore shed much light on Singapore's defence strategy. Singapore drove a hard bargain. Initially, Singapore wanted Britain, Australia and New Zealand to pay rent but subsequently waived it for the British. As Lord Carrington said, given the amount of real estate and assets that the British were giving to Singapore for free, "it would be intolerable to pay rent to Singapore and such a course could not be defended in Parliament".[108] Canberra and Wellington felt very strongly that all ANZUK forces

---

[105] From the [UK] FCO to Singapore, Telegram Number 838, 18 Dec. 1970 (Confidential), FCO 24/657, National Archives of Singapore, Microfilm Number NAB 1260.
[106] See From Kuala Lumpur to Department of External Affairs, Canberra, Renewal of British Presence, 27 July 1970 (Secret), A4359, Item 221/4/31/4 PART 1 for a similar Australian comment that Samad Noor "seldom has the last word".
[107] From Singapore to the Foreign and Commonwealth Office, Telegram Number 1038, 23 December 1970 (Confidential), FCO 24/657, National Archives of Singapore, Microfilm Number NAB 1260.
[108] Meeting between the UK Defence Secretary [Lord Carrington] and the New Zealand High Commissioner, 31 March 1971 (Confidential), FCO 24/980, National Archives of Singapore, Microfilm Number NAB 1402; Interview with J.K Hickman, CMG by D.M. McBain, 18 December 1995, at http://www.chu.cam.ac.uk/archives/collections/BDOHP/Hickman.pdf.

should be treated equally, a view that London shared.[109] On this, Lee differed. In his letter to the New Zealand High Commissioner, Lee explained that the position of the British was different from that of the Australians and New Zealanders: First, the British built the facilities in Singapore and were due to hand them over under the Dudley Agreement (1968) as part of an overall programme which included some 50 million pounds of aid to mitigate the effects of the rundown. Second, "the British have been and are here. We wanted them to remain here", whereas Singapore had wanted the Australians and New Zealanders to stay in Terendak (in Malaysia). Third, after the ANZUK forces moved to Singapore and, before the British elections brought about a change of policies, Singapore was negotiating "something less than market rentals".[110] The Australians and New Zealanders however had a different interpretation of Lee's third point. They claimed that they were negotiating "utilities and beneficial services but not rent". British High Commissioner Falle put it all down to "a slight element of misunderstanding". According to Falle, Singapore might claim that a fixed sum for beneficial service was a form of rent and that Australia and New Zealand "were arguing about words rather than actual intent".[111]

The record of conversations that Lee Kuan Yew and Goh Keng Swee separately had with Australian, British and New Zealand officials provides a composite Singaporean perspective on the rent issue and the real reasons behind the quibble over rent. Lee was initially adamant about charging Australia and New Zealand and came across as being un-persuaded and un-persuadable by any counterarguments. To Lee, the "readiness to pay rent or the reverse was an indication of their determination to stay".[112] Lee also told New Zealand Prime Minister Sir Keith Holyoake that he was worried that if Singapore agreed to the "extravagant" ANZUK real estate bid, it would simply be helping "to speed up

---

[109] "Five Power Defence Arrangements (for inclusion in the PUS's Monthly Newsletter)", FCO 24/981, National Archives of Singapore, Microfilm Number NAB 1402.
[110] Office of the High Commissioner, New Zealand, Telegram Five Power Defence – Real Estate, Text of Letter from Lee Kuan Yew, addressed to the High Commissioner, delivered by Messenger late afternoon of 10 April 1971 (Confidential), FCO 24/999, National Archives of Singapore, Microfilm Number NAB 1476.
[111] From the British High Commission, Singapore to Kuala Lumpur, Canberra and Wellington, "Real Estate", 13 April 1971 (Confidential), FCO 24/999, National Archives of Singapore, Microfilm Number NAB 1476.
[112] From the British High Commission, Singapore to UK FCO, 3 April 1971 (Confidential), FCO 24/999, National Archives of Singapore, Microfilm Number NAB 1476.

the day when the British would withdraw for good". In his view, a "modest British presence" would "have a good chance of surviving for many years to come".[113]

The Singapore position was concisely put across by Goh at a meeting between Lord Carrington and his Australian, New Zealand and Singapore counterparts in London on 15 April 1971. Goh made the following points: (a) while there was a clear case for the British to continue occupying facilities in Singapore without payment of rent as in the past, Singapore had to charge Australia and New Zealand because "Singapore was a small island and badly needed the available accommodation for her own Forces" and "the only way to give an incentive to other countries to be economical in their payments for space was to make them pay". One solution, about which "Singapore would be quite happy" was for the ANZUK ground troops not to be stationed in Singapore; (b) ANZUK air and naval presence was important but "the value of the ANZUK brigade was political rather than military"; (c) Singapore felt "aggrieved" that it was not receiving equal treatment: Malaysia would not accept Singapore units at the Jungle Warfare Centre and had rejected requests for the use of ranges in Malaysia; (d) Singapore had asked Australia for training space but had received no reply. There could be a quid pro quo: if Australia were prepared to make a training area available, he might be able to persuade his colleagues "to take a more flexible attitude in other matters".[114]

At a meeting with New Zealand diplomat Norm Farrell on 28 April 1971, Goh told him that he was "prepared to be accommodating on the rent issue as far as New Zealand was concerned". Whatever the amount, it would be offset against the assistance New Zealand had given Singapore in the past. But Goh was "quite adamant about his need to get from the Australians a commitment on training facilities". Farrell got the firm impression from the meeting that no headway would be made regarding real estate until Canberra responded positively to Singapore's requests. Goh explained Singapore's long-term concern about "the emergence of an ill-disposed regime in Indonesia or, possibly Malaysia", a concern which Lee Kuan Yew also spoke about when he met Sir Keith Holyoake in May.[115] Goh hoped that this would not happen and there was no indication at present of

---

[113] "Five Power Defence: Conversation between the New Zealand and Singapore Prime Ministers at Singapore Airport, 4 May 1971 (Secret)", FCO 24/1000, National Archives of Singapore, Microfilm Number NAB 1476.

[114] Meeting between the UK Defence Secretary [Lord Carrington] and Australian, New Zealand and Singapore Ministers, Ministry of Defence, Whitehall, London, 15 April 1971 (Confidential), FCO 24/999, National Archives of Singapore, Microfilm Number NAB 1476.

[115] "Five Power Defence: Conversation between the New Zealand and Singapore Prime Ministers at Singapore Airport", 4 May 1971 (Secret), FCO 24/1000, National Archives of Singapore, Microfilm Number NAB 1476.

such a possibility but "Singapore had to be prepared to meet it if necessary". Goh added that the government "did not believe that Britain, Australia or New Zealand would be willing to help much, in the military sense, if such a development did occur". Singapore thus had to be ready to "go it alone" to ensure its long-term security, which is why it attached so much importance to the issue of training, particularly for tanks, artillery and strike aircraft.

Goh emphasised that Singapore was "fully committed to the Five-Power concept" but apart from the integrated air defence system, it was evident that Malaysia was not willing to give Singapore any assistance. He was not prepared, despite the urgings of his military advisers, to ask the Malaysians formally for such assistance because he knew, from the soundings he had taken, that these requests would be refused. In Goh's assessment, the Malaysian political situation was presently "very difficult" and "it would be counter-productive for Singapore to press the issue". He hoped that over time the Malaysians would "mellow and become more helpful" but in the meantime, Singapore had to secure other arrangements. Goh was aware that Kuala Lumpur would be "upset" if Australia and New Zealand provided the military training facilities that Singapore wanted. But he felt that Kuala Lumpur "must realise that Singapore's needs were urgent and surely they would prefer them to be provided by Australia (which they knew had considerable influence in Singapore) rather than by a non-Commonwealth country such as Israel". Apart from the issue of military training, Goh also complained that the size of the ANZUK bid for real estate was "excessive". (In an earlier 12 March conversation also with Farrell, Goh described the bid as "exorbitant".) Farrell reported that Goh spoke "at some length, and convincingly" about the difficulties Singapore was having in finding barrack accommodation for its own needs. Singapore just could not afford to let its own military requirements be hamstrung by an ANZUK bid for more than was needed. What could New Zealand do to help? Farrell said that while in Kuala Lumpur, he would urge Prime Minister Razak "to be a little more sympathetic to Singapore's needs" and he would also suggest to his New Zealand colleagues that they study any proposals from Singapore regarding training facilities in New Zealand. Goh said it would be useful but added that "by far the most useful thing New Zealand could do, at this stage, would be to urge the Australian government to look favourably on Singapore's request for training facilities". In sum, the critical issue for Singapore was training facilities. While the size of the ANZUK real estate bid was another bugbear, according to Goh it could be resolved quite quickly.[116]

---

[116] From Singapore to Wellington, "Five Power Defence – Talk with Singapore Minister of Defence, Dr Goh, from Minister of Defence (NZ)", 28 April 1971 (Secret), FCO 24/999, National Archives of Singapore, Microfilm Number NAB 1476.

The record of a meeting between Goh Keng Swee and Nicholas Parkinson (Australian High Commissioner to Singapore) on 8 June 1971 is both stark and revealing. The Defence Minister had wanted to meet Parkinson to check whether the Australian side had received Singapore's training requests. Goh wanted Parkinson to understand "what the game was all about" concerning rent and training. In Goh's words, the "whole Five Power business was a toothless paper tiger". There were only two possible threats to Singapore, and they were Indonesia and Malaysia, for both of which the FPDA would be of no help. Thus, if Canberra would not accede to Singapore's request for training facilities, "you can go home". Singapore would inform him of the requested rental charges shortly and he hoped that the Australians would find the rent demand "exorbitant" and realise that the only option was to accede to Singapore's training requests or "go home". If Australia provided the training facilities, Singapore would waive "the rent altogether". Singapore would also pay for all training requirements in Australia. Most important to Singapore were air and armour training. When Parkinson reiterated the difficulties that Australia faced in agreeing to Singapore's requests, Goh retorted that what he needed was "constructive help" and not constant harping on the difficulties. It was useless asking Singapore to seek facilities from Malaysia as "Singapore knew perfectly well that Malaysia would not allow Singapore tanks or aircraft to train in Malaysia". Parkinson asked Goh whether he should tell Canberra that the Singapore Government would opt out of the FPDA unless Australia acceded to Singapore's request. Goh's reply was "Yes... Tell them that bluntly". Goh had in fact moved his position from "provide us with training or pay rent" (which was what he told Australian Defence Minister John Gorton when they met in London in April 1971) to the extreme position of "provide us with training or go home". Parkinson, in his report, said he was sure there was some "bluff and overstatement" in what Goh said but it was difficult to judge how much.[117] The follow-up letter from Goh was more moderate in tone although the intention remained unchanged. In his letter of 10 June, Goh explained Singapore's request: *"Basically, the proposal is to station a small amount of military hardware in training areas in Australia, together with maintenance crews, and to rotate operational personnel and train them in the use of these weapons and equipment".*[118]

Finally, Goh told British High Commissioner Falle that it would "not be satisfactory" from the Singapore point of view if Canberra agreed to pay rent

---

[117] From Singapore to the Department of External Affairs, Canberra, 8 June 1971 (Secret), A4359, Item 221/4/31/4 PART 3.
[118] Even if the letter was written in less stark terms compared to the 8 June conversation, the thrust was essentially the same. See the memo "From Singapore to Department of External Affairs, Canberra", 10 June 1971 (Secret), A4359, Item 221/4/31/4 PART 3.

but did not provide training facilities. Rent would be reviewed in two or three years and the Singapore government might then decide that it was unsatisfactory. But if the Australians offered training facilities, "the permanence of the 5-Power arrangements would be assured". If Singapore could not get training in Australia, Singapore might have to seek assistance from a non-Commonwealth country.[119]

The British side was gravely concerned about the situation. As Lord Carrington had said, an ANZUK presence without ground troops would not be considered credible by the British. It would be a serious matter if one of the ANZUK countries withdrew its contingent from Singapore as it would cast doubt on the overall Five Power concept. It would cause Britain to reconsider its position.[120] Goh had told the British that aerial and armoured training was what Singapore needed most urgently.[121] In their discussions with the Australians, they expressed hope that Canberra could accede to many, if not all, of Singapore's training requests. London would also do what it could to help Singapore with its training needs. In the British assessment, the Indonesians and the Malaysians would not strongly oppose it.[122] Canberra was not unsympathetic to Singapore's needs but had to consider "domestic political problems…in a bid for training over such a large area on a semi-permanent basis" as well as Malaysian and Indonesian concerns.[123] The Indonesians did not express too much concern although Australian officials based in Jakarta (and Kuala Lumpur) recommended strongly against acceding to Singapore's request "as it is not in Australian interests to support the 'Israel of Southeast Asia'".[124] The Malaysian view was that they placed "great value" on the Five-Power Defence Cooperation and wished it to continue; they had "grave reservations" about the aerial and armoured training Singapore had requested; they "deplored the tactic of blackmail" adopted by Singapore; the decision was for the Australians to take but "as Malaysia had been approached, it wished to note that the Singaporean requests had not been made in the 5-Power

---

[119] From the British High Commission in Singapore to the Foreign and Commonwealth Office (FCO), "5-Power Defence", 15 June 1971 (Secret), FCO 24/1001, National Archives of Singapore, Microfilm Number NAB 1476.
[120] Meeting between the Defence Secretary and Australian, New Zealand and Singapore Ministers, Ministry of Defence, Whitehall, London, 15 April 1971 (Confidential), FCO 24/999, National Archives of Singapore, Microfilm Number NAB 1476.
[121] From the British High Commission in Singapore to the FCO, "5-Power Defence", 15 June 1971.
[122] From London to Department of External Affairs, Canberra, "Five Power – Singapore Training and Real Estate", 12 June 1971 (Secret), A4359, Item 221/4/31/4 PART 3.
[123] From the British High Commission, Canberra to the FCO, "Five Power Defence".
[124] From the British High Commission in Singapore to the FCO, "Real Estate", 27April 1971 (Confidential), FCO 24/999, National Archives of Singapore, Microfilm Number NAB 1476.

context and that to give way to them would not augur well for future 5-Power cooperation".[125]

The chief Malaysian objection, the Australians surmised, was tank training.[126] Having assured Kuala Lumpur that they would not make any training arrangements with Singapore which were not acceptable to the Malaysians, on 3 July, Australian Prime Minister William McMahon announced in Canberra that the Australian Government had agreed to a request by Singapore for their troops to train in Australia. McMahon further added that Kuala Lumpur had not made a similar request; if there were any, it would be considered under the terms of the FPDA. However, Lee Kuan Yew in his memoir recalled that in the 1970s when Singapore asked Australia for permission to use their training areas for military exercises, Canberra was "not forthcoming" till the 1980s. In contrast, New Zealand "readily agreed".[127] He probably meant that Canberra did not accede to all of Singapore's requests. Australian Foreign Minister Leslie Bury explained at a press conference in Kuala Lumpur in July 1971 that the reason for Singapore's request was that there was very little training space on the island and it was heavily populated. He further revealed that Malaysia was "not altogether delighted but was reasonably reconciled" to Singapore troops training in Australia.[128] The settlement of the training issue paved the way for the resolution of the rent negotiation which in turn made it possible for officials to dot the i's and cross the t's of the Notes and Annexes of the FPDA document.

In 1966 Goh Keng Swee remarked, "If the Governments of Singapore and Malaysia are unable effectively to cooperate in their common defence, this must adversely affect the efficacy of the defence arrangements with Britain, Australia and New Zealand who are expending large sums of money and men in retaining their military commitments in this region. So cooperate we must, but this cooperation must be as between two sovereign States and not as big brother and his satellite".[129] The Anglo–Malaysian Defence Agreement (AMDA) was eventually terminated

---

[125] From Canberra to London, Kuala Lumpur, Singapore and Wellington, "Five Power Defence", 16 June 1971 (Secret), FCO 24/1001, National Archives of Singapore, Microfilm Number NAB 1476.

[126] Australian Embassy, Jakarta, Inwards Cablegram from Kuala Lumpur, "Singapore Rent and Training", 19 June 1971 (Secret), A4359, Item 221/4/31/4 PART 3.

[127] Lee Kuan Yew, *From Third World to First, The Singapore Story: 1965–2000* (Singapore: Times Editions, 2000), p. 430. See also Tim Huxley, *Defending the Lion City: The Armed Forces of Singapore* (Sydney: Allen & Unwin, 2000), pp. 201–8.

[128] Australian Embassy, Jakarta, Inwards Cablegram from Kuala Lumpur, *Straits Times* Report of 10 July, 10 July 1971, A4359, Item 221/4/31/4 PART 3.

[129] Singapore Government Press Statement, MC. FE. 29 (Defence): Statement by Dr. Goh Keng Swee, Minister of Defence, at the Singapore Parliament, on 23 Feb. 1966.

on 1 November and the FPDA came into force on the same day as intended.[130] According to S.R. Nathan (Deputy Secretary, Ministry of Foreign Affairs at the time), the value of the Five Power arrangements from the Singapore point of view was that it enabled Singapore to go ahead and build its own economy. This was important to prevent the spread of communism. Nathan cited the example of Japan "which had built up a strong economy to the detriment of communist influence".[131] During his visit to New Zealand in 1975, Lee Kuan Yew gave credit to the FPDA for the "steadying influence" which it exerted. According to Lee, while it was no longer necessary to maintain ground forces in Singapore, "there was psychological value in perpetuating the concept of the Arrangements".[132]

Those were the critical years of the formation of the FPDA. Fifty years later, Singapore still sees relevance in the FPDA. As Lee Hsien Loong wrote in a Facebook post, "the FPDA is the second-oldest military partnership in the world (after NATO). I'm glad it is still active and relevant today. This cooperation fosters peace and security in the region, and Singapore continues to support it in a very different world".[133]

However difficult the relationships between Singapore and its immediate neighbours might be at times, it is worth recalling what Goh Keng Swee said on the topic in 1971. According to Goh, many people were inclined to draw similarities between Singapore and Israel, and indeed there were some points of resemblance, such as standard of living and the level of technology as compared to Singapore's neighbours. But it would be "dangerous to read too much into the similarities" between the two countries. There were at least four fundamental differences: (a) while Singapore's neighbours might dislike and envy Singapore, they "do not hate" Singapore in the way the Arabs hate Israel; (b) the superpowers were not competing as in the Middle East with the Russians supporting the Arab cause and the Americans supporting Israel; (c) the Singapore economy, unlike Israel's, is extremely vulnerable to economic blockades. The imposition of a naval blockade would be regarded by Singapore as sufficient *casus belli*; and (d) unlike

---

[130] "Five Power Defence Arrangements Come into Effect" (Statement by the Australian Minister of Defence, David Fairbairn), 1 Nov. 1971 (For Press), A4359, Item 221/4/31/4 PART 3.
[131] From the Australian High Commission in Singapore to the Department of External Affairs, Canberra, "Record of Conversation held between Mr. S.R. Nathan, Deputy Secretary, Ministry of Foreign Affairs, Singapore, and Mr. A.G.D White, First Secretary, Australian High Commission", 9 Jan. 1970, A 1838/318, Item 3024/12 (Part 1), NAB 780.
[132] From the British High Commission in Wellington to the FCO, "Visit to New Zealand of the Singapore Prime Minister", 9 April 1975, FCO 15/2025.
[133] Lee Hsien Loong, Facebook post, 17 Oct. 2021 (accessed 17 Oct. 2021); see also Transcript of Doorstop Interview with Minister for Defence Dr Ng Eng Hen at Marina Barrage for FPDA 50 Flypast, 18 Oct. 2021, at https://www.mindef.gov.sg/web/portal/mindef/news-and-events/latest-releases/article-detail/2021/october/18oct21_transcript (accessed 19 Oct. 2021).

Israel which was established as a Jewish state, Singapore is multi-racial despite its Chinese majority population. Every attempt to turn Singapore into another "China" is strenuously resisted. In Goh's prognosis, he did not think that there is "any realistic danger of war" between Singapore and her neighbours unless a "madcap regime" were established in either or both these countries. But since Singapore cannot be certain that this would not happen, "it is necessary for us to continue to develop our military strength".[134]

Addressing the issue of finding a meaningful role for Singapore in Southeast Asia, Goh said, "if we come down to brass tacks, this really means getting on better terms with our two neighbours, Malaysia and Indonesia, and establishing meaningful ties with other countries in the region". He went on to say that "in spite of universal acceptance of the benefits of regional cooperation…we all know that the position is far from good". He cautioned, "if we are not careful, it will get worse as the gap between our standard of living and theirs widens in the seventies".[135] It is worth quoting a now declassified 1967 "Top Secret" British report in some detail here. According to British assessment, Singapore had "no significant natural resources and hitherto her undoubted prosperity by Asian standards has depended on her position as the entrepôt point for a large part of Malaysia's international trade; the entrepôt trade with Indonesia and other countries in Southeast Asia; and the presence of the British base". However, since the separation, Malaysia had begun "to look increasingly to her own resources for her international trade…and has shown no interest in the creation of a common market with Singapore". The report further noted that it was not clear whether Singapore's entrepôt trade with Indonesia could be re-established at anything like the pre-Confrontation level. In summary, the British report noted that "though the growth rate in Singapore in recent years had been impressive, the underlying trends are far from encouraging and cast doubt as to whether in the long-term Singapore could maintain a viable economy at the present standard of living".[136] The Singapore economy now, as everyone knows, has surpassed all expectations.

---

[134] Closing Address by Dr. Goh Keng Swee, Minister of Defence, at the 3rd Singapore Command and Staff College (SCSC) Course, 19 Nov. 1971. This is one of the most important speeches to read for an understanding of the thinking behind the military dimension of Singapore's Grand Strategy. See also Lee Kuan Yew, *Hard Truths To Keep Singapore Going* (Singapore: Straits Times Press, 2011), pp. 322–3.
[135] Text of Speech by the Minister for Defence, Dr. Goh Keng Swee, at the Adult Education Board Forum on "Qualities Required in the Seventies" at the University of Singapore, 22 Nov. 1970.
[136] Defence Review Working Party to Cabinet, "Politico-Military and Economic Implications of Proposed Force Reductions in the Far East", 4 April 1967 (Top Secret), FCO 24/45, NAB 1276 018.

CHAPTER 2

The Lee Kuan Yew Years (1965–90): Singapore and the World

I

In Chapter 1, we focused on what Lee Kuan Yew described as dealing with "more urgent matters first": Singapore's strategy with regards to its immediate and most important neighbours Malaysia and Indonesia, as well as the critical matter of defence. In this chapter, the focus is on Singapore's strategy and its navigation through the complex environment beyond its immediate surroundings in the early years of independence and particularly on the United States and China.

Singapore became independent during the twin periods of Decolonisation and the Cold War, some may say, the height of the Cold War. "The primary task of our foreign policy", in the words of Singapore's first Foreign Minister, S. Rajaratnam, "will always be to safeguard our independence from external threats. We shall try to do this by establishing friendly relations with all countries, particularly those nearest to us".[1]

Immediately upon independence, Singapore declared itself "non-aligned". Rajaratnam explained that this was not "simply a case of Singapore following a current Afro-Asian fad". There was a logic to Singapore's non-alignment choice. Lee Kuan Yew had on various occasions described Singapore as "the hub of Southeast Asia", "the cockpit of a big power conflict between East and West", "the heart" and "linchpin" of Southeast Asia.[2] As Rajaratnam explained, Singapore

---

[1] Speech by the Minister of Foreign Affairs (Mr. S. Rajaratnam), 16 Dec. 1965.
[2] Transcript of the Proceedings (slightly edited) of a Meeting of Singapore and Malaysian PAP Leaders, with a Following Press Conference at the Cabinet Office, City Hall, 12 Aug. 1965; Transcript of an Interview given by the Prime Minister, Mr. Lee Kuan Yew, to Four Foreign Correspondents, 14 Aug. 1965, at the Studio of Television Singapura.

was seen by the world and by its neighbours as a "strategic key" in the region. As such, Singapore's foreign and defence policy must ensure that the country did not become "the pawn of an outside power" and would not "increase tensions and fears amongst [its] neighbours". Choosing "Alignment" would jeopardise its recently won independence: "when a small country like Singapore aligns itself with a big power, there is no doubt as to who keeps in step with whose policies…a policy of alignment with a big power means promotion not of our national interests but those of the big power".[3] In another speech a decade later, Rajaratnam compared the influence of a major power to the gravitational pull of the sun: "when there are many suns the gravitational pull of each is not only weakened but also, by a judicious use of the pulls and counterpulls of gravitational forces, the minor planets acquire a greater freedom of navigation". Thus, Singapore's capacity "to resist big power pressure would be greater if there were a multiplicity of powers present in the region".[4]

While the above position is valid to a point, Lee Kuan Yew qualified that while Singapore would be "non-aligned as far as power-bloc conflicts are concerned", "I am not neutral where my survival is concerned". Lee said that when Singapore had settled "more urgent matters first", he still had to explain his position in regard to "our relationship with the Afro-Asian countries…because some of the Afro-Asian countries although they know me and they know that I am not a little puppet, may be a bit unhappy about the [British] bases". Lee's explanation was that Singapore could not "make a concession" with regard to the bases because "this is my survival". "If they can devise a formula" to ensure the survival of Singapore and Malaysia as well ("because the nexus is too tight" [being] "my water and my hinterland"), Lee said he was prepared to consider it but "there is no alternative…there must be some defence arrangement which will prevent a bigger neighbour with a vaster army, much greater fire power from just over-running us". This point was reiterated by both Rajaratnam and Toh Chin Chye during their two-month tours of the Afro-Asian countries, the Soviet Union and Yugoslavia.[5] The objectives of the tour, following Singapore's admission as the 117th member of the United Nations on 21 September 1965, were to assure these countries that:

---

[3] Speech by the Minister of Foreign Affairs (Mr. S. Rajaratnam), 16 Dec. 1965.
[4] Qtd. in Terence Chong and Darinee Alagirisamy, "Chasing Ideals, Accepting Practicalities, Banishing Ghosts", 2 July 2021, *Intellectuals SG*, at https://sgintellectuals.medium.com/chasing-ideals-accepting-practicalities-banishing-ghosts-f8840992aac1 (accessed 10 Jan. 2023).
[5] Transcript of an Interview Given by the Prime Minister, Mr. Lee Kuan Yew, to Four Foreign Correspondents on 14 August 1965, at the Studio of Television Singapura.

(a) the British bases in Singapore were essential for its security and survival, and would not be used for "aggressive purposes"; the continued presence of the bases thus did not make Singapore a 'neo-colonialist' state;
(b) Singapore intended to expand trade with Communist China and the Soviet Union, thus confirming its non-aligned posture;
(c) the Afro-Asian countries should acknowledge Singapore's independence by supporting Singapore's bid to attend the forthcoming Afro-Asian Conference;
(d) Singapore must trade with all to survive.[6]

As Rajaratnam explained in Parliament on 17 December 1965, since Singapore was a country economically dependent on trade, the promotion of trade with as many countries as possible would be a major objective of Singapore's foreign policy. "The only criterion for trade is whether trade with another country is in our economic interest, because promotion of our economic interest is promotion of our national interest". There could however be occasions when "economic interests may have to be sacrificed to safeguard some important political interests".[7]

Singapore's strategy with regards to non-alignment is however complex. As Kawin Wilairat has noted, the "initial overture" to this group of newly decolonised countries was "essentially motivated by the need to gain international recognition and acceptance, especially among the nonaligned countries", of which the Afro-Asian bloc formed the majority. These countries, though not all, were "sceptical" about Singapore's independence and the "continuing presence of British naval bases".[8] Lee Kuan Yew was able to win them over, particularly the African nations. As Peter Boyce has noted, no country challenged Singapore's admission to the United Nations and "the welcome from Africa was particularly warm". Indeed, speaking on behalf of the African group of countries, the Tanzanian delegate said that Singapore was "destined to play a positive part in the liberation of peoples who are still under colonial yoke".[9]

The American consulate in Singapore astutely noted that while the Singapore leadership managed to establish their non-aligned image—for example, Singapore's relation with Cambodia during the early years of independence was

---

[6] From the American Consulate to the US Department of State, 2 Oct. 1965, RG 59, Box 2651, POL 2-1 Singapore 1/1/65.
[7] Speech by the Minister of Foreign Affairs (Mr. S. Rajaratnam), 17 Dec. 1965.
[8] Kawin Wilairat, *Singapore's Foreign Policy: A Study of the Foreign Policy System of a City-State*, unpublished PhD dissertation, Georgetown University, 1975, p. 305.
[9] Peter Boyce, *Malaysia & Singapore in International Diplomacy: Documents and Commentaries* (Sydney: Sydney University Press, 1968), p. 41.

"particularly close"—Singapore was actually "pro-western in fact and non-aligned in image". That was Singapore's usefulness, "for were we to seek to 'commit' Singapore or otherwise erode that non-aligned image, Singapore's usefulness as a bridge would be lost". The February 1966 policy paper recommended that the United States should "therefore resist any temptation to press too hard in the direction of 'improving relations', recognising, rather, that if Singapore can maintain a British base and offer us R&R and purchasing facilities for Vietnam while still preserving a potential for influence with the non-aligned countries, we should consider ourselves fortunate indeed".[10] Another comment, written towards the end of 1966, mentioned that Lee Kuan Yew had become disillusioned with the concept of Afro-Asian solidarity.[11] Kawin Wilairat noted that because of the different pace and forms of economic development as well the different political priorities between Southeast Asia and Africa, Singapore concluded that "the most that can be expected from Afro-Asian relations is the occasional airing of views and support for similar ideological concerns". Closely connected to Afro-Asia is the Non-Aligned Movement of which Singapore also became very critical. Lee was of the view that the Non-Aligned Movement should focus more on "real issues of economic development" rather than indulge in "political rhetoric". By 1971, according to Wilairat, "Singapore's foreign policy had undergone a major shift—the Afro-Asian symbols and slogans had been dropped, and a decidedly pro-Western stance adopted".[12]

II

This is perhaps the appropriate place to bring both the United States and Communist China into the discussion of Singapore's Grand Strategy. To understand the evolution of Singapore's attitude towards the United States, we must begin with this passage from Lee's memoirs: "Britain and the empire constituted the world that I had known all my life, a world in which the British were central to our survival; while we wanted freedom to decide what we should do with our lives, we also wanted and needed our long historical, cultural and economic ties to be maintained".[13]

---

[10] From the American Consulate in Singapore to the US Department of State, "Singapore Policy Assessment", 25 Feb. 1966, RG 59, Box 2451, POL 6 – Singapore 1/1/65.
[11] From the American Embassy in Singapore to the Department of State, "Singapore Government's Attitudes toward Asian Regional Organizations", 16 Sept. 1966, RG 59, Box 2652, POL 8 – Singapore 1/1/66.
[12] See Wilairat, *Singapore's Foreign Policy*, pp. 423, 442–7.
[13] Lee Kuan Yew, *The Singapore Story* (Singapore: Singapore Press Holdings, 1998), p. 455.

In comparison, in August 1965, the Singapore leadership was unfamiliar with the United States. As the American Consul General noted, all the senior Singapore officials spoke Anglo-English and had been schooled under British rule: "their direct knowledge of the United States is practically nil... Their orientation is Afro-Asian, not Western, and the political environment in Singapore is fertile ground for anti-American barbs". Most were hesitant to associate publicly with the United States although in private conversations, they showed "lively interest in the United States and in ways in which the American experience or individual Americans and private American institutions might be helpful to Singapore and Malaysia".[14] Both George (G.G.) Thomson (Director of Political Study Centre, Singapore) and Devan Nair (Secretary General, National Trade Union Congress) both believed that Lee had a distorted view of US foreign policy.[15]

Similarly, the Americans were also unfamiliar with Singapore and did not know Lee Kuan Yew well, if at all. Henry Thayer (US Ambassador to Singapore, 1980–84) recalled that before 1980, the United States knew little of Singapore and had very "limited access" to the Singapore leadership. Thus, one of his principal tasks as ambassador was "to find out what the Singapore leadership, from Prime Minister Lee on down, was thinking".[16] Although Lee was not a communist, he and the People's Action Party (PAP) were "treated with suspicion".[17] Until 1968 when the British announced the decision to withdraw "east of Suez", Washington had left the security of Malaysia and Singapore in the hands of London. It was a burden-sharing arrangement between the United States and Britain to ensure that the region did not fall into the communist orbit. Unsurprisingly, like Lee, the US did not welcome the British retreat. Indeed, in a 19 September 1966 conversation between Goh Keng Swee and William Bundy (Assistant Secretary of State, Bureau

---

[14] From the American Consulate in Singapore to the Department of State, "Singapore Government Officialdom and Attitudes towards the United States", 21 Dec. 1964, RG 59, Box 2452, POL 15-1 Malaysia.

[15] From the American Consulate in Singapore to the Department of State, 21 May 1964, RG 59, Box 2452, POL 15-1 Malaysia.

[16] The Association for Diplomatic Studies and Training (ADST), Foreign Affairs Oral History Project, "Ambassador Harry E.T. Thayer, interviewed by Charles Stuart Kennedy" (1990), the pdf can be accessed through the link to his name at https://adst.org/oral-history/oral-history-interviews/#gsc.tab=0 (accessed 4 Jan. 2023).

[17] Philip Hsiaopong Liu, "Love the Tree, Love the Branch: Beijing's Friendship with Lee Kuan Yew, 1954–1965", *China Quarterly* 242 (June 2020): 557. Liu cites documents from the US National Archives, College Park, Maryland. The Americans believed Lee would create a "Socialist Malaya oriented towards mainland China". See also James J. Halsema (Information Officer, USIS, Singapore 1949–52), ADST Oral Histories: " Lee was regarded with rather a great deal of suspicion…because he was considered pretty far over to the left…"; the source can be found in a pdf at the ADST Foreign Affairs Oral History Project website (see fn 16) by the link to his name.

of East Asian and Pacific Affairs [US]), Bundy had assured Goh that Washington "would do everything possible" to get the British to stay.[18]

An October 1965 US Department of State analysis revealed that prior to Singapore's separation from Malaysia that year, Lee "seemed to consider [the] US worth cultivating" because he hoped that the Tunku would realise that he had to come to terms with Lee and his People's Action Party if the Commonwealth and the United States "presented him with [a] common front". The US was however reluctant to become involved and this was apparently misinterpreted by Lee as a US attempt to "reserve [the US'] position in event it became necessary to substitute US for UK presence". Lee "seems to have concluded" that while the US had been "potentially useful before separation", it had now become "a real threat", especially given its hostility to non-alignment and the "pro-US stance of the Malaysian government". Lee had reportedly told several people of the "real danger" to Singapore of a US "intervention on the side of the Malaysian government in the event of a racial conflict in Malaysia". This was one reason for the delay in acceding to the US request on 22 November 1965 to elevate the Consulate General in Singapore to Embassy status. According to E.W. Barker (Minister for Law), the Singapore government had decided that it was necessary to "build a fire" under Washington.[19] Lee was also concerned about the normalisation of Malaysian–Indonesian relations post-Confrontation and its possible ramifications (revival of Maphilindo) for Singapore. He was convinced that the US would throw its support behind "Pan-Malayan regional cooperation" and "sacrifice" the overseas Chinese which the Americans regarded as "politically unreliable" anyway.[20] Lee related that news reporters in New York had asked Foreign Minister Rajaratnam if Singapore would eventually become a "province of China", considering that "90 per cent of its population is Chinese".[21] Lim Kim San (Singapore's Minister of Finance) also alleged that the US was "anti-Chinese" and that it looked upon Singapore as an "unreliable 'Third China'". The US Embassy in Singapore reported that Lim "appears attached to this belief, which is fairly pervasive among GOS [Government of Singapore] leaders".[22]

---

[18] Memorandum of Conversation, 19 Sept. 1966, RG 59, Box Number 2652, POL Singapore – A.
[19] From the American Consulate in Singapore to the Department of State, 10 Dec. 1965, RG 50, Box 2651, POL 2-1/Singapore 10/16/65.
[20] From the American Consulate in Singapore to the Department of State, 15 Oct. 1965, RG 59, Box 2652, POL 15-1/Singapore 1/1/65.
[21] From the American Consulate in Singapore to the Department of State, 5 Oct. 1965, RG 59, Box 2653, POL – Political Affairs & Relations/Singapore-US.
[22] From the American Embassy in Singapore to the Department of State, 7 July 1966, RG 59, Box 2652, POL 15-1/Singapore 1/1/65.

Washington recognised that given Lee's attitude towards the US, the Americans' lack of direct communication with Lee would only feed on itself, accentuate Lee's isolation and produce "inevitably further strains" in Singapore–US relations. But Washington also did not want to encourage "Lee's misconception" that US strategic interest in Singapore placed him "in the dominant position and [the US] can be brought to heel by hardnosed bargaining and threats of Barisan take-over".[23]

The above may help us better understand Lee Kuan Yew's well-known diatribe against the US on 31 August 1965 which he repeated on 14 September. During a "carefully planned" press conference on 31 August, Lee "made public for the first time anti-American views which he has frequently expressed in private". He described the US conduct of its foreign relations as shallow and lacking in wisdom. He emphasised that "if the British bases go, there will be no American bases in Singapore".[24] US officials believed that Lee "exploited three personal incidents as grist for his larger purpose"; this was "a calculated ploy to attain membership in the Afro-Asian club and appeal to Indonesia, while at the same time reminding the Commonwealth that there can no substitute for their continuing presence in Singapore".[25] George Bogaars (Permanent Secretary of Defence) met with US consulate officials soon after Lee's 31 August press conference and conveyed the following points. He hoped the US "understood the motivation behind" Lee's anti-US diatribe, which was to "gain Afro-Asian acceptance" and timed to "set the stage" for the forthcoming Afro-Asian tour by the deputy Prime Minister and Foreign Minister. Lee also felt that it was necessary to make "incontrovertibly clear" that Singapore was in control of the bases. Lee also wanted to "squelch" the opposition (Barisan) efforts to exploit the base issue. Bogaars believed that Lee would continue to make "anti-American noises", particularly with reference to the usage of the Singapore bases. It is worth noting here that on 15 August 1965, Lee had told James Bell (US Ambassador to Malaysia) that he was "under some pressure" regarding the British bases. He also asked to meet Bell privately to discuss Singapore's foreign policy. Lee said he preferred to talk to Bell given their

---

[23] From the Department of State to the American Embassy in Kuala Lumpur, Malaysia, RG 59, Box 2652, POL 15-1/Singapore 1/1/65.
[24] From the American Consulate in Singapore to the Department of State, 4 Sept. 1965, RG 59, Box 2651, POL 2-1/Singapore 1/1/65; from the American Consulate in Singapore to the Department of State, 18 Sept. 1965, RG 59, Box 2651, POL 2-1/Singapore 1/1/65. See also Daniel Chua, *US-Singapore Relations, 1965–1975: Strategic Non-Alignment in the Cold War* (Singapore: NUS Press, 2017), pp. 63–72.
[25] From the American Consulate in Singapore to the Department of State, 4 Sept. 1965, RG 59, Box 2651, POL 2-1/Singapore 1/1/65

previous friendship rather than the Consul General. Bell drove to Singapore to meet Lee the next day.[26]

Bogaars also reconfirmed that the Ministry of Defence would not interfere with the existing British–US arrangement of transporting South Vietnamese officers to Singapore for training at the Johore Jungle Warfare School.[27] E.W. Barker (Minister of National Development and acting Foreign Minister while Rajaratnam was on his Afro-Asia tour) who was "visibly embarrassed by Lee's continued sniping at the US" told the American Consul General that Lee knew what he was doing but added his assurance off the record that the Singapore government was well aware it "cannot afford to intimidate the US".[28] It is worth noting that the American side chose not to respond to Lee's attacks.

Lee indeed was cognisant of the indispensability of US power in the region. He told Surenda Singh (Indian High Commissioner to Singapore), that while he had his own difficulties with the US and had often been critical of US policies, "anyone who was not a communist and wanted to see the US leave Southeast Asia was a fool". Lee said that while larger countries such as Japan and India could "afford to indulge themselves in aloofness from the struggle", smaller nations "understand that should the Americans withdraw from Southeast Asia, the Chinese will promptly fill the vacuum" and that "this would be the end of their independence".[29]

Lee Kuan Yew met US Ambassador Extraordinary and Plenipotentiary James D. Bello on 26 March 1966; this was the "first time Lee had asked to see any US official since August 1965". According to Lee, he had asked to see the Ambassador in a spirit of letting "bygones be bygones" and to signal the opening of a "new era in US–Singapore relations".[30] On 4 April 1966, the Consulate General of the USA in Singapore was finally elevated to the status of an Embassy. A press release on the same day announced the establishment of full diplomatic relations.[31] Meanwhile, both countries had reached agreement on the modalities

---

[26] From the American Embassy in Kuala Lumpur, Malaysia to the Department of State, 15 Aug. 1965, RG 59, Box 2653, POL 7 Singapore.
[27] From the American Consulate in Singapore to the Department of State, 1 Sept. 1965, RG 59, Box 2653, POL – Political Affairs & Relations/Singapore-US.
[28] From the American Consulate in Singapore to the Department of State, 5 Oct. 1965, RG 59, Box 2653, POL – Political Affairs & Relations/Singapore-US.
[29] From the American Embassy in New Delhi, India to the Department of State, 12 Sept. 1966, RG 59, Box 2651, POL 7 – Visits & Meetings/Singapore 1/1/65.
[30] From the American Consulate in Singapore to the Department of State, 3 April 1966, RG 59, Box 2651, POL 22-1/Singapore 1/1/66.
[31] From the American Embassy in Singapore to the Department of State, 10 April 1966, RG 59, Box 2651, POL 22-1/Singapore 1/1/66.

of a Vietnam Rest and Recreation (R&R) programme in Singapore on 19 March 1966 and the first R&R group, comprising 74 men, arrived in Singapore on 31 March and departed on 5 April, without incident.[32] Henceforth, except for the periodic hiccups expected in all relationships, Singapore–US relations have been smooth. That said, the Carter administration (1977–81) was a low-point given President Carter's focus on human rights and lack of interest in Southeast Asia; this was a period, thankfully brief in the view of the Singapore leadership, where the interests of both countries did not coincide.

III

Of the early speeches Lee Kuan Yew delivered in the immediate years after Singapore became independent, perhaps the most memorable, if not the most significant, is that entitled "Big and Small Fishes in Asian Waters", delivered on 15 June 1966, not long after the opening of a "new era in US–Singapore relations". This speech, delivered in anticipation of the end of Indonesia–Malaysia Confrontation, was preceded by Lee's response to a question regarding Singapore as a "nut" and Malaysia and Indonesia together as the "joined-up nutcracker". In his response, Lee recalled reading an account in Milovan Djilas's book, *Conversations with Stalin* of a conversation between Stalin and Tito. Stalin told Tito, "Why not swallow Albania?" But the shrewd Tito did not do that because according to Djilas, if Yugoslavia had done it, it might not be still there. Lee provided a fish allegory: "The big fish says to the medium-sized fish, 'Why not swallow up the small one?' And the medium-sized fish if it is sufficiently unthinking goes and does it. Then, the big fish will eat not only the medium one, but he will also have the smaller one! And I think that would be a more satisfactory meal all around because both will be eaten up in one gulp".[33] It is obvious who the small, medium and big fish are to which Lee was referring.

US officials, amongst others, read the speech very carefully: "Lee spoke in parables, conveying his meaning clearly enough but making himself a difficult target for anyone who found [his] speech objectionable".[34] This was a wide-ranging/sprawling speech which set out Lee's reading of the nature of international

---

[32] Ibid.
[33] "Transcript of a Press Conference Given by the Prime Minister, Mr. Lee Kuan Yew, at City Hall to Local and Foreign Correspondents, 2 June 1966".
[34] From the American Embassy in Singapore to the Department of State, 17 June 1966, RG 59, Box 2652, POL 15-1/Singapore 1/1/65.

relations.[35] Pertaining to the subject of Singapore's grand strategy, two related points are worth highlighting:

(a) According to Lee, while the best recourse for small fishes is to be "friends with both medium and big fish", he cautioned that we should never take the future for granted or believe that decolonisation meant reverting to "some idyllic, romantic past; that before the white man came, we were all Asians together, loving each other, living in peace and helping each other and that all were happy". In fact, before the white man came, "there were bigger fish chasing small fish and smaller fish chasing shrimps" (from a Chinese proverb, "Big fish eat small fish; small fish eat shrimps"). Without saying so, he implied that Singapore, being the smallest in the region, was a shrimp. But "there are various types of shrimps. Some shrimps stay alive…Species in nature develop defence mechanisms. Some shrimps are poisonous: they sting. If you eat them, you will get digestive upsets". Thus, Singapore has got "to discover its own survival techniques".

(b) There needed to be a new balance of power in the region which must be non-racial or multi-racial and underpinned by some external powers, e.g. the US, Britain and others. If problems in the region were resolved along ethnic lines, it would be the "big fishes that will dominate Asian waters in the sense that ultimately the demographic boundaries will be decided by the big fishes in Asia". Thus, what should emerge would be "a new power structure in which the legitimate interests of the big powers are conceded, and the legitimate interests of the middle and smaller powers are respected". Lee was concerned that the US and Britain might not be able to maintain their commitments in the region for more than another decade, and there would be pressure to get the West out of Asia.

The British decision to withdraw from the region (see the previous chapter) heightened the importance of the United States in Singapore's grand strategy and expedited Singapore's engagement with the US. Lee Kuan Yew visited the US for the first time in October 1967; the main objective of the visit was, in his words, "to try to persuade the United States Government that it was needed in Southeast Asia and that the countries of the region did not have the power to go it alone".[36] Rajaratnam in a 1968 speech echoed Lee's sentiments when he said that a country

---

[35] "Transcript of a Talk Given by the Prime Minister, Mr. Lee Kuan Yew, on the Subject 'Big and Small Fishes in Asian Waters' at a Meeting of the University of Singapore Democratic Socialist Club at the University Campus, 15 June 1966".

[36] From the Australian Embassy in Washington DC to the Australian Department of External Affairs, 26 Oct. 1967, "Visit of Prime Minister of Singapore", A1838, Item 3024/11/161 Part 2, Singapore-Relations with United States of America.

of America's size and strength could not opt out of Asia and that if America stopped worrying about Asia, other countries would do so because the region is "too big, too rich and too important a chunk of territory to be forgotten".[37] Lee's belief that the region needed a balance of power explains Singapore's lack of support for the Malaysian idea of ZOPFAN (Zone of Peace, Freedom and Neutrality) although Singapore signed the "aspirational" declaration in the name of ASEAN solidarity.

We now know from declassified American and Australian archival documents that the US was interested in using the naval base facilities in Singapore and used the Australians as the go-between/middleman in the discussions. The Australians were apparently unsure how far Singapore "would be prepared to go with direct United States involvement". They noted that Singapore had so far shown "a considerable willingness to have an American presence and contact provided it is discreet and out of sight". The Australians were of the view that it would be easier for Singapore to accept American presence "if it could be done under some form of joint control, preferably with a Commonwealth flavour".[38] At the same time, Singapore was also keen to purchase military equipment from the United States. Not all of Singapore's requests/wish lists were granted or approved immediately.[39]

While Lee believed a balance of power was necessary for the security of Singapore and the region, and he was interested both in allowing the US to use Singapore's naval facilities and in establishing closer commercial relations with the United States, he was clear that in the long-term interests of the region there should not be any "permanent occupation or permanent establishment of American occupation forces or armed forces in South and Southeast Asia". He remained consistent in his view even though, in 1971, his relationship with the US had improved considerably. "We do not want a US base in Singapore...I do not want a Russian base, nor do I want a US base", he stated categorically.[40]

In our discussion of the role of the United States in Singapore's grand strategy, we cannot avoid mentioning the Vietnam War. Lee Kuan Yew had spoken frequently about the war from 1965 to the end of the war in 1975. His

---

[37] Text of the speech by the Minister of Foreign Affairs and Labour, S. Rajaratnam, at a dinner organised by *Time* magazine, 6 Oct. 1968.

[38] From the Australian High Commission to the Department of External Affairs, Canberra, 4 June 1968, A1838, Item 3024/11/161 Part 2, Singapore -Relations with United States of America. Documents in this folder/file deal mainly with American interest in the Singapore naval base and Singapore's interest in purchasing military hardware from the United States.

[39] See documents in A1838, Item 3024/11/161 Part 2 and Part 3, Singapore-Relations with United States of America.

[40] Transcript of interview with Prime Minister Lee Kuan Yew by Mims Thomson, UPI, 19 March 1971.

views were complex; he had been critical of the American conduct of the war but basically, he had supported the American position[41] yet he did not wish to lose his non-aligned credentials. For Lee, American involvement in Vietnam was buying time for Southeast Asian countries including Singapore to develop. It also contributed to stiffening the resolve of the non-communist Southeast Asian countries to resist Communism.

However, in 1966, during the dialogue session of his "Big and Small Fishes in Asian Waters" speech, he cautioned against assuming that the United States would always consider South Vietnam fundamental to its prestige and to the security of Southeast Asia. It was therefore unrealistic to believe that the Americans would keep pouring in troops and resources indefinitely. He reckoned that if the Johnson administration did not succumb to domestic pressure to pull out before 1968, the election in 1972 could decide the matter. "Even if it didn't happen in 1972, it would come in 1976, which is only 10 years away". Thus, it was necessary to be realistic and think beyond that. "But whilst we buy time, if we just sit down and believe people are going to buy time for ever after for us, then we deserve to perish", he concluded.[42]

IV

We now turn to the People's Republic of China (PRC), or Communist China for short. In his speech on 16 December 1965, Foreign Minister S. Rajaratnam pointed out that while Singapore, "generally speaking", was "sincere in our wish to be friendly with all countries which want to be friends with us, in the hard world of international realities, there are bound to be degrees of friendship between countries". Those closest were naturally the countries "whose foreign policy principles and deeds coincide with our national interests and our basic aspiration".[43] The PRC during this period certainly did not belong to this category of countries. But Rajaratnam went on to say that things could change, and "in international politics, it is not wise to formulate foreign policies on the basis of permanent enemies".[44]

---

[41] For details, see Ang Cheng Guan, *Southeast Asia and the Vietnam War* (London: Routledge, 2010); Ang Cheng Guan, "Singapore and the Vietnam War", *Journal of Southeast Asian Studies* 40, no. 2 (June 2009): 1–32.
[42] "Transcript of a Talk Given by the Prime Minister, Mr. Lee Kuan Yew, on the Subject 'Big and Small Fishes in Asian Waters' at a Meeting of the University of Singapore Democratic Socialist Club at the University Campus, 15 June 1966".
[43] Speech by the Minister of Foreign Affairs (Mr. S. Rajaratnam), 16 Dec. 1965.
[44] Ibid.

Singapore from very early on had recognised the strategic importance of the PRC: "The whole world has got to live with 'Mainland China' as you call it... The countries in Southeast Asia are not big enough to come to terms with China on their own. It will have to be up to the major powers to come to some accommodation... Then the countries of Southeast Asia can find accommodation with China within the framework of the United Nations, I hope...".[45] In Lee's analysis, one big power that would never lose interest in Southeast Asia was China and we could not "afford to forget that". The border regions surrounding China were "vital to her and they should be neutral, if not positively friendly. And if you get weak and unstable situations, the manipulation that is possible—not with any military effort, just sheer economic manipulation and...[thrown] in with the ideological subversion, this would become quite a Balkanised situation".[46] He believed the Chinese were "determined, as a people, to unify and build a modern, wealthy Chinese nation". When China became prosperous, "good luck to me, because I will be much safer".[47] In an October 1967 American TV interview, he said that having lost China, they "have got to live with it". China was now run by a group of men who wanted China to become a great power. "Why shouldn't they be great?" he asked. "You can't stop them".[48]

A 1967 comment on China by Goh Keng Swee is worth quoting for its prescience: "The great problem that China poses and to which we in Asia have yet to find a solution is this. If, by the 1990s or in the early decades of the 21st century, the Communist system in China were to produce a modern industrial state equipped with all the technological advances, what will happen to the rest of Asia if it fails to achieve similar progress?"[49]

There was another reason for the importance of the PRC to Singapore, which was not publicly stated: the "very long-term possibility that China could eventually offer Singapore some sort of protection against Malay nationalism". In the short and medium term, however, China, because of its promotion of

---

[45] Interview (Hugh D.S. Greenway, *Time/Life* Bureau Chief, Southeast Asia) with the Prime Minister, Mr. Lee Kuan Yew, 10 June 1969.
[46] Transcript of an interview with Lee Kuan Yew by Anthony Rendell, London, Australian Broadcasting Commission, 17 Sept. 1966.
[47] *Meet the Press,* NBC (US), 22 Oct. 1967.
[48] Ibid.; see also Henry Kamm, "Interview with the Prime Minister", *New York Times*, 26 May 1971 for a very detailed analysis of China by Lee; see also text of speech by Mr. S. Rajaratnam, Minister of Foreign Affairs and Labour, at the International Press Institute World Assembly Luncheon, Hong Kong, 18 May 1970 for a similar view of China being "determined to sustain its claim to be a global power".
[49] Goh Keng Swee, *The Economics of Modernisation* (Singapore: Federal Publications, 1972), p. 23.

the communist ideology and the continued risk of internal subversion, was still perceived as "a threat".[50] An Australian 1968 report noted that while Lee Kuan Yew and his ministers knew that they "could not long survive in a chauvinistic and pro-Peking Singapore", "they do not rule out the possibility that future generations may choose to align closely with China if the balance of power should swing against the West in Southeast Asia". The report further observed that Singapore's approach was "to adopt a correct policy towards Peking (short of recognition) refraining from public criticism of Chinese policies and indeed avoiding, so far as possible, making any statements about Communist China at all". It is worth noting that Chinese Ministry of Foreign Affairs archival documents suggest that for a brief period before 1965, Lee Kuan Yew "exploited overseas Chinese loyalties to win Beijing's support".[51]

The establishment of diplomatic relations between Singapore and China was thus "absolutely inevitable", Lee said. But considering the concerns of Singapore's neighbours, Singapore would wait until after the other Southeast Asian countries had done so.[52] As Kawin Wilairat noted, "the question of establishing formal ties with China is one which requires the most careful and sensitive handling by Singapore. The potential repercussions, internal and external, of such a move cannot be downplayed for a country which has in the past been called a Third China and whose Southeast Asian identity has been questioned by her neighbours".[53] Indeed, Indonesia reportedly "greatly feared" Beijing "gaining [a] dominant position in Singapore" which was likened to a "dagger pointed at the heart of Indonesia".[54]

Beijing had apparently wanted to recognise Singapore but was "prevailed upon to withhold recognition out of deference to Indonesia". American officials believed that Chinese strategy was to cultivate Lee Kuan Yew and elements in the

---

[50] From the British High Commission in Singapore to the UK Foreign and Commonwealth Office (FCO), 12 Nov. 1970, FCO 24/887, NAB 1504. See also Yuan-li Wu, *The Strategic Land Ridge: Peking's Relations with Thailand, Malaysia, Singapore, and Indonesia* (Stanford University, CA: Hoover Institution Press, 1975), p. 58.
[51] "Aspects of Singapore's Foreign Relations", June 1968, A1838/318, Item 3024/12 (Part 1), NAB 780. See also Liu, "Love the Tree, Love the Branch: Beijing's Friendship with Lee Kuan Yew, 1954–1965", pp. 550–72. During his visit to Cambodia in 1962, Lee contacted the Chinese ambassador "to express his understanding of Chinese policy and his warm feeling for China as an overseas Chinese", cited in Tan Kok Chiang, *My Nantah Story: The Rise and Demise of the People's University* (Singapore: Ethos Books, 2017), p. 58.
[52] Transcript of press conference given by the Prime Minister in Tokyo, 11 May 1973.
[53] Wilairat, *Singapore's Foreign Policy: A Study of the Foreign Policy System of a City-State*, p. 511.
[54] From the American Embassy in Jakarta to the Department of State, 1 September 1965, RG 59, Box 2652, POL 16 – Independence & Recognition/ Singapore.

PAP to "encourage them to develop some sort of relationship with Jakarta".[55] Rajaratnam thought that the report that Chinese Foreign Minister Chen Yi had sought to persuade the Indonesians to recognise Singapore was "concocted to win favour here". In his analysis, China probably wanted to avoid antagonising Singaporeans "against the day when circumstances would favour an attempt to increase China's influence in the island".[56]

We now know from Chinese Ministry of Foreign Affairs archival documents that after independence, there were "at least two major diplomatic exchanges" to get Beijing to formally recognise Singapore's independence: the first on 18 August 1965 when Ko Tek Kin (Singapore's first High Commissioner to Malaysia) met Qi Feng (deputy Director, Xinhua News Agency) in Hong Kong, and the second when Toh Chin Chye, S. Rajaratnam and Ong Pang Boon (Singapore's Minister of Education) met PRC ambassadors, Wang Yutien and He Ying in Kenya and Tanzania, respectively.[57] By the time Jakarta recognised Singapore in June 1966, Chinese foreign policy had turned ultra-left while Singapore had turned towards the United States. As Philip Hsiaopong Liu noted, "from a Beijing perspective, Lee had sided with China's 'most serious danger' and was no longer pro-China or anticolonial".[58]

At a press conference on 15 September 1965, before Rajaratnam and deputy Prime Minister Toh Chin Chye left for the United Nations General Assembly meeting New York, Toh said that if Singapore were admitted into the UN, it "would support [Communist] China's admission to the UN".[59] On 17 November 1965, Lee said that Singapore's policy towards Communist China "was still an open question". The only decision Singapore had decided on was that it would support Communist China's "unconditional entry" into the UN "on a simple vote of members". Since 1965, Singapore had consistently voted against the US resolution ("Important Question Resolution") that characterised the question of Chinese representation as an "important" matter that required a two-thirds majority vote. Washington was able to keep Beijing out of the UN for a decade

---

[55] From the American Consulate in Hong Kong to the Department of State, 20 Sept. 1965, RG 59, Box 2652, POL 16 – Independence & Recognition/ Singapore; from the American Embassy in Jakarta to Department of State, 30 Aug. 1965 and 1 Sept. 1965, RG 59, Box 2652, POL 16 – Independence & Recognition/ Singapore.
[56] From the Australian High Commission in Kuala Lumpur to the Department of External Affairs, 28 August 1965, A1838, Item 3024/7/1 Part 1, Singapore – Political – Foreign Policy.
[57] See Liu, "Love the Tree, Love the Branch: Beijing's Friendship with Lee Kuan Yew, 1954–1965", pp. 550–72.
[58] Ibid., p. 567.
[59] From the American Consulate in Singapore to the Department of State, 18 Sept. 1965, RG 59, Box 2651, POL 2-1/Singapore 1/1/65. Singapore joined the UN on 21 Sept. 1965.

(until 1971) through this procedural device. Lee dismissed talks that Singapore was pursuing a "two-China policy" and expressed doubts that such a policy was "right" or in Singapore's interests. The question of Taiwan's status could be decided after Beijing had taken its seat in the UN.[60] Lee was exercising damage control to further clarify Singapore's position.

A month earlier, on 17 October, the government issued a statement in response to news reports, specifically one entitled "Abu Bakar Takes Two-China Line" summarising Abu Bakar bin Pawanchee's remarks on China and Taiwan in his 14 October UN speech.[61] Abu Bakar was Singapore's first permanent secretary at the Ministry of Foreign Affairs, who moved on to become Singapore's first permanent representative to the UN. The Singapore government was apparently "embarrassed" by the two paragraphs on Singapore's China policy. The government statement pointed out that while Singapore's foreign policy was one of non-alignment, any statement made at this stage on "major problems of long standing" represented only attitudes and not fixed policy. On the issue of whether Singapore supported one or two Chinas, it would have to be "examined more carefully".[62] At the UN General Assembly meeting in September 1965, Singapore, as a new (the 117th) member state of the UN, had voted in support of the Albanian Resolution to transfer the UN seat from the Republic of China (ROC)/Taiwan to the PRC. The US and others interpreted this as a tactical move aimed at consolidating identification with the non-aligned countries.[63] The following year and for the next years until 1971, Singapore abstained from voting on the resolution to expel the ROC. Apparently, Singapore did not feel that the time was ripe for a final resolution of the issue of Chinese representation at the UN. American officials based in Singapore noted that "like many other Afro-Asian nations, Singapore is caught between its desire to be recognised or at least accepted as a nation by Communist China and its reluctance to set a dangerous precedent by denying Taiwan the right of self-determination. Singapore's position

---

[60] From the US Consulate in Singapore to the Department of State, 22 Nov. 1965, RG 59, Box 2651, POL 2-1/ Singapore 10/16/65.
[61] For the full text of Abu Bakar's speech, see UN General Assembly 20th Session 1362nd Plenary Meeting, at https://undocs.org/en/A/PV.1362 (accessed 12 Dec. 2022), particularly paragraphs 6 and 7. See also the news report "S'pore Tells UN: Admit China", *The Straits Times*, 16 Oct. 1965.
[62] From the American Consulate in Singapore to the Department of State, 23 Oct. 1965, RG 59, Box 2651, POL 2-1/ Singapore 10/16/65. See the full text of the Singapore Government Press Statement, 16 Oct. 1965; NAA (National Archives of Australia) A1838/2, 3024/11/87 Part 1.
[63] From the American Embassy in Singapore to the Department of State, 24 Sept. 1966, RG 59, Box 2651, POL 2-1/Singapore 8/3/66.

is further complicated by fear that Communist China might actively seek to block Singapore's admission to the Afro-Asian Conference in November [1965]". In addition, there was the "perennial political requirement in this predominantly Chinese state that the GOS avoid any actions or statement which might lend substance to left-wing charges that the Government is following the 'US–UK anti-China line'".[64]

Almost a year after Singapore became independent, Beijing had still not recognised it. But China also did not condemn the country. The Chinese had expressed their wish to trade with Singapore, to which Lee did not object.[65] Singapore was interested in any country that wanted to trade with it, be it Taiwan or China. Referring to Taiwan in 1968, he said that Taiwan had a bustling little economy which was bigger than Singapore's, and that "we are extremely anxious to increase our cooperation with them".[66] In 1969, Taiwan established a trade office with consular functions/representative office in Singapore. In 1970, Beijing still categorised Singapore as part of British Malaya. Thus, while economic relations with China were "very good", political relations were not.[67] But, in Lee's view, while Taiwan was influential in economic terms, unlike China, its strategic importance was dependent on American strategic aims.[68] As for China, both Lee and Rajaratnam had drawn attention to Beijing's "increasing importance both as a world force and a regional power". Lee had also echoed Malaysia's second deputy Prime Minister, Tun Dr Ismail's view that "there cannot be a lasting peace in Southeast Asia without China's concurrence".[69]

The record of a conversation between the New Zealand High Commissioner and S. Rajaratnam in June 1971 provides a glimpse of Singapore's thinking on the issue of the admission of China to the UN, or at least that of the Foreign Minister. Apparently, Rajaratnam had refused to talk very much about China publicly for some time. Asked how Singapore planned to vote on the Chinese representation issue in 1971, Rajaratnam said that Singapore "would wait until

---

[64] From the American Consulate in Singapore to the Department of State, 26 Oct. 1965, RG 59, Box 2651, POL 2-1/ Singapore 10/16/65.
[65] "Transcript of a Press Conference Given by the Prime Minister, Mr. Lee Kuan Yew, at City Hall to Local and Foreign Correspondents, 2 June 1966".
[66] "Transcript of General Press Conference Given by the Prime Minister, Mr. Lee Kuan Yew, at TV Centre, 21 December 1968".
[67] "Transcript of Question-and-answer Session Following the Prime Minister's Luncheon Address at the Reception Given him by the French Diplomatic Press Association, at the Hotel George V, Paris, 25 September 1970".
[68] From the British High Commission in Singapore to the FCO, 12 November 1970, "Singapore-China Relations", FCO 24/887, NAB 1504.
[69] Ibid.

the last possible moment to make up its mind". The primary concern was not to offend any of the "big boys". Rajaratnam said he thought the best solution would be for the Beijing supporters to put forward just the first half of the Albanian resolution. This, in his view, would ensure a "very substantial majority" of votes. The difficulty at present was that many countries, including Singapore, did not want to face the embarrassment of having to vote for the Albanian resolution, which would mean expelling Taiwan. But if only the first half of the Albanian resolution were voted on, Beijing would certainly take over the Chinese seat and "the Formosans finding no seat left for them would quietly disappear... The Formosans don't need to be in the United Nations—but we do need the Communist Chinese in if there is to be any chance of getting them to behave better in this part of the world". Elaborating his argument, Rajaratnam suggested that for all those who wished to see Taiwan remain as a separate entity if the country were out of the UN, someone, perhaps Japan, should tell Chiang Kai Shek to give up all pretensions to reclaiming the mainland and declare Formosa a separate independent state. There were already sufficient American assurances to deter Beijing from trying to take over Taiwan by force—"Taiwan was as safe as anyone in this area can reasonably expect". After declaring independence, Taiwan could then embark upon a campaign to join the UN. In this scenario, Rajaratnam thought there was a good chance for Taiwan to succeed in getting a seat in the UN after a few years; Beijing would probably turn a blind eye having secured its main objective of being the sole representative of the Chinese nation in the UN. Beijing would not like independent Formosa and would never recognise it but knowing they could not take over Formosa by force and having bigger fish to fry, they would tacitly agree that other countries could maintain relations with both Beijing and Taipei. Having sketched the above solution, Rajaratnam agreed that there was not much chance of persuading Chiang Kai Shek to look at the issue from this perspective. "That's the pity if it", he said, "for once the old man dies that's the way things are going to evolve"; the mainlanders in Taiwan were an ageing group and their influence would be reduced. The second generation had little desire to have anything to do with the Mainland. He hoped that Chiang could look to the future and realise that now was the time for Formosa to make a bid for long-term independence for "if he messes this one up it will make it much more difficult in the future to get any reasonable solution".[70]

Not long after the June conversation with Rajaratnam, the world was informed on 15 July 1971 that US President Richard Nixon would be visiting China the following year from 21–28 February. Washington also indicated that

---

[70] From the New Zealand High Commission in Singapore to the Secretary of Foreign Affairs, Wellington, 23 June 1971, "Singapore and China", FCO 24/1203, NAB 1290.

it would not oppose the seating of Beijing in the Security Council and was prepared to let UN members decide on Chinese representation. But it wanted to keep Taiwan in the General Assembly, which was in fact, "legally untenable".[71] On 25 October 1971, Singapore, for the second time since 1965, voted for the Albanian Resolution. It is worth noting that in Southeast Asia, only the Philippines voted against, Thailand and Indonesia abstained. On the Important Question Resolution, Thailand, the Philippines, Indonesia and Cambodia voted in favour. The US argued for the PRC to be admitted separately from the ROC, in short, dual representation, but this proposal was defeated. UN General Assembly Resolution 2758 which recognised the PRC as "the only legitimate representative of China to the United Nations" was passed with 76 votes for, 35 against and 17 abstentions.

If our knowledge of Singapore–PRC relations during the Cold War years is limited, we know even less about Singapore–ROC relations. Singapore's vote for the Albanian Resolution which contributed to the expulsion of Taiwan from the UN apparently did not negatively affect the bilateral relationship. Under a 1973 agreement, Taiwanese advisers were first sent to Singapore to train its military pilots and subsequently assisted in building the Singapore navy. Singapore's first Air Force and Navy chiefs originally served in the Taiwanese military. It is public knowledge that the Singapore Armed Forces have trained in Taiwan under "Project Starlight", which was "an umbrella agreement allowing infantry, artillery and armoured training at battalion scale and beyond on Taiwanese soil".[72] Secret discussions began in 1967 and Project Starlight was eventually approved in 1975. It was not surprising that Taipei (indeed, it would have been surprising if the Taiwanese had not) tried or hoped to obtain a quid pro quo from Singapore: training facilities in exchange for support of the ROC in the UN, which Singapore was both unable and unwilling to give. Nevertheless, Project Starlight "formed the cornerstone of early defence cooperation and [bound] the two sides together even in the

---

[71] See Khurshid Hyder, "China's Representation in the United Nations", *Pakistan Horizon* 24, no. 4 (1971): 75–9; "People's Republic of China In, Taiwan out, at U.N.", *The New York Times*, 27 Oct. 1971; "Foreign Relations of the United States, Document 167: Editorial Note in Foreign Relations of the United States, 1969–1971", Volume XVII, China, 1969–72, at https://history.state.gov/historicaldocuments/frus1969-76v17 (accessed 25 March 2021); *Yearbook of the United Nations, 1971, Volume 25* (New York: Office of Public Information, United Nations, 1974), pp. 126–37.

[72] Alan Chong, "Singapore's Relations with Taiwan 1965–2005: From Cold War Coalition to Friendship under Beijing's Veto", in *Ensuring Interests: Dynamics of China-Taiwan Relations and Southeast Asia*, ed. Ho Khai Leong and Hou Kok Chung (Kuala Lumpur: Institute of China Studies, 2006), p. 182.

absence of formal diplomatic relations".[73] Lee Kuan Yew himself visited Taiwan regularly from 1973 and had a good relationship with Taiwanese Premier (and later President) Chiang Ching-kuo. As Pasha L. Hsieh noted, "As an 'open secret', the scale of defence cooperation between Taiwan and Singapore is rarely seen in non-diplomatic relations".[74] As Rajaratnam recalled, there were pressures from both the Americans and Taiwanese "to join them to exclude China". But Singapore had to "devise [its] own policy...We were not anti-Taiwan, but we didn't want to be pro-Taiwan either. So, we decided to have good relations discreetly with the Taiwanese and with the People's Republic of China without antagonising either".[75]

If 1966 marked the beginning of Singapore's relations with the US, Deng Xiaoping's visit to Singapore in November 1978 is often hailed as the beginning of Singapore's relations with the PRC, although both countries established formal diplomatic relations only in October 1990, the last Southeast Asian country to do so, after Indonesia. As in the case with the United States, apart from some episodic hiccups, the relationship has generally been smooth. As Lee said in a speech at Victoria University in Wellington, New Zealand on 11 March 1965, the world's small nations could survive only by finding a "coincidence of interests with the big Powers".[76]

V

The end of Confrontation paved the way for the formation of ASEAN in August 1967. This is the appropriate place to describe Singapore's attitude towards multilateralism during its formative years.

Both Rajaratnam and Goh Keng Swee were initially somewhat sceptical about whether the region was ready for any regional cooperation structure. While Rajaratnam called for "a reversal of the present tendency to base regional efforts on political cooperation" and instead refocus on economic cooperation first and other fields later, he said he was not referring to the ASA (the Association of

---

[73] I-wei Jennifer Chang, "Taiwan's Military Ties to Singapore Constrained by China", *The Global Taiwan Brief* 5, no. 9 (6 May 2020), at https://globaltaiwan.org/2020/05/vol-5-issue-9/ (accessed 10 Jan. 2023).
[74] See Pasha L. Hsieh, "The Quest for Recognition: Taiwan's Military and Trade Agreements with Singapore Under the One-China Policy", *International Relations of the Asia-Pacific* 19, no. 1 (2019): 89–115.
[75] "Raja on Early Days of 'Do-it-yourself' Foreign Policy", *The Straits Times*, 2 April 1987.
[76] "'Pawns' in Conflict", *Wellington Dominion*, 12 March 1965. Lee would reiterate this point often. See for example Lee Kuan Yew, "The Fundamentals of Singapore's Foreign Policy: Then & Now", S. Rajaratnam Lecture, 9 April 2009 (Singapore: MFA Academy, 2009).

Southeast Asia) or any other concept because creating elaborate structures without first developing a sense of regionalism through practical experience in cooperation would result only in failure.[77]

Asked why Singapore was so loath to contemplate political associations in the region, Rajaratnam explained that Singapore could not afford political relationships since these could be seen as hostile to others in the region. For example, Malaysia would suspect closer ties between Singapore and Thailand, even more so between Singapore and Indonesia. The way ahead for Singapore's security, according to Rajaratnam, was to look rather for associations "in the economic and non-political fields". Nobody could object to this. But even so, he felt that Singapore "could not risk unfavourable attention by seeking to take initiatives". He was "doubtful" about the extent to which the type of regional organisation he had spoken of would progress. In fact, he came across as "rather gloomy about Singapore's prospects amid the political conflicts likely to develop within the region".[78]

Goh Keng Swee, in the aforementioned conversation with Secretary Bundy on 19 September 1966 in response to Bundy's suggestion that Southeast Asian countries could form an OAS-type of regional organisation and that the US might participate in such an organisation, expressed the view that countries in Southeast Asia, with the exception of Thailand and possibly Cambodia, lacked "the necessary experience to form and maintain such an organization". "ASA falls down on staff work", he said. Furthermore, since the communist threat in the area was primarily from indigenous forces, he felt that it would be extremely difficult for a regional-type organisation to know when the danger had reached the point where it would be necessary to step in and act.[79]

Lee Kuan Yew, on the other hand, was much more, if still cautiously, optimistic. Readers may recall from the previous chapter that peace talks between Jakarta and Kuala Lumpur began in May 1966. In the same month, Jakarta and Manila held consultations on the setting up of a regional organisation to replace the abortive Maphilindo concept, which in the view of Singapore, augured the possibility of a Malaysian–Indonesian rapprochement sooner rather than later.[80]

---

[77] From the American Embassy in Singapore to the Department of State, 17 Sept. 1966, RG 59, Box 2651, POL 2-1/ Singapore 8/13/66.
[78] From the Australian High Commission in Singapore to the Department of External Affairs, Canberra, 6 July 1966, A1838/2, Item 3024/7/1 Part 2.
[79] Memorandum of Conversation, 19 September 1966, RG 59, Box Number 2652, POL Singapore – A. Bundy however disagreed with Goh's views.
[80] From the American Embassy in Singapore to the Department of State, 22 May 1966, RG 59, Box 2651, POL 1/ Singapore 5/1/66.

The "surprise" arrival of an Indonesian military goodwill mission in Kuala Lumpur in June 1966 aroused some concerns in Singapore. Privately, several Singapore officials expressed concern over the "one race, one religion" atmosphere in Kuala Lumpur during the goodwill visit, which Singapore officials "fear[-ed] may presage a revival of Maphilindo or some form of pan-Malayanism".[81] Also in June, both sides agreed in principle to a peace agreement which was eventually signed on 12 August.

Lee's "Big and Small Fishes in Asian Waters" speech on 15 June 1966, which coincided with the above developments, provides a clear view of Singapore's attitude towards multilateralism in the region. In that speech, there is a part worth quoting in some detail. Lee said he was supportive of "a large Southeast Asia Union...if you can bring what are relatively, in Asian terms, diverse peoples together". But not Maphilindo because "it implies Malayness, which means Indonesianess because they are the largest part of Southeast Asia. And it implies Islam and it implies the Malay language... And the Tengku had quite rightly said—I am not saying this, the Tengku is saying this—'Forget it. It is a waste of time'. Why does he say that? It is as if a Chinese foreign minister from Peking were to proclaim, 'let's have a big union of China, Taiwan, and Singapore'...based on what? On Chineseness!" In short, Lee was highlighting the dangerous implications of playing the ethnic card. He went on: "But if you say, 'Look, let's have the Thais in too... This gives a broader spectrum to Southeast Asian cooperation'...And then I say we look beyond to a wider horizon still—Thailand, Indonesia, Philippines, Yes. Burma, Laos, all the Buddhist states—there, I would say, is a very good admixture to a large Southeast Asian whole for economic, cultural, social cooperation. And eventually, what we want to do is to try and establish, within the decade, some semblance of a balance which can be maintained with the minimum of outside under-pinning".[82]

To Lee, "the self-contained national unit, national self-sufficiency, is old-fashioned and out-of-date. It does not work unless you are a really big land mass like the United States of America or the USSR". Thus, with regional cooperation, "you lump together 300 million people, and everybody stands to gain". He envisaged that Singapore "could be the catalyst that could speed up the course of economic development" and act as "a spark plug" for economic progress and development in the region. But first, all the countries had to agree that "nobody

---

[81] From the American Embassy in Singapore to the Department of State, 5 June 1966, RG 59, Box 2651, POL 1/Singapore 5/1/66.
[82] "Transcript of a Talk Given by the Prime Minister, Mr. Lee Kuan Yew, on the Subject 'Big and Small Fishes in Asian Waters' at a Meeting of the University of Singapore Democratic Socialist Club at the University Campus, 15 June 1966".

can swallow up the whole and we have to cooperate".[83] Geographical proximity is a necessary but not sufficient condition for "if blind persons get together you are unlikely to get anywhere", Lee said. Regional cooperation for economic development needed leadership, which was a sensitive issue during the period.[84]

Besides economics, Lee also envisaged some form of multilateral security arrangements in Southeast Asia. By this, he did not mean that he supported the presence of foreign troops in Singapore, although as we have noted, in 1966, Singapore's security depended on the "burly Englishmen" and "sturdy Gurkhas". Lee was interested in "cooperation for the protection it might offer to small states in the region", a point he made during his state visit to India in September 1966. It was reported that the Indians listened "politely to him but [were] very cautious in committing [themselves] concerning such a regional approach". An article in the *Hindustan Times* argued that Lee's views concerning multilateral security arrangements should be taken more seriously by India because "the time may come, when the US will decide to stop underwriting Asia against China; at that time, the countries of Asia will need to recognise that security has its military side and free Asia must sooner or later provide for its own defence".[85] Lee was clearly not expressly thinking of China when he expressed his idea. Asked by an interviewer for his views on regional defence cooperation in 1969, Lee replied that "when [the] Americans talk about defence arrangements in Southeast Asia they usually mean defence against China". But Lee did not believe that China had a "predatory expansionist policy" and did not expect the "Chinese People's Liberation Army fanning out through Southeast Asia".[86]

Lee's multilateral security arrangement idea was ahead of its time. It did not receive much support within ASEAN, except perhaps from Indonesia. President Suharto broached the idea that besides economic, social and cultural cooperation, ASEAN could be made more effective by adding military cooperation. But nothing came out of it and generally the Indonesians continued to stress more "the non-security aspects of regional cooperation while at the same time seeking to avoid foreclosing defence cooperation in the future". As an October 1970 US study of ASEAN noted, "the subject of a future defence role for ASEAN remains

---

[83] Ibid.; interview with Lee Kuan Yew by Hugh D.S. Greenway, *Time/Life* Bureau Chief, Southeast Asia, 10 June 1969.
[84] Ibid.
[85] From the American Embassy in New Delhi to the Department of State, "Singapore PM's Visit to India", 9 Sept. 1966, RG 59, Box 2451, POL 6 – Singapore 1/1/65. See also Eugene R. Black, *Alternative in Southeast Asia* (New York: Frederick A. Praeger, 1969), p. 58. Black described Lee as having "floated a trial balloon..." but was ignored.
[86] Interview with Lee by Greenway, 10 June 1969.

one of the touchiest issues among member states".[87] In the meantime, member states were free to cooperate militarily amongst themselves. Singapore's policy towards ASEAN was that the association should concentrate in the first place on economic and social projects within the framework of its present membership, then consider the question of widening its membership and finally of increasing the scope of its discussions.[88] Singapore's long-term goal was the creation of an ASEAN "Common Market".[89] Indeed, S. Rajaratnam, in his oral answers in Parliament to questions pertaining to the inaugural ASEAN Foreign Ministers' Conference in Bangkok in August 1967, said that "a common market" was one of Singapore's objectives and that ASEAN was "a scheme for economic cooperation" and not military.[90]

Eugene Black, who played a key role in the formation of the Asian Development Bank in November 1966, visited Singapore that year in his capacity as Special Adviser to President Lyndon Johnson for the Economic and Social Development of Southeast Asia. In his 1969 book, *Alternative in Southeast Asia*, Black wrote the following about Singapore: "Lee Kuan Yew knows that Singapore's future safety and prosperity depend on regional cooperation within Asia. 'I would like to see an Asia', he said recently, 'particularly my immediate part of Asia, largely self-sustaining, interlocked...in trade, commerce, and industrialisation programmes, economic growth and mutual security with a minimum of direct support of intervention from the outside'. But, as one of his chief lieutenants put it to me recently, 'We have so much to gain that we cannot get out in front'". Black had the impression that although Singapore was one of the five founding members of ASEAN, "given the hostility of Malaysia and Indonesia...Lee has little leverage and little opportunity to play a constructive role". "I suspect", Black added, "he [Lee] is glad that ASEAN has been formed, if only for the participation of Thailand and the Philippines, which tends to diminish somewhat the influence of the other two members".[91]

---

[87] Barbara French Pace, *Regional Cooperation in Southeast Asia: The First Two Years of ASEAN – 1967–1969*, Study I in *The Guam Doctrine: Elements of Implementation*, Report RAC-R-98-2, Oct. 1970.

[88] From the Australian High Commission in Singapore to the Department of External Affairs, Canberra, "Singapore – Foreign Policy", 23 Sept. 1970, A 1838/318, Item 3024/12 (Part 1); from the Australian High Commission in Singapore to the Department of External Affairs, Canberra, Record of Conversation held between Mr. S. R. Nathan, Deputy Secretary, Ministry of Foreign Affairs, Singapore, and Mr. A.G.D. White, First Secretary, Australian High Commission, 9 Jan. 1970, A 1838/318, Item 3024/12 (Part 1), NAB 780.

[89] From the American Embassy in Singapore to the Department of State, 5 June 1968, Box 2324, POL Malaysia-Singapore.

[90] ASEAN Foreign Ministers' Conference at Bangkok, Oral Answers to Questions, 9 Aug. 1967, Singapore Parliament Reports (Hansard).

[91] Black, *Alternative in Southeast Asia*, pp. 57–8.

CHAPTER 3

The Lee Kuan Yew Years (1965–90): Transforming/The Making of Singapore's Defence Strategy

I

This chapter leads up to the 1980s, the final decade of Lee Kuan Yew's administration (1959–90). As an introduction to this theme, the chapter delves deeper into the issue of Singapore's defence strategy and the introduction of "Total Defence". The introduction of such a defence strategy signals that Singapore had perhaps finally put all the pieces of its Grand Strategy into place. The chapter further explains Singapore's robust response to the Vietnamese invasion of Cambodia, which was seen as posing an existential threat to Singapore.

A series of British reports pertaining to Singapore's defence provides a glimpse of Singapore's defence strategy and development in the 1970s. Despite not having a military tradition, Singapore's efforts to fast-pace its defence capability were developing well. According to a British assessment in 1972, "the SAF could take the first thrust of a potential enemy but could not hold out for long";[1] this was understandable given that compulsory military service was introduced only in 1967. We recall from Chapter 1 that in 1975, Lee said that there was no longer any need for foreign ground forces in Singapore.

Some key findings of a 1974 professional study, which was described as "very comprehensive and valuable", by the Defence Adviser to the British High Commissioner in Singapore, for the years 1974–80 of the composition and capabilities of the Singapore Armed Forces (SAF) are worth highlighting here:

---

[1] "Singapore: Annual Review for 1972", 1 Jan. 1973, FCO 24/1778.

(a) A major objective of introducing National Service was to develop "a sense of national consciousness and identity". Ministers and senior officials generally admit quite readily that the SAF was valued "as a means of nation building and not merely for the orthodox purposes of defence against aggression and the maintenance of internal security".

(b) Progress has been "considerable", considering Singapore's lack of indigenous personnel with any military experience and the traditional Chinese disdain of military life. The report noted that "for a country of small size, SAF is a large organisation with a widespread capability".

(c) Dr Goh Keng Swee, who is described as "able and energetic" and who read "voluminously on military subjects and on occasions has confounded his expatriate advisers and visiting senior officers with his knowledge of a particular subject", was given a great deal of credit for the development of the SAF. Goh was "fascinated by technology" (which we will describe below).

(d) The SAF was however deficient in logistical support and its operational capability was still limited. Singaporeans would "probably put up a good fight" if the country were attacked. In the assessment of the British, "the possibility of an attack on Singapore by either of its neighbours seems at the present time as unrealistic and improbable as a Singapore attack on them" despite the "gossips alleging secret plans by one side or the other and occasional reports of threatening remarks by Singapore or Malaysian politicians".

(e) There were two views: the optimistic and the pessimistic. Both sides might have contingency plans against remote eventualities but "whilst there are stable and responsible governments in Kuala Lumpur, Jakarta and Singapore, and especially whilst ASEAN is providing a forum for increased consultation and cooperation", there was no need to further develop the SAF's "orthodox military capability". The pessimists, on the other hand, argued that the situation in Southeast Asia could deteriorate, the FPDA[2] provided no real safeguard and therefore Singapore must develop the capability to defend itself.

(f) The British assessment was that given the limitations of size and geographical position, "no force could defend Singapore indefinitely against a strong attack from neighbouring territories". All Singapore could do "would be to fight a holding action and the SAF already seems to have the strength and equipment necessary for this". Should deterrence fail, the SAF had "the military capability to prevent foreign occupation". Thus, rather than expand

---

[2] The Five Power Defence Arrangements comprising Australia, New Zealand, Britain, Malaysia and Singapore, signed in 1971.

further, the British view was for "a period of consolidation" which "would enable Singaporeans to gain experience and take over from expatriates and also to improve the SAF's logistic and command organization".[3]

Two observations from the above study require elaboration. The first is Goh Keng Swee's interest in technology. If Lee Kuan Yew's 1966 speech "Big and Small Fishes in Asian Waters" is the key speech to read for an understanding of Singapore's Grand Strategy and the thinking behind it, Goh's 1971 speech, "What Kind of War?", is the speech to read for an understanding of the military dimension of the Strategy.[4] In this speech, Goh addressed the question of the options "open to Singapore in the prosecution of war against much larger countries". Singapore's physical size "makes it even more imperative to fight defensive battles outside the country". This meant that the sea "must be regarded as a vital means of movement of troops". In addition, "air supremacy must be achieved over a sustained period". In Goh's view, if Singapore could achieve "air supremacy and have the means of sea transport", the "geography of the archipelago" would confer "a decisive advantage upon Singapore". Given Singapore's population size, it should at all costs avoid "a rifleman's war" because Singapore would not be able to bear the attrition of manpower compared to countries with large populations. Therefore "technology" is important. Goh referred to Israel as an example to show that a small country with "a high level of technological and scientific standards can inflict a shattering military defeat on nations more than fifty times her size". Technology is also important because modern weapons, even simple ones, "require a minimum level of technology and training for their operation...and maintenance". Speaking from the perspective of 1971, Goh noted that Singapore's military build-up had been "quite unbalanced". While the Army was making "good progress", he acknowledged the much slower development of the Air Force and the Navy as "these two services are particularly difficult to establish" given that "their demand on technology is very exacting".

Goh was adamant that the edge the SAF needed was in "technology" and that "open warfare was only the external manifestation of a war that was really being

---

[3] From the British High Commission in Singapore to the FCO, "Singapore Armed Forces", 18 March 1974, FCO 15/1912. For details, see "Singapore Armed Forces Military Capability, Report by Defence Adviser, British High Commission Singapore", January 1973, FCO 15/1912. See also British High Commission in Singapore to FCO, "Singapore's Defence: The End of an Era", 2 April 1976, FCO 15/2159.
[4] Goh Keng Swee, Closing Address at the 3rd Singapore Command and Staff College (SCSC) course, 19 Nov. 1971.

fought in secret laboratories".[5] We now know that in 1970, Goh set up a top-secret team to conduct research on electronic warfare, the precursor of DSO [Defence Science Organisation] National Laboratories, which is today Singapore's largest defence research and development organisation. Goh was "worried that merely importing equipment was not enough. It had to be internally modified to give Singapore the edge in battle", according to then-DSO chairman Professor Lui Pao Chuen in 2002.[6] S.R. Nathan, who was Director of the Security and Intelligence Division (SID) and to whom the small top-secret team reported, pointed out that those who sold the equipment to Singapore could be the worst source of leaks about its capability.[7] It is worth noting that Goh Keng Swee was not the only one in the leadership who stressed the importance of technology. S. Rajaratnam too declared, presciently, in a context which goes beyond defence, that "the only certainty I am prepared to vouch for in this so-called Age of Uncertainty is that the future belongs only to those nations which are prepared to serve as partisans of the new Technological Society emerging out of the crumbling structure of the First Industrial Revolution".[8]

The May 1969 riots in Malaysia, the Vietnam War and its aftermath reinforced the pessimists' view that Singapore needed to urgently upgrade its armed forces. Even as the SAF continued in its relentless pursuit, in his "What Kind of War?" speech Goh cautioned that Singapore needed "to avoid taking measures which could be considered provocative by our neighbours". He cited the example of the purchase of the French AMX-13 light tank which aroused much concern from Singapore's neighbours. Goh said that there were "other more sensitive weapon systems which we would like to procure... But we cannot, at this stage at any rate, ignore the reaction of our build-up with our neighbours, for to do so may mean foregoing a decided advantage in that we would unnecessarily give them time to plan for, produce and train in the use of counter-measures". Unnecessarily precipitating an arms race could inadvertently lead to "a military conflict with relatively rational governments with whom we want to be on peaceful terms". Thus, the timing of the introduction of new weapons and weapon systems "is one of the more crucial decisions which the Singapore Government has to make". Indeed, countries which Singapore

---

[5] Source of quotation still cannot be disclosed.
[6] For DSO, see "About DSO", at https://www.dso.org.sg/about/ (accessed 23 Nov. 2022).
[7] For an account of the early years and the evolution by those who were involved, see "The Man with a Secret", *Today*, 5–6 Oct. 2002.
[8] Speech at the opening of the FIDIC [Fédération Internationale des Ingénieurs Conseils/International Federation of Consulting Engineers] Annual Conference, Singapore, 14 June 1982.

approached to buy arms, such as the United States and Australia, were concerned about indirectly triggering an arms race. Goh reiterated that Singapore's military preparations were "against the eventuality that one or both [the neighbouring] governments [were] replaced by irrational regimes".

Finally, there was the issue of cost, the economic dimension of the acquisition of defence capabilities. Goh reminded his audience that since most of the weapons had to be purchased from "modern industrial countries", they did not come cheap. A country would need to have the purchasing power, especially if it wanted to acquire technologically-advanced weapons: "the means to do so therefore constitute an important military resource". Asked whether his political belief and economic theory were based on "the primacy of economic growth", Goh's adamant reply was "Yes! Unless you have economic growth, you die".[9]

Lee Kuan Yew had said that defence and economics were equally important.[10] The view of the political leadership in the early years was that defence had a slight edge over economic growth. Lim Kim San (who had taken over the Minister of Defence portfolio from Goh) pointed out in 1968 that "without this defence build-up, there may come a time when all the economic growth in the world will not stand us in good stead, because we would be captured and it would be too late to regret that we should have given priority to our defence build-up first".[11] It is never a straightforward choice. Lee qualified his premise that "defence and security [are] indivisible from trade and industry" by adding that this premise "will have to be left over for some time until the meaning percolates through".[12] Years later, he would describe the nexus as two sides of the same question as "you cannot have a strong defence unless you have a strong finance. And you cannot have strong defence and strong finance unless you have a strong, unified, well-educated and increasingly cohesive society. They are all part of one whole".[13]

Because of the impending, in fact accelerated, withdrawal of British forces, Singapore's defence expenditure for the financial year 1 January 1969 to 31 March

---

[9] Melanie Chew, *Leaders of Singapore* (Singapore: Resource Press, 1996), p. 149. See also Goh Keng Swee, *The Practice of Economic Growth* (Singapore: Federal Publications, 1997), pp. vii–viii. Goh noted that defence ministries world-wide consume enormous resources. To Singapore's credit, the defence build-up years did not necessitate any increase in taxes as the balance of payments continued to be strong despite the purchase of military hardware; see also Chin Kin Wah, "Singapore: Threat Perception and Defence Spending in a City-State", in *Defence Spending in Southeast Asia*, ed. Chin Kin Wah (Singapore: ISEAS, 1987), pp. 203–12.
[10] Transcript of a press conference to a group of foreign correspondents, 11 Dec. 1965.
[11] The Minister of Defence (Mr Lim Kim San), Estimates of Expenditure for Financial Year, 1 Jan. 1969 to 31 March 1970, 18 Dec. 1968, Singapore Parliament Reports (Hansard).
[12] Transcript of a press conference to a group of foreign correspondents, 11 Dec. 1965.
[13] Lee Kuan Yew, *Hard Truths To Keep Singapore Going* (Singapore: Straits Times Press, 2011), p. 32.

1970 increased exponentially to the extent that Goh Keng Swee (who assumed the position of Minister of Finance in 1967) felt it necessary to spend a substantial portion of his speech at the presentation of the annual budget statement in Parliament on 3 December 1968 on explaining this budget component.[14] In fact, he wasted no time: the opening sentence was on the defence budget. Goh noted that a forecast of defence expenditure reaching some ten per cent of GNP (Gross National Product) would inevitably require tax increases. The public had "a right to know what we are spending the money on, what they can expect to get in return for it and whether they are getting value for their money". Goh then went on to describe in some detail the defence build-up of the three services (Navy, Air Force and Army) over the next few years up till 1971. The details need not delay us here. The key take-away from this speech which is relevant for our present study is the following: there were two views on the defence build-up, which according to Goh were both incorrect. The first was that Singapore was too small, both in land and population size, to defend itself against armed attack by countries bigger in size. To this, Goh's response was that Singapore's National Servicemen were well-trained to the "highest professional standards" and "equipped with the best weapons money can buy". In addition, there was still a reserve service liability for ten years after completing two years of National Service, giving a total of 12 years. This, plus the full-time army though "comparatively small", presented a "substantial force by any standard" and "should be adequate to protect Singapore against any foreseeable military threat".

The second view was that the government was over-spending on defence by "arming ourselves in a precipitate manner and to an extravagant degree". To this accusation, Goh's counterargument was that even at the current pace, "it would not be until 1979, that is, the end of the next decade, that we would reach the full potential of the order of battle", and that was assuming that Singapore could continue to "provide weapons, ammunition, equipment and transport for each and every Reserve Battalion". Singapore must also be able to keep its "options open for faster build-up should this prove necessary".

There was no doubt that Singapore was spending a lot of money on defence. Goh admitted as much in a 1972 speech. It was necessary: "If history has one lesson to teach us, it is that we can hope to live in peace if we maintain strong defences. Small countries generally have no other desire than to be left in peace to develop their potential. But until a new international order is created whereby small nation states can have an assurance that their territory and independence will always be

---

[14] Speech delivered at the presentation of the Annual Budget Statement in Parliament on 3 Dec. 1968, *Wealth of East Asian Nations: Speeches and Writings by Goh Keng Swee*, ed. Linda Low (Singapore: Federal Publications, 1995), pp. 3–22; See also Chin, "Singapore: Threat Perception and Defence Spending in a City-State", pp. 206, 211.

respected, there is no choice than the example of Switzerland and Sweden".[15] It was also, he said in a 1974 speech, because of this spending that "further reduction of the military presence of friendly countries would not produce any adverse effect, either on our economy or on the climate of confidence". In the financial year 1971–72, 25.2 per cent of the budget went to defence. In the financial year, 1974–75, defence expenditure declined to 15.6 per cent. "This is as it should be", Goh explained, "It does not make sense when everything in Southeast Asia is relatively calm and stable, to keep spending more and more money on defence". In terms of defence expenditure as a percentage of GNP, Goh said it had been around ten per cent for some years and "had been steadily dropping till now [1974] when it is just over 5 per cent, which is what many countries keep their defence expenditure at", exceptions aside.[16] As Chin Kin Wah noted, because the Singapore economy had been performing well over the years and wealth had been accumulated, Singapore "was spared the stark choice between defence and economic development".[17]

II

In their account of Singapore's Defence, Ho Shu Huang and Samuel Chan noted that, by the early 1980s, the Singapore Armed Forces (SAF) had become "a credible fighting force". Indeed, the military historian John Keegan in 1983 described the SAF as "one of the best forces in Southeast Asia, well-trained and well-armed".[18] In 1984, the leadership was ready to introduce the concept of "Total Defence" although as early as 1966, Lee Kuan Yew had already noted that security went beyond the protection of one's borders. In his words, "it was a multi-coloured question".[19]

"Total Defence" was a natural progression from 1967 when National Service was inaugurated, and the Singapore Armed Forces was formed. It took several years before Singaporeans internalised National Service as a way of life, after which the government began to focus on the next logical area—the role of reservists—a critical component of Singapore's overall military strength and one to which Goh

---

[15] Speech at the Commissioning Ceremony of the 10th Batch of Infantry Officer Cadets, SAFTI, at the Istana, 19 July 1972. Goh was again Minister of Defence from 1970 to 1979.
[16] Speech at the Commissioning Ceremony of SAF Officers at the Istana on 12 July 1974.
[17] Chin, "Singapore: Threat Perception and Defence Spending in a City-State", p. 211. Although Chin was referring to the period of his study, from 1965 to round about mid-1980s, it is true also for the period after it.
[18] Qtd. in Ho Shu Huang and Samuel Chan, *Singapore Chronicles: Defence* (Singapore: Straits Times Press, 2015), p. 13.
[19] Ibid.

Keng Swee had alluded in his 1968 budget speech mentioned above. As the Defence Minister Goh Chok Tong (1982–91) explained in his Ministry of Defence budget speech in Parliament on 16 March 1984, "having spent many years to educate the general public concerning military defence...it is now time to cover the other potential weak spots in Singapore's security. Hence, the mass effort on civil defence starting last year [1983], and greater effort to educate the public on total defence. Otherwise, we...can be caught unawares and Singapore can go down without an aggressor even having to mount a military campaign against Singapore because we are not prepared even psychologically, socially, and in the fields of economics and civil defence".[20] "Total Defence" when first introduced thus comprised five key pillars/dimensions: military ("securing Singapore against a foreign attack"), civil (management of "local disasters and crises"), economic (building a strong and resilient economy), social ("promoting harmony across ethnic, social, cultural or religious differences") and psychological ("development of national fortitude"). In the words of Teo Chee Hean (Minister of Defence, 2003–11), in a 2005 speech, it has since become a "key component in Singapore's defence strategy": "we need more than the military for a strong defence" and "every Singaporean has a part to play to make us more resilient and strengthen the country's ability to protect itself from threats, whatever form they may take, and to overcome them".[21] We recall what Rajaratnam had told a cohort of officer cadets in 1982: at the end of the day, it is "men" not weapons that win wars. For a relatively prosperous Singapore, its acquisition of hardware presents no insurmountable problems but "you cannot buy software without which the hardware is useless junk. Only in the hands of men with requisite resoluteness, a sense of high purpose, a definition of personal honour...only then do the weapons he wields acquire the magic of invulnerability".[22]

This is the appropriate place to pause and introduce a critical component/element of Singapore's Grand Strategy, which is, to borrow Daniel Goh's phrase, "multiculturalism and the problem of solidarity".[23] Much has been written on multiculturalism and its various manifestations in Singapore by political scientists,

---

[20] Goh Chok Tong, "Main and Development Estimates of Singapore for the Financial Year 1st April [1984] to 31st March 1985", *Singapore Parliament Reports (Hansard)*, at https://sprs.parl.gov.sg/search/#/topic?reportid=011_19840316_S0002_T0004 (accessed 21 Dec. 2022).
[21] "Strategies for a Small State in Turbulent World", Excerpt from a Speech by Defence Minister Teo Chee Hean to the Singapore Press Club, 21 April 2005, *The Straits Times Interactive*, 23 April 2005; Ho and Chan, *Singapore Chronicles: Defence*, p. 12.
[22] Speech by Mr. S. Rajaratnam, Second Deputy Prime Minister (Foreign Affairs) at the 1/82 Officer Cadet Course held at the Officer Cadet School Main Auditorium, Pasir Laba Camp, 23 March 1982.
[23] Daniel P.S. Goh, "Multiculturalism and the Problem of Solidarity", in *Management of Success: Singapore Revisited*, ed. Terence Chong (Singapore: ISEAS, 2010), Chapter 30.

sociologists and others. There is no need to retrace all that has been said and written in the scholarly literature. Three points are relevant for this study: (a) "race" as an existential issue to Singapore; (b) the deliberate efforts by the government to create a distinct Singapore identity based on the unity of the different races in Singapore; and (c) the difference between the intent and the outcome of the policies.[24]

When Singapore became independent on 9 August 1965, Lee Kuan Yew assured Singaporeans that "we are going to have a multiracial nation in Singapore. We will set the example. This is not a Malay nation; this is not a Chinese nation; this is not an Indian nation. Everybody will have a place: equal; language, culture, religion..." In the same press conference, Lee specifically spoke to the Malays: "And I ask the Malays: don't worry. This was the Government that believed in multiracialism and brought Singapore away from chauvinism into multiracialism, Pity [it] turned out that we could not achieve multiracialism and integration in Malaysia. But we will achieve it in Singapore".[25] Multiracialism was written into the Singapore constitution. This is the internal/domestic dimension.

There were apparently two visions of or approaches to achieving multiracialism in Singapore; some would describe them as a "realist" versus a "idealist" approach.[26] Daniel Goh noted three phases of multiracialism in Singapore: (a) "Melting Pot" (1950s–70s), very much associated with S.

---

[24] See Daryl Choo, "Rooting Out Everyday Racism", *Today*, 29 June 2022, at https://www.todayonline.com/big-read/big-read-short-rooting-out-everyday-racism-1932656 (accessed 24 Nov. 2022); Nabilah Awang, Ng Jun Sen and S.M. Naheswari, "High Time to Talk about Racism, but Singapore Society Ill-equipped after Decades of Treating it as Taboo", *Channel News Asia*, 21 June 2021, at https://www.channelnewsasia.com/singapore/the-big-read-racism-singapore-society-race-interracial-1955501 (accessed 24 Nov. 2022); Kelly Ng, "The Policies that Shaped a Multiracial Nation", *Today*, 10 Aug. 2017, at https://www.todayonline.com/singapore/policies-shaped-multiracial-nation (accessed 24 Nov. 2022).

[25] "Transcript of a Press Conference Given by the Prime Minister of Singapore, Mr. Lee Kuan Yew, at Broadcasting House, Singapore", 9 Aug. 1965, at https://www.nas.gov.sg/archivesonline/speeches/record-details/740acc3c-115d-11e3-83d5-0050568939ad (accessed 6 Jan. 2023).

[26] For a discussion of S. Rajaratnam's view of multiracialism, see Norman Vasu, "Locating S. Rajaratnam's Multiculturalism", in *S. Rajaratnam on Singapore: From Ideas to Reality*, ed. Kwa Chong Guan (Singapore: World Scientific, 2006), pp. 125–58; see also "In His [Lee Kuan Yew's] Own Words: 'Equality is an Aspiration, it is not Reality, it is not Practical'", *The Straits Times*, 19 Aug. 2009 (this speech is described in the headnote to the transcription as one of Lee Kuan Yew's last major speeches in Parliament). PM Lee Hsien Loong, in his 2015 S. Rajaratnam Lecture ("Choice and Conviction") discussed in a later chapter, said that "Our foreign policy is a balance between realism and idealism. We know we have to take the world as it is and not as we would wish it to be. But we believe that we can and must defend ourselves and advance our interests".

Rajaratnam; (b) "Mosaic Approach" (1980s–90s); and (c) "Multiculturalism" (new millennium). The last is a combination of the first two.[27] According to Goh, as Singaporeans moved in the age of globalisation, having developed "a strong sense of racial identity that is tied to religion" (brought about by the "mosaic approach" of the previous two decades), "the problem emerges when the balance between the feelings associated with racial-religious cleavages and the sentiments of mechanical solidarity [is] disrupted by global events".[28] One example is given by the events of 11 September 2001 ("9/11"). In recent years, the rise of China has given rise to concerns that ethnic Chinese Singaporeans (the majority in Singapore), "showing sympathy and sentimentality for China", could "undermine the multiracial and multicultural character of Singapore". Bilahari Kausikan believes that Singapore's social cohesion has already been stressed,[29] although it must be said that Singaporeans overall still value racial harmony and political order.

Multiracialism, if not successfully managed, would be the Achilles heel of Singapore's Grand Strategy. The government has acknowledged that racism exists in Singapore but denies that it is systemic. While more needs to be done to strengthen social cohesion and policies need to be tweaked with the changing times, much progress has been made since 1965.[30] As former Chief Justice of Singapore Chan Sek Keong noted, "Singapore's achievement is in being able to use multiculturalism to foster social cohesion and as a building block of a new nation… Multiculturalism is here to stay because we do not have and cannot afford a dominant or a homogeneous culture. The espousal of any racial or religious community will destroy Singapore".[31]

Finally, there is an external aspect of multiracialism which is often overlooked in its discussion. Lee Kuan Yew explicated this in his 15 June 1966 "Big and Small Fishes" talk when he said that there needed to be a new balance of power in the

---

[27] For a discussion of the pros and cons of the three approaches, see Goh, "Multiculturalism and the Problem of Solidarity", in *Management of Success: Singapore Revisited*, ed. Chong, Chapter 30.
[28] Qtd. in ibid., p. 572.
[29] "Negotiating Clashing Chinese, Singapore Identities amid China's Growing Influence", *The Straits Times*, 2 May 2022.
[30] "Managing the Tensions of Tribal Politics: Lawrence Wong", *The Straits Times*, 24 Nov. 2021; "'Take the Extra Step' to Make Minorities Feel Comfortable, says Lawrence Wong in Speech Discussing Racism in Singapore", *Channel News Asia*, 25 June 2021; "Singapore has Made Much Progress on Race Issues: Lawrence Wong", *The Straits Times*, 18 April 2021.
[31] Chan Sek Keong, "Multiculturalism in Singapore: The Way to a Harmonious Society", *Singapore Academy of Law Journal* (2013), at https://journalsonline.academypublishing.org.sg/Journals/Singapore-Academy-of-Law-Journal/e-Archive/ctl/eFirstSALPDFJournalView/mid/495/ArticleId/500/Citation/JournalsOnlinePDF (accessed 5 July 2022).

region which must be non-racial or multi-racial and underpinned by some external powers, for example, the UK, the US and others. If problems in the region were resolved along ethnic lines, it would be the "big fishes that will dominate Asian waters in the sense that ultimately the demographic boundaries will be decided by the big fishes in Asia".[32]

On 15 February each year, Singapore commemorates the anniversary of the 1942 Fall of Singapore to the Japanese in World War Two as Total Defence Day. I return to the subject of "Total Defence" in subsequent chapters. Here, it suffices to say that "Total Defence", like "Total War", is an operation/activity "from which nothing and no one is exempt, and 'to which all resources and the whole population are committed'".[33] The prerequisite for the success of "Total Defence" is a unified citizenry (thus the importance of multiracialism as described above).

III

In December 1978, Vietnam invaded Kampuchea, ostensibly to save the country from the horrors of the Pol Pot regime. Singapore expended much time, energy and resources on the Cambodian issue in the 1980s, specifically from 1979 to 1988, almost a decade. And it is to this issue we now turn to understand Singapore's response to the Vietnamese invasion and its connection with Singapore's Grand Strategy.[34]

The Cambodian problem is a very significant issue in the history of the international politics of Southeast Asia, with important implications for the survival of Singapore as well as the growth and development of the Singapore Foreign Service. Former Foreign Minister S. Dhanabalan described the Cambodian issue as "the key issue for the Ministry" and "the centerpiece of ASEAN diplomacy" during the 1970s and 1980s.[35] Former Deputy Prime Minister Goh Keng Swee described the Cambodian problem as "a life-and-death struggle, the outcome of which will have [a] profound effect on the Republic".[36]

---

[32] Transcript of a talk at a meeting of the University of Singapore Democratic Socialist Club at the University campus, 15 June 1966.

[33] Paul K. Saint-Amour, "On the Partiality of Total War", *Critical Inquiry* 40, no. 2 (Winter 2014): 420; the embedded quotation is from the OED.

[34] For details, see Ang Cheng Guan, *Singapore, ASEAN and the Cambodian Conflict 1978–1991* (Singapore: NUS Press, 2013). The following narrative is extracted from the book which was written based on Singapore MFA archival documents.

[35] Tommy Koh and Chang Li Lin, eds., *The Little Red Dot: Reflections by Singapore's Diplomats* (Singapore: World Scientific, 2005), p. 41. S. Dhanabalan was Singapore's Foreign Minister from 1980 to 1988.

[36] From First Deputy Prime Minister to Mr Eddie Teo, Director SID, 13 December 1984 (Secret).

Why was the Kampuchean issue so important to Singapore? The answer was clearly explained by then Permanent Secretary, Ministry for Foreign Affairs, S.R. Nathan: "the Kampuchean issue was central to Singapore's policy. The principle involved was that no foreign military intervention should be allowed to overthrow a legally constituted regime. If this principle were violated, it would create a dangerous precedent. Foreign forces could go into Thailand and depose the current Thai government and put up a regime under the Communist Party of Thailand. Singapore had to work on the worst possible outcome... Singapore [thus] could not compromise".[37]

One would have expected small states such as Singapore to adopt a "low profile approach to foreign policy". Singapore however adopted a very "high profile" on the Cambodia issue, not, as S. Rajaratnam explained, because it had "an exaggerated capacity to influence Soviet policy". In fact, Rajaratnam quipped that what "Singapore says...is of no consequence to the Soviets". But "only a high-profile policy offers small nations the possibility of bringing influence to bear on great and powerful nations". How? Not by acting alone but by "articulating their fears openly and loudly...the collective voice of small nations" could Singapore "have an impact on the policy of a great power". Indeed, in one of his memorable lines, Rajaratnam said that "even an indifferent student of history will tell you the meek far from inheriting anything have invariably disappeared from the earth".[38] Singapore's condemnation, in both words and deed, of Russia's invasion of Ukraine in February 2022 reminds one of the responses to the Vietnamese invasion some forty years ago. By imposing sanctions on Russia, the only Southeast Asian country to do so, Singapore is under no illusion that it can alter Russia's actions, but it was important for Singapore to make a point, just as it did in the 1980s, that it 'cannot accept one country attacking another country... without justification".[39]

In the inaugural S. Rajaratnam Lecture in 2008, 30 years after the invasion of Cambodia, S.R. Nathan (who had risen to be the President of Singapore) recalled how "together with other ASEAN delegations, for a decade, Singapore diplomats helped lead the challenge to the position of Vietnam and its allies both in regional as well as international fora". Many of Singapore's career ambassadors,

---

[37] "Extract of Notes of Conversation between 1PS and Mr David Dodwell, Financial Times correspondent, MFA, 30 Oct. 1979".
[38] Speech by Mr. S. Rajaratnam, Second Deputy Prime Minister (Foreign Affairs) to the Democratic Socialist Club at the National University of Singapore, 21 Dec. 1981.
[39] Warren Fernandez, "Why Singapore Had to Take a Strong Stand against Russia's Attack on Ukraine", *The Straits Times*, 26 March 2022, at https://www.straitstimes.com/singapore/why-singapore-had-to-take-a-strong-stand-against-russias-attack-on-ukraine (accessed 24 Nov. 2022).

such as Tommy Koh, Kishore Mahbubani and Tony Siddique, and senior MFA officials cut their teeth and learnt their trade during this period. The Cambodian conflict was, in the words of Singapore diplomat Barry Desker, "the defining issue for a generation of Foreign Service officers and helped to build a strong *esprit de corps*".[40] Nathan further recalled that "in the Non-Aligned Movement and in the UN General Assembly, our stand, and that of our ASEAN colleagues, enabled us to move the matter to the 'Paris Conference on Cambodia' and helped the restoration of Cambodia's independence".[41]

In his study of Singapore's foreign policy, Michael Leifer noted that "the Cambodian conflict...was a defining period for ASEAN. It was the critical episode over and during which the Association attained and demonstrated the quality of a diplomatic community able to conduct itself up to a point, as unitary international actor. Equally significant was the way in which Singapore assumed an increasingly active diplomatic role within the Association in upholding a corporate solidarity in challenging Vietnam's military occupation of Cambodia and the legitimacy of the government carried into Phnom Penh in the saddlebags of its army".[42]

Indeed, on 12 January 1979, soon after the Vietnamese invasion of Kampuchea, a special ASEAN Foreign Ministers' closed-door meeting was convened in Bangkok. This meeting was called by Thai Prime Minister Kriangsak Chomanan to discuss the Vietnamese invasion, but it was initiated by Singapore's Foreign Minister S. Rajaratnam.[43] According to S.R. Nathan, this meeting turned out to be very significant as "it was not just a matter of ASEAN's response specifically to the Vietnamese invasion of Cambodia, although this was very important as well. It also marked the beginning of a longer phase of intense activity by Singapore's MFA in opposing the occupation".[44] Singapore diplomat Tan Seng Chye described it as a "very significant meeting" as it was during this meeting that ASEAN decided how it would respond to the Vietnamese occupation.[45] There

---

[40] Email correspondence with Barry Desker, 4 January 2010.
[41] S.R. Nathan, *Singapore's Foreign Policy: Beginnings and Future* (The Inaugural S. Rajaratnam Lecture, 10 March 2008, MFA Diplomatic Academy), pp. 27–32.
[42] Michael Leifer, *Singapore's Foreign Policy: Coping with Vulnerability* (London: Routledge, 2000), pp. 84–5. Although Leifer did not have access to the official documents, it is clear from his study that he had interviewed many officials involved in the making and execution of Singapore's foreign and defence policies who, in his words, "would almost certainly not wish to be identified".
[43] Lee Kuan Yew, *From Third World to First: The Singapore Story: 1965–2000* (Singapore: Times Editions, 2000), p. 347.
[44] S.R. Nathan, *An Unexpected Journey: Path to the Presidency* (Singapore: Editions Didier Millet, 2011), p. 385.
[45] Author's email correspondence with Tan Seng Chye, 12 June 2009.

was uncertainty in Thailand whether to come to terms with the Vietnamese.[46] Rajaratnam rallied his ASEAN colleagues. The Thais thus valued the support of Singapore in encouraging international support and rallying all ASEAN members to stay on course to oppose the Vietnamese.[47] Singapore took a strong stand against the Vietnamese because it had an "affinity of feelings" for Cambodia as "Cambodia's problems could become Singapore's problems in the future".[48]

While the resolution of the Cambodian problem is generally considered a diplomatic triumph for ASEAN, it tested ASEAN's solidarity from 1978 to 1991.[49] Over those years, there was broad agreement within ASEAN, but there were also deep divisions. According to Lee in mid-1982, Singapore shared 90 per cent of Thailand's objectives. Singapore managed to persuade Malaysia to share about 80 per cent of the objectives. Indonesia gave just about 50 per cent support and the Philippines about 55–60 per cent.[50] As the problem dragged on unresolved, the Indonesians in particular, and the Malaysians as well, became impatient with what they saw as Thailand's rigid position and began to pursue their own initiatives, which were essentially motivated by their fear of China. Indeed, in 1985, both Kuala Lumpur and Jakarta were rivals for support of their respective initiatives. In the typical ASEAN Way, the association accepted Indonesia's two-track policy towards Vietnam—one strictly bilateral and the other consistent with ASEAN policy. ASEAN also agreed that Indonesia in 1984, as well as Malaysia in 1985, could serve as "interlocutors" for ASEAN in discussions with Vietnam. The long simmering differences between Indonesia and Thailand became more obvious from 1986, but as Kishore Mahbubani stressed, the differences within ASEAN should not be exaggerated. Responding to the observation that the plethora of ASEAN statements proved that there were disagreements within the association, he retorted that "there was disgruntlement everywhere, even in Hanoi. What

---

[46] See also Alan Dawson, "Implications of a Long-term Conflict on Thai-Vietnamese Relations", in *Confrontation or Coexistence: The Future of ASEAN–Vietnam Relations*, ed. William S. Turley (Bangkok: Institute of Security and International Studies, Chulalongkorn University, 1985), pp. 154–5.
[47] Email correspondence with Tan, 12 June 2009.
[48] "Notes of Conversation between PS Mr. Chia Cheong Fook and Mr Sam Rainsy (Advisor to Prince Sihanouk)", MFA, 4 March 1983; "Notes of Dinner Conversation between Son Sann, 1DPM and 2DPM, Sri Temasek", 2 April 1983.
[49] Lee, *From Third World to First: The Singapore Story: 1965–2000*, p. 374.
[50] Brief for Prince Sihanouk's visit to Singapore (2–6 Sept. 1981), *Brief on Kampuchea* Aug.1981 (Secret); Notes of Conversation between PM and Prince Sihanouk, Istana Annexe, 28 June 1982 (Secret).

was important was that ASEAN's official stand remained unchanged".[51] And as Viji Menon explained: "All the ASEAN countries shared the same objective with regard to the Cambodian problem: the withdrawal of Vietnamese forces from Cambodia and self-determination for the Cambodian people. There were, however, differences in nuances and emphasis as to how the problem should be solved. It was difficult for all six different countries to totally agree on one approach. The differences in geo-political perceptions, history, culture and other factors should be considered. However, these factors had not prevented ASEAN from acting as a united body".[52]

Singapore's response, working in tandem with its fellow ASEAN members, to the Cambodian issue thus illustrated, in practice, two precepts of Singapore's foreign policy as described by Bilahari Kausikan, then Second Permanent Secretary, MFA: "We can, we must and we do cooperate with our neighbours. This is an imperative". "We must [however] cooperate without illusions. Problems will inevitably occur from time to time and there will be ups and downs in relationships. We must accept this and manage them. We should regard events with a certain psychological equilibrium, not becoming euphoric or complacent when things are good, and not panicking or become despondent when things are bad. We need patience, stamina, steady nerves and a long-term view, taking things one step at a time and standing firm on fundamentals... We are inescapably and forever part of South-east Asia. But we must also never be limited or be trapped by South-east Asia.... We must always reach beyond our immediate region and maintain a lifeline to the world at large".[53]

The Cambodia episode also showed Singapore's attitude towards China and the United States, the two most important countries outside the region.

There were fundamental differences between the ASEAN countries (Singapore included) and China. The ASEAN countries were disturbed by Beijing's continued support for the communist parties in the region and its assertion of a special relationship with the overseas Chinese, which they viewed as "dangerous subversion".[54] For ASEAN therefore, Cambodia must not come

---

[51] "Notes of Conversation between DD/INTL 4, K. Mahbubani and Ms Lim Yoon Lim, Straits Times, MFA, 25 March 1981". For an excellent summary of the Southeast Asian perception of the Cambodia issue, see Kishore Mahbubani, "The Kampuchean Problem: A Southeast Asian Perception", *Foreign Affairs* (Winter 1983/84): 401–25. Mahbubani was then Deputy Chief of Mission of the Singapore Embassy in Washington.
[52] "Extracts of Notes of Meeting between DD/D1, Miss Viji Menon and the Yugoslav Counsellor, Mr. Risto Nikovski, MFA, 18 November 1986" (Confidential).
[53] Bilahari Kausikan, "Some Fundamentals of Singapore's Foreign Policy", in *The Little Red Dot: Reflections by Singapore's Diplomats*, ed. Koh and Chang, pp. 104–5.
[54] Lee, *From Third World to First: The Singapore Story: 1965–2000*, pp. 664–5.

under China's influence and control.[55] Both Bangkok and Beijing did not always share similar objectives. As Nathan explained, unlike China, it was not ASEAN's objective to humiliate Vietnam.[56] From the outset Singapore was aware that eventually Vietnam's interest would have to be taken into consideration. As Kishore Mahbubani pointed out in a 1981 conversation, "Singapore did not want Vietnam to be bled until it collapsed and became a satellite of the PRC. That would be even more disastrous for ASEAN than the present situation". [57] Singapore wanted a strong, independent, and prosperous Vietnam. The fear of Vietnam, Mahbubani said in another conversation, was due only to its invasion of Kampuchea; once Hanoi withdrew its forces, Vietnam would no longer be perceived as a threat.[58]

The Chinese launched an attack on Vietnam on 17 February 1979 "to teach Vietnam a lesson" for its invasion of Kampuchea.[59] While the ASEAN countries felt that Vietnam could not be let off without repercussions, none could officially support the Chinese action for the same reason that they could not support Vietnam's invasion of Kampuchea.[60] S.R. Nathan recalled that having strongly opposed the Vietnamese invasion of Cambodia, the ASEAN countries had a problem in "coming to terms" with the Chinese invasion. ASEAN "could not reasonably endorse" the Chinese action. But luckily the Chinese troops withdrew a month after the attack "and so ASEAN was let off the hook".[61]

As for the United States, Singapore believed that the US was the only country whose aid to the non-communist side could match that of the USSR to Vietnam or China to the Khmer Rouge.[62] Singapore would have liked an arrangement whereby China backed the Khmer Rouge (a fact) and the US and ASEAN would

---

[55] "Notes of a Conversation between Minister Dhanabalan and the Hungarian Minister for Foreign Affairs, Mr. Peter Varkonyi, Hungarian Ministry of Foreign Affairs, Budapest, 16 September 1985" (Confidential).
[56] "Notes of Conversation between 1PS [Nathan] and Mr Wongsanith, Former Cambodian Ambassador to Singapore, City Hall, 16 April 1981" (Secret).
[57] "Extract of Notes of a Conversation between DD/INTL Kishore Mahbubani and Mr. Ray Burghardt, US Deputy Director of East Asian Affairs, 15 September 1981".
[58] "Notes of a Conversation between DD/INTL 4, K. Mahbubani and Mrs. Lim Yoon Lim, *Straits Times*, MFA, 25 March 1981", S017:261/13/1.
[59] For a more recent account of Chinese decision making on the Sino–Vietnamese War (1979), see Zhang Xiaoming, "Deng Xiaoping and China's Decision to Go to War with Vietnam", *Journal of Cold War Studies* 12, no. 3 (Summer 2010): 3–29.
[60] Interview with S. Dhanabalan, 1994, *Senior ASEAN Statesmen* (Oral History Centre, National Archives of Singapore, National Heritage Board, 1998).
[61] Nathan, *An Unexpected Journey: Path to the Presidency*, p. 386.
[62] Visit of PM Son Sann to Singapore (9–14 March 1984), *Information Note on Kampuchea*, 22 March 1984.

back the non-communists. Lee Kuan Yew said in a *New York Times* 1989 interview, "there would be a vague understanding that we should not fight one another while the Vietnamese are in Cambodia". But what eventuated was that "China co-opted both the Khmer Rouge and non-communists", and ASEAN "pitched in to give the non-communists a boost, but without a big backer".[63]

There were few expectations of an American role at the initial stage. The US had not overcome the "Vietnam syndrome" and American officials were not only doubtful of the capabilities of the non-communist forces, but also sceptical of ASEAN's ability to stay the course. Washington also did not want to complicate US–China relations despite Singapore's repeated argument that the US should do more to increase Thai options and reduce Bangkok's dependence on the Chinese for its security against Vietnam. In general, the Carter administration (1977–81) had little if any interest in Southeast Asia.

After 1981 (under the new Reagan administration), Singapore started lobbying for increased American assistance to the non-communist forces. The top priority was to initiate the flow of funding and then attempt to gain commitments from Washington. Both Rajaratnam and Dhanabalan, during their visits to the US capital, stressed to American leaders and officials the vital role of the US in building up a credible non-communist force in Cambodia.[64] At a one-on-one meeting with President Reagan in June 1981, Lee told him that the Soviets had been causing trouble in Southeast Asia, and that Deng Xiaoping's view was that China did not want satellite states around it and was prepared to accept whichever party won a free vote in Cambodia. This, according to Lee, helped win the support of Reagan who was "absolutely against the Vietnamese and the puppet regime". However, a conversation with Assistant Secretary of State for East Asia and the Pacific, John Holdridge, in November led Lee to conclude that a Heng Samrin victory (backed by Hanoi) was as unacceptable to the Americans as it was to the Chinese.[65] In December 1981, the Reagan Administration for the first time agreed to provide the non-communist Khmers with "administrative and financial propaganda and other non-lethal assistance". The amount was however insignificant compared to US aid to other parts of the world.[66] Washington also did not want to dispense aid directly. When the Coalition Government of Democratic Kampuchea (CGDK) was formed in 1982, Washington welcomed its

---

[63] Steven Erlanger, "Singapore Chief Fears for Cambodia", *The New York Times*, 25 Oct. 1989.
[64] "US Support for Non-communist Khmer Groups", *Information Note on Kampuchea*, 23 Oct. 1981, Issue No. 57/81 (Secret).
[65] Lee, *From Third World to First: The Singapore Story: 1965–2000*, p. 378.
[66] "US Assistance to the Non-communist Cambodian Resistance", *Information Note on Kampuchea*, 4 July 1984, Issue No. 87/84 (Secret).

formation but did not recognise it. In a nutshell, Washington generally adopted a rather lukewarm attitude towards the Cambodian issue. US Department of State officials dealing with Southeast Asia preferred a passive, minimal involvement and a low-risk US policy towards Cambodia.[67]

During talks with Foreign Minister Dhanabalan on the sidelines of the ASEAN Post-Ministerial conference in Jakarta in July 1984, US Secretary of State George Schultz confirmed his country's commitment to provide non-lethal aid to the non-communist Khmer resistance.[68] However, American policy started to shift slightly only in 1985.[69] Reagan's reaffirmation of US backing for ASEAN during his day-long visit with President Suharto in Bali in May 1986 boosted the hitherto lukewarm support for ASEAN's effort to free Kampuchea from Vietnamese occupation.[70] When they met in Manila on 27 June 1986, US Secretary of State George Shultz told Dhanabalan that current US policy on Cambodia was to provide extensive security assistance to Thailand, and a programme of support of not more than 50 per cent of the aid going to the non-communist resistance (NCR). ASEAN should provide the other 50 per cent. Washington would continue to leave the management of the Cambodia problem in ASEAN's hands.[71] In October 1986, Singapore's Ambassador to the United States reported that Washington was not committed to the NCR per se, "but supported the NCR only as a means of supporting ASEAN".[72]

Singapore's active involvement in the Vietnam–Cambodia conflict, as then-Minister of Foreign Affairs, Wong Kan Seng said much later (2011), was not about Singapore's relations with Vietnam. The bilateral relationship quickly improved soon after the resolution of the Cambodia issue. It was a matter of principle: "Vietnam's invasion of Cambodia was a clear case of violation of international borders and an act of external aggression, which would have established an undesirable precedent for international relations if let unopposed. It was external interference on the basis of internal developments". Singapore thus "had to respond" for "anything less would have undermined our credibility

---

[67] "US Attitude towards the Cambodian Government (CG)", *Information Note on Kampuchea*, S017: 146/21(7), 11 Nov. 1982, Issue No. 134/82 (Secret); "American Attitudes towards the Cambodian Problem", *Information Note on Kampuchea*, 22 June 1983, Issue No. 84/83 (Secret).
[68] Author's email correspondence with Mr. Mushahid Ali, 28 Oct. 2009.
[69] "Current US Position on Cambodia", *Information Note on Kampuchea*, 28 Sept. 1985, Issue No. 114/85 (Secret).
[70] Author's email correspondence with Mr. Mushahid Ali, 29 Aug. 2009.
[71] Extract of notes of breakfast meeting between Minister Dhanabalan and US Secretary of State George Shultz, Manila, 27 June 1986.
[72] From Bilahari Kausikan to Mr. Robert Chua (AD/VLC), 31 Oct. 1986.

and posed serious implications for our security".[73] This has been a consistent position of Singapore. For example, when Russia annexed Crimea in 2014 and invaded Ukraine in 2022, the Singapore Foreign Ministry declared that "Singapore opposes the annexation of any country or territory as it contravenes international law. We also object to any unprovoked invasion of a sovereign country under any pretext".[74] Indeed, Singapore was the first Southeast Asia country to openly express its unequivocal concern about the Russian invasion.[75]

It is necessary now to mention Singapore's response to Indonesia's invasion of East Timor in December 1975, just three years before the Vietnamese invasion of Kampuchea. Declassified British archival sources reveal that Singapore shared Indonesia's fear of East Timor being used by both Soviet and Chinese communists. Singapore's ambassador to Indonesia apparently told the British that Lee Kuan Yew had given Suharto "carte blanche" since "the unity of ASEAN was worth a blind eye". Rajaratnam, while he "accepted Indonesia's fear that Timor could end up 'like Cuba'", cautioned Suharto against "overt military intervention" as "it could create a diplomatic 'albatross'". Rajaratnam thought that "covert subversion" and patience would be a more effective approach. A Wikileaks cable has revealed that Tan Boon Seng (Deputy Secretary of Singapore's Ministry of Foreign Affairs) explained that the decision to abstain on the Timor vote was taken "at the highest level" and for three reasons: Singapore fundamentally opposed armed intervention by any country and did not think an exception could be made in this case. The forcible takeover of Timor might set a precedent for Malaysia to do the same to Brunei or even Singapore if a regime hostile to Singapore controlled Malaysia. Singapore wanted to impress on Indonesia that the city-state was not going to support "every twist and sudden turn of Indonesian diplomacy".[76]

Singapore's abstention in the 1975 UN vote on Indonesia and East Timor was "seen by the Indonesians as a major betrayal of ASEAN" and briefly affected Indonesia's relations with Singapore. In 1977, Singapore changed its vote in

---

[73] Wong Kan Seng, *Lessons for Singapore's Foreign Policy: The Cambodian Conflict* (S. Rajaratnam Lecture, 23 Nov. 2011, MFA Diplomatic Academy), pp. 14–16. Singapore also voted against the US-led invasion of Grenada in 1983.

[74] "Singapore Opposes Crimea Annexation: MFA", *The Straits Times*, 22 March 2014, at https://www.straitstimes.com/singapore/singapore-opposes-crimea-annexation-mfa; Davina Tham, "Ukraine's Sovereignty, Territorial Integrity 'Must be Respected', says Singapore as Russia Recognises Breakaway Regions", *Channel News Asia*, 22 Feb. 2022.

[75] Sebastian Strangio, "Why have Southeast Asian Governments Stayed Silent over Ukraine?", *The Diplomat*, 23 Feb. 2022.

[76] The WikiLeaks Cable is cited in Laura Southgate, *ASEAN Resistance to Sovereignty Violation: Interests, Balancing and the Role of the Vanguard State* (Bristol: Bristol University Press, 2019), pp. 55–6.

support of Indonesia.[77] This episode is an illustration of what Rajaratnam said in his primer on Singapore's foreign policy in Parliament on 17 December 1965: "the pursuit of national interests cannot be absolute in a world where the fact of national independence has to be balanced against the reality of interdependence between nations... Interdependence cannot therefore be on the basis of national interests without regards to the national interests of one's partners and friends. There will arise occasions when we have to make some sacrifice of our national interests for the long-term interests of the nation".[78]

IV

It is generally agreed that the Cambodia issue was "the greatest diplomatic success of ASEAN's first quarter century".[79] This could have been achieved only with the five ASEAN members working/coordinating closely with each other. One would have thought that, given what we know about Singapore–Malaysia–Indonesia relations (see Chapters 1 and 2), it would be very challenging for them to work well together. In fact, and surprisingly, if one looked at Singapore's relations with its two most significant neighbours from the 1960s through the 1990s (discussed in Chapter 4), one would conclude that the 1980s were perhaps the most promising decade in their relationships.

Mahathir Mohamad, who succeeded Hussein Onn as Prime Minister of Malaysia in July 1981, visited Singapore in December that year. Lee Kuan Yew, in his welcoming speech for the visiting Malaysian Prime Minister, said that because so much of both countries' past was intertwined, it had been difficult for Lee's generation to consider themselves completely different from Malaysians. It took about ten years before Malaysia and Singapore were able to establish an equable and less emotional approach to each other and to begin to have a better understanding of each other's differences: "These differences are manageable and may even bring mutual benefits if we know how to use the comparative advantage we enjoy in our different fields to complement the other's economic developments. Then we shall increase the total well-being of both people".[80]

---

[77] Lee Jones, *ASEAN, Sovereignty and Intervention in Southeast Asia* (London: Palgrave Macmillan, 2012), pp. 70–1. The author based his account on British archival sources and oral interviews, specifically with Singapore diplomats Bilahari Kausikan, K. Kesavapany and Barry Desker.
[78] Speech by the Minister of Foreign Affairs (Mr. S. Rajaratnam), Yang Di-Pertuan Negara's Speech: Debate on the Address, 17 Dec. 1965, Singapore Parliament Reports (Hansard).
[79] Ang, *Singapore, ASEAN and the Cambodian Conflict, 1978–1991*, pp. 168, 171, fn. 63.
[80] "Speech by Prime Minister Lee Kuan Yew at the Welcoming Banquet for Dato Seri Dr Mahathir Mohamad and Datin Seri Siti Hasmah", Istana, 17 Dec. 1981.

The visit was described as a "great success". Agreement was reached on the division of the territorial waters in the Straits of Johor. Mahathir even went as far as to praise Singapore's economic success and its contribution to Malaysia's economy. Vice-Premier Musa Hitam visited Singapore in February 1983 and both sides signed a slew of cooperative agreements. On 27 November 1990, just before Lee Kuan Yew stepped down as Prime Minister, both sides signed a Point of Agreement which resolved the issue of the railway land owned by the Malaysian government in Singapore. Not that there were no problems in the bilateral relationship, the most notable being the November 1986 visit of the President of Israel, Chaim Herzog, to Singapore which triggered strong protests in Malaysia.[81] Another was Second Minister of Defence Lee Hsien Loong raising the sensitive issue of the loyalty and patriotism of Malays in the SAF in Parliament, which led the Malaysians to accuse Singaporean military personnel of espionage in Johor.[82]

Regardless of how much relations with its neighbours improved, Singapore's mind-set is conditioned by the view that in foreign relations, "your best friends are never your immediate neighbour", a point which Lee Kuan Yew reiterated on several occasions. "Your neighbours are not your best friend, wherever you are", Lee declared in a speech on the subject of "International Relations". "This is because... your neighbour's hedge grows and infringes on your part of the garden and the branch of his fruit tree covers your grass and your roses do not get enough sunshine and so many things happen. And therefore our best friends, as has happened with so many other countries, are those who are farther afield with whom we can talk objectively".[83] Thus, he felt that with Malaysia, both sides should forget about sentiments and just do business with each other because "if we go into sentiments,

---

[81] See Bilveer Singh, *The Vulnerability of Small States Revisited: A Study of Singapore's Post-Cold War Foreign Policy* (Yogyakarta: Gadjah Mada University Press, 1999), pp. 213–4.

[82] Philippe Régnier, *Singapore: City-State in Southeast Asia* (Honolulu: University of Hawaii Press, 1987), pp. 158–61; Norman Vasu and Nur Diyanah Binte Anwar, "The Maligned Malays and National Service", in *National Service in Singapore*, ed. Ho Shu Huang and Graham Ong-Webb (Singapore: World Scientific, 2019), Chapter 9; "A Close and Difficult Relationship", *Today*, 23 March 2015.

[83] "Broadcast Excerpts from an Address Given by the Prime Minister, Mr. Lee Kuan Yew, on 'Changing Values in a Shrinking World' at the Political Study Centre", at https://www.nas.gov.sg/archivesonline/speeches/record-details/73d5f696-115d-11e3-83d5-0050568939ad (accessed 21 Dec. 2022); the talk was given on 13 July 1966 and broadcast on 18 July. See also the transcript of a speech by the Prime Minister, Mr. Lee Kuan Yew, at a seminar on "International Relations", held at the University of Singapore, 9 Oct. 1966.

emotions, feeling, there is going to be a great deal of antipathy...you can go into real orgies of bitterness and hate".[84]

In Singapore–Indonesia relations, the 1980s also witnessed significant improvement and cooperation, such as the agreement to develop Batam and other trade-related agreements.[85] President Suharto visited Singapore in 1983. A new Indonesian Embassy was opened in Singapore in 1985. Singapore's Chief of Defence Force, Winston Choo, recalled that General Benny Murdani (Commander-in-Chief of the Indonesian National Armed Forces, 1983–88) in conversation with him as well as openly to the Temasek Society had said that he did not see the SAF as a threat. On the contrary, a strong SAF would be good for Indonesia, and together Choo and Murdani worked towards closer military cooperation; the opening of the air range in Siabu is just one example. According to Murdani as recalled by Winston Choo, the distance from Jakarta to Singapore is nearer than that from Jakarta to the extreme portions of Indonesia. Thus, what happens in Singapore would have a greater impact on Jakarta than what happens in other parts of Indonesia. Murdani saw that the SAF was developing professionally and assessed that opening training areas to Singapore was also an opportunity for the Indonesian air force to learn from its Singaporean counterpart, and both sides would benefit.[86] Singapore–Indonesia relations, specifically Indonesia under Suharto, could be summed up by the title of an article by former Singapore ambassador to Indonesia, Barry Desker: "Lee Kuan Yew and Suharto: Friends Till the End".[87]

V

We have earlier identified two speeches which are essential to understanding Singapore's Grand Strategy: Prime Minister Lee Kuan Yew's "Big and Small Fishes in Asian Waters" speech on 15 June 1966 and Defence Minister Goh Keng Swee's 19 November 1971 speech "What Kind of War?". To conclude this chapter, this

---

[84] Transcript of a television interview with the Prime Minister, Mr. Lee Kuan Yew, by three foreign press correspondents, Creighton Burns of *The Age* [Melbourne], Nihal Singh of *The Statesman* [India] and Dennis Bloodworth of *The Observer* [London], recorded at the studios of Television Singapura, 28 July 1966; transcript of a speech by the Prime Minister, Mr. Lee Kuan Yew, at a seminar on "International Relations", held at the University of Singapore, 9 Oct. 1966.
[85] Régnier, *Singapore: City-State in Southeast Asia*, pp. 161–4.
[86] Loke Hoe Yeong, ed., *Speaking Truth to Power: Singapore's Pioneer Public Servants* (Singapore: World Scientific, 2020), p. 275.
[87] Barry Desker, "Lee Kuan Yew and Suharto: Friends Till the End", *The Straits Times*, 8 April 2015, at https://www.straitstimes.com/opinion/lee-kuan-yew-and-suharto-friends-till-the-end (accessed 12 Dec. 2022).

is perhaps the appropriate point to introduce the third important speech, that by Lee Hsien Loong at the Singapore Institute of International Affairs (SIIA) on 16 October 1984, in his capacity as Political Secretary in the Ministry of Defence. The younger Lee retired from the military and entered politics that year. A month or so before his SIIA speech, it was announced that he would be one of the PAP candidates in the forthcoming general election. He was subsequently elected as a Member of Parliament in the Singapore General Election in December and rose to become the Prime Minister of Singapore in August 2004.

The speech, entitled "Security Options for Small States",[88] made the following key points: (a) international relations resemble the law of the jungle and "in the international jungle, justice and righteousness are concepts which are edifying, resonant, but inoperative. The game is survival, and the stakes are life and death"; (b) small countries, such as Singapore, have "disabilities" which "appear overwhelming", for example, economically, they cannot be self-sufficient; militarily, they are usually outnumbered, and often lack strategic depth, "their front will also be their rear"; politically, they have relatively more difficulty in sustaining a high-quality leadership over time given a much smaller talent pool. In sum, small countries face the danger of "gambler's ruin", a mathematical problem which is "to calculate how long a gambler with a fixed initial capital can last at a casino before going bankrupt, and what are the chances that he will bust the bank instead". Ruin is more often than not the result. However, the message the younger Lee wanted to convey in his speech was that "there is, however, hope": the fate of small states and their future are "neither predestined nor dismal". Those states "with the will and the wits will survive". Like small animals in the real jungle, small countries can survive and thrive in the "international jungle". Lee Hsien Loong's "jungle" analogy echoes the elder Lee's "Big fish eats small fish" analogy.

The critical question is how? The price for survival is, in his view, "eternal vigilance" but vigilance is not enough. There are four sets of strategies that small states should apply to assure their security: "development" which he defined as "the strengthening of the nation internally, by building up a stable and cohesive society, establishing social bonds, encouraging economic growth, and strengthening political institutions"; "diplomacy" which is "the totality of a state's relations with other states in the international system"; "deterrence" and "defence" which are required because "diplomacy is no substitute for strength" and "to believe that peaceful diplomatic means can replace immoral military ones is to pursue a chimera".

---

[88] Speech at the Singapore Institute of International Affairs, Singapore, 16 Oct. 1984.

These strategies "are not mutually exclusive, and the way to survive is to apply as many of them as possible". Lee however devoted much space in his speech to expanding on the last strategy. A credible deterrence must be based on a viable defence, meaning having "a strong-armed force": The "choice confronting the nation, no matter how dire the threat, must never be suicide or surrender". One should never concede in advance, for to do so "would be to invite trouble, whereas if one is willing to pay, one may never have to pay. It is sometimes rational to be unpredictable". Small nations which hoped not to be attacked must make the costs of aggression "visibly and credibly exorbitant" by showing that "they value their freedom more than the aggressors would value their servitude". If a small state must fight, it must fight to win, but not "in the sense of overthrowing the enemies, and wiping them off the map". "It can defeat the aggressor's forces in battle, thereby defending the integrity of its boundaries, and compelling a favourable peace". Finally, small nations must learn to apply advances in "knowledge, in technology", and "in the art of war".

A somewhat subtle change is notable. With the improvement of the SAF, by the mid-1980s, the "fatalism" of the "poisonous shrimp" deterrence strategy was replaced by a new metaphor, that of a "porcupine", which in the words of Ho Shu Huang and Samuel Chan, is "a harmless creature if left on its own" but which is able to "inflict pain on an aggressor, and still survive the attack".[89]

---

[89] Ho and Chan, *Singapore Chronicles: Defence*, p. 55. For a discussion of the metaphors, see also pp. 49–64 and Ho and Ong-Webb, eds., *National Service in Singapore*, pp. 53–6; Pak Shun Ng, *From "Poisonous Shrimp" to "Porcupine": An Analysis of Singapore's Defence Posture Change in the Early 1980s*, Working Paper No. 397, Strategic and Defence Studies Centre, Canberra, Australia, April 2005.

CHAPTER 4

The Goh Chok Tong Years (1990–2004): Singapore Enters the Post-Cold War Era

I

This chapter recounts Singapore's Grand Strategy under the premiership of Goh Chok Tong from 1990 to 2004. The focus is largely on the economics–security nexus of Singapore's strategy. It also discusses the developments in Singapore's relations with its two most important pairs of relationships: the US and China; and Malaysia and Indonesia.

By the end of the 1980s, the leaders who conceptualised and crafted Singapore's Grand Strategy, except for Lee Kuan Yew, had left the political scene. Goh Keng Swee and S. Rajaratnam, who featured so prominently in the first three chapters of this book, retired from active politics in 1985 and 1988, respectively. Lee stepped down as Prime Minister in November 1990 and assumed the position/title of Senior Minister. He was succeeded by Goh Chok Tong who, at the age of 49, was eighteen years younger than Lee. As Ho Khai Leong commented, "the first thing to note about the two generations of Singapore's leadership is that the circumstances in which Lee and Goh took office were markedly different. Lee's priorities on assuming office in the late 1950s and early 1960s were to build a new nation which had been ruled by a declining imperial power for a hundred years, to compete for legitimacy with the powerful pro-communist factions, to ensure the nation's survival after the British colonial administration had left, and to maintain the island-state's competitiveness in a region that was largely hostile and suspicious". Goh, on the other hand, "inherited from Lee a nation on the verge of entering the first league, that of a developed nation. Goh would also become Prime

Minister just as the world entered the post-Cold War period".[1] Whereas therefore the Cold War was the setting for the first three chapters, the setting for this chapter on Goh Chok Tong years' premiership from 1990 to 2004, overlaps with the first post-Cold War decade.

One of the most significant features of the post-Cold War period is globalisation.[2] Globalisation of course did not begin in 1990 but "the end of the Cold War propelled such economic interdependence forward".[3] The idea that security lies in trade ties was received wisdom in the post-Cold War era. This view is being challenged as I write but it still holds true for Singapore. This is a view that the Singapore leadership (from the first generation to the current) holds close to heart. As Lee Kuan Yew said on the hundredth day of Singapore's independence, "a foreign policy must be designed to bring the surest guarantee of Singapore's survival and our prosperity"; in short, "trade and industry" are as important as "defence and security".[4] He reiterated this in 2011: "Without a strong economy, there can be no strong defence".[5] We recall, from Chapter 3, Goh Keng Swee's terse remark, "unless you have economic growth, you die". It is therefore to the subject of Economics in Singapore's Grand Strategy that we now turn. By the time Goh Chok Tong became Prime Minister in late-1990, the Singapore economy "had already achieved a relatively advanced state and was primed for further growth".[6]

II

It is necessary to begin with some background to put Singapore's economics–security strategy post-1990 into context.

As mentioned at the end of Chapter 1, a section which focused on Singapore in a 1967 report presented to the British cabinet on the "politico-military and economic implications of the proposed force reductions in the Far East" is

---

[1] Ho Khai Leong, "Prime Ministerial Leadership and Policy-making Style in Singapore: Lee Kuan Yew and Goh Chok Tong Compared", *Asian Journal of Political Science* 8, no. 1 (2000): 91–123.
[2] Prasenjit Duara, *The Crisis of Global Modernity: Asian Traditions and a Sustainable Future* (Cambridge: Cambridge University Press, 2015), p. 254.
[3] Maximilian Terhalle, "The 1970s and 2008: Theorizing Benchmark Dates for Today's Decentred Global Order", *International Studies* 56, no. 1 (2019): 1–27, p. 9.
[4] Transcript of an interview with the Prime Minister by Jackie Sam of the *Straits Times* Press and Wu Shih *of Sin Chew Jit Poh*, 16 Nov. 1965.
[5] Qtd. in Han Fook Kwang, "Is Lee Kuan Yew's Strategic Vision for Singapore Still Relevant?". *East Asia Forum*, 10 April 2019.
[6] Bridget Welsh et al., eds., *Impressions of the Goh Chok Tong Years in Singapore* (Singapore: NUS Press, 2009), p. 201.

pertinent here to our present discussion. The study noted that Singapore had no "significant natural resources" and "hitherto her undoubted prosperity by Asian standards has depended on her position as the entrepôt point for a large part of Malaysia's international trade; the entrepôt trade with Indonesia and other countries in Southeast Asia; and the presence of the British base". But since the separation, the future of Singapore as an entrepôt point for Malaysia has become "highly uncertain". Kuala Lumpur, for example, "has shown no interest in a common market with Singapore". Singapore also lost "virtually" the whole of the entrepôt trade with Indonesia because of Confrontation. This "has not yet been recovered nor is it clear whether it can be established at anything like the former level". The report further noted that it was not likely that the development of markets for products manufactured in Singapore could sufficiently support a viable economy. Some "unexpected developments" could transform Singapore's economic prospects, such as a rapprochement with Malaysia and a quick recovery of the Indonesian economy, both which were most unlikely. Therefore, the authors of the report concluded that while the growth rate in recent years had been impressive, "the underlying trends are far from encouraging and cast doubt as to whether in the long-term Singapore could maintain a viable economy at the present standard of living even if there were no question of the rundown of the British base". The economic problem Singapore faced was complicated by "the rapid growth of the working population and the already high rate of unemployment". The report concluded that if no corrective action were taken, there could be economic, social and political chaos in the country even before the British military withdrawal was completed.[7]

Goh Keng Swee had made a similar point in a 1967 speech. Asian cities, according to Goh, had a "vital role to perform" which was to "transform themselves under their independent national governments into beachheads of a dynamic modernisation process to transform the countryside". But Singapore was "completely untypical of Asian cities" for the "simple reason...that the hinterland of Singapore lies in other national cities and not within the territorial boundaries of the Republic of Singapore". Singapore thus cannot assume the role of modernising the populations of its economic hinterland. Therefore, "what we do is follow a good-neighbour policy towards our neighbours and accommodate their wishes as far as this is possible and continue to provide efficient services by

---

[7] Defence and Oversea Policy (Official) Committee, Defence Review Working Group, "Politico-Military and Economic Implications of Proposed Force Reductions in the Far East", 4 April 1967, FCO 24/45, NAB 1276. See also Chan Chin Bock et al., *Heart Work: Stories of How EDB Steered the Singapore Economy from 1961 into the 21st Century* (Singapore: Singapore Economic Development Board and EDB Society, 2002), Chapter 1 ("The Birth of the EDB").

way of trade relations, finance, insurance, shipping, communications, banking and development capital". However, he pointed out, it was "within the rights of these governments to dispense with" Singapore's services "if they do desire and if they wish to pay the price for providing their own services". And there is nothing Singapore could do to stop that.[8] Indeed, during the years under the premiership of Goh Chok Tong (1990–2004), the period saw Singapore's competitive positioning in the region being "eroded" as its neighbours, particularly Malaysia, began to compete more directly with Singapore, just as Goh Keng Swee had predicted/anticipated.[9]

We recall from Chapter 2 that Singapore's main interest in ASEAN is in its economic potential, an ASEAN "common market". Lee Kuan Yew tried to emphasise this point. According to Ben Harun (Assistant Under Secretary, Malaysian Ministry of Foreign Affairs), "a free trade area was not on the cards for a long time to come, but the habit of talking about economic matters was a good one to have started". Lee tried again at the second ASEAN Summit in 1977 for a firmer commitment to economic cooperation and intra-ASEAN free trade, also with much success. It was only 15 years later, at the fourth ASEAN Summit in 1992, that an agreement was reached to establish an ASEAN Free Trade Area (AFTA). Singapore worked behind the scenes to make this happen. Goh Chok Tong was able to persuade then-Thai Prime Minister Anand Panyarachun "to champion the proposal".[10] Fast forward, the ASEAN Economic Community (AEC) was established in 2015.[11] As Koichi Ishikawa observed, "evaluations of ASEAN's economic integration have been mixed".[12]

Given the critical importance of the economy to Singapore's security, it is not surprising that it forms a significant aspect/dimension of Singapore's Grand Strategy. In the same 1967 speech by Goh Keng Swee mentioned above, he said that while Singapore "would do everything possible to retain" its trade links with its hinterland, it would be "prudent" for Singapore "to try to broaden" its

---

[8] Speech Delivered at the Inauguration of the World Assembly of Youth (WAY) Asian Regional Seminar on "Urbanisation" at the National Trade Union Congress Hall on 16 April 1967, in Goh Keng Swee, *The Economics of Modernisation* (Singapore: Federal Publications, 1972), Chapter 2.
[9] Welsh et al., eds., *Impressions of the Goh Chok Tong Years in Singapore* (Singapore: NUS Press, 2009), p. 204.
[10] Ibid., pp. 120–1.
[11] Nicholas Tarling, *Southeast Asian Regionalism: New Perspectives* (Singapore: ISEAS, 2011), pp. 84, 91; Ang Cheng Guan, *Southeast Asia after the Cold War: A Contemporary History* (Singapore: NUS Press, 2019), p. 812.
[12] Koichi Ishikawa, "The ASEAN Economic Community and ASEAN Economic Integration", *Journal of Contemporary East Asian Studies* 10, no. 1 (2021): 25.

external economic ties by "attempting to provide services and goods to countries outside the immediate region". Goh did not think a "Southeast Asian common market" was a "practical proposition in the foreseeable future".[13] Given Singapore's limitations as described above, Goh offered four guiding points: (a) Singapore must plan its industrial growth principally on the basis of markets in developed countries; (b) Economic growth in the neighbouring countries is to Singapore's economic advantage and "to the extent that Singapore is able to assist such growth, it should do so"; (c) Singapore should make "greater efforts in cooperative endeavours between governments in non-economic fields"; and (d) Singaporeans "must know more about" neighbouring countries. (Goh observed that Singaporeans were "insular in [their] outlook to an extraordinary degree" as they knew very little about the customs, history, and the general way of life "of the enormously rich diversity of peoples in Southeast Asia". They also had very little interest in finding out.[14])

Goh Keng Swee's four points were also made, albeit differently, by S. Rajaratnam. In his first National Day message one year after Singapore's independence, Rajaratnam described Singapore as "an overcrowded island with no natural resources of its own". Singapore's prosperity and well-being depended "primarily on our being able to trade with and render services to other countries". This meant that Singapore's economic health was dependent on the economic health of its neigbouring countries. In short, Singapore could not on its own "decisively influence all the factors relating to the state of its economy". This being so, Singaporeans needed to "develop new attitudes" regarding politics and economics as the country's political and economic future would be "decisively affected by developments in the region and beyond"; Singaporeans must thus "get out of the habit of thinking and acting as though Singapore is the world". They must become more sensitive to events outside Singapore and particularly in Southeast Asia. It is in Singapore's national interest "to foster any measure to promote peace, progress and prosperity in the region". The more prosperous and peaceful Southeast Asia becomes, the greater the prospects for peace and prosperity in Singapore. In short, Singaporeans "cannot afford to think in terms of Singapore interests alone".[15]

In the previous three chapters, we have highlighted three speeches which are essential to understanding Singapore's Grand Strategy. The fourth must be

---

[13] "'Regional Cooperation in Southeast Asia', Speech Delivered at the Annual Dinner of the University of Singapore on 24 January 1970", in Goh Keng Swee, *The Economics of Modernisation*, Chapter 12.

[14] Ibid., pp. 110–1.

[15] National Day Message from the Minister for Foreign Affairs, Mr. S. Rajaratnam, 8 Aug. 1966.

S. Rajaratnam's 1972 speech entitled "Singapore: Global City" which intentionally focused on the economic dimension.[16] Rajaratnam began his speech by asking the question "why has not an independent Singapore as yet not collapsed?". After all, the conventional wisdom had been that "a small city state, without a natural hinterland, without a domestic market and no raw materials to speak of, has a near-zero chance of survival politically, economically or militarily". His answer was that Singapore was transforming itself in a "Global City". Rajaratnam, like his colleague Goh Keng Swee, anticipated that Singapore could not rely on entrepôt trade to survive as its neighbours "take over much of the trade themselves". If one accepts the view that Singapore's prosperity was the consequence of the failure of its neighbours to realise their full economic potential, "when they do so they would dispense with the services that Singapore has traditionally performed. Then it will be curtains for Singapore". But, in his analysis, "if we view Singapore's future not as a regional city but as a Global City, then the smallness of a hinterland, or raw materials and a large domestic market are not fatal or insurmountable obstacles". For a Global City, with the help of modern technology, "the world is its hinterland". Rajaratnam then gave a list of examples which Singapore could become or become a part of, including the international maritime and air communication and international financial centre networks, linking up with international and multi-national corporations and plugging into the internationalised production chain. While there were dangers in globalisation, "Singapore must be prepared to undertake these risks simply because the alternative to not moving into the global economic system is, for a small Singapore, certain death". Rajaratnam was a strong advocate of the necessity, indeed the reality of globalisation. ("Today, only the most economically primitive country can insulate itself from the international economy", he said.[17]) This reality involved the "free flow of trade internationally and a fair competition" and the "interdependency of nations",[18] which Lee Kuan Yew also prescribed.

---

[16] "Singapore: Global City", Text of address by Mr. S. Rajaratnam, Minister for Foreign Affairs to the Singapore Press Club, 6 Feb. 1972. See also Yee-Kuang Heng, "A Global City in an Age of Global Risks: Singapore's Evolving Discourse on Vulnerability", *Contemporary Southeast Asia* 35, no. 3 (Dec. 2013): 423–46.

[17] "Speech by Mr. S. Rajaratnam, Second Deputy Prime Minister (Foreign Affairs) at the opening of the Times Conference held at the Shangri-La Hotel", 4 Sept. 1984.

[18] See for example Rajaratnam's speeches on the following occasions: at the 33rd session of the United Nations General Assembly in New York, 29 Sept. 1978; at the Opening of the Times Conference on "Investment Opportunities in Turbulent Times" held at the Shangri-La Hotel, Singapore, 24 March 1983; at the International Conference on "The Future of Asia" held at the Mandarin Hotel, Singapore, 23 Aug. 1983; and at the opening of the Times Conference held at the Shangri-La Hotel, Singapore on Tuesday, 4 Sept. 1984.

This is perhaps a good place to pause and call attention to the transformation of Singapore into a global financial centre/hub. The sense of "apprehension and insecurity" post-independence led the government to adopt many policies to promote economic development to ensure the survival of Singapore, of which a key initiative was "growing a financial services centre as an engine of growth".[19] Furthermore, as Lee Kuan Yew often said, small states such as Singapore must make themselves relevant and useful so that "other countries have an interest in our continued survival and prosperity as a sovereign and independent state".[20] As J.J. Woo observed, "a specific group of cities, most of them housing successful IFCs [international financial centres], has emerged to serve as important nodes in the global economy...These 'global cities' are effectively 'command centres' for the global economy by virtue of their role in facilitating global economic transactions and acting as 'base points' in the spatial organization and articulation of production and markets".[21]

Singapore's beginnings as a financial centre date back to the colonial period. Its entrepôt trade shipping activities contributed to the formation of financial services in Singapore. But it was only with the independence of Singapore that its development as a global financial centre "took on a more systematic approach with the government taking active steps towards establishing a financial services industry in Singapore". Woo identified five phases: 1960s (Beginnings), 1970s (Growth and Expansion), 1980s (Internationalisation and Consolidation), 1990s (Liberalisation and Consolidation) and 2000s (Diversification). Apparently, the momentum for reforms of Singapore's financial sector ("towards a more transparent and accountable regulatory approach") in order to be "internationally competitive" was initiated by Lee Kuan Yew before the Asian Financial Crisis (1997). The Monetary Authority of Singapore (MAS) led the review under the guidance of Deputy Prime Minister Lee Hsien Loong.[22] Some 60 years since

---

[19] J.J. Woo, *Singapore as an International Financial Centre: History, Policy and Politics* (London: Macmillan Palgrave Pivot, 2016), p. 38; Ralph C. Bryant, "The Evolution of Singapore as a Financial Centre", in *Management of Success: The Moulding of Modern Singapore*, ed. Kernial Singh Sandhu and Paul Wheatley (Singapore: ISEAS, 1989), chapter 16, p. 338.

[20] Qtd. in Yvonne Guo and Woo Jun Jie, "The Secrets to Small State Survival", *The Straits Times*, 23 Sept. 2013, at https://www.straitstimes.com/singapore/the-secrets-to-small-state-survival (accessed 4 July 2022). The quotation is from Lee's 9 April 2009 S. Rajaratnam Lecture, at https://www.mfa.gov.sg/Newsroom/Press-Statements-Transcripts-and-Photos/2009/04/Speech-by-Minister-Mentor-LKY-at-the-S-Raj-lecture-at-shangri-la-hotel-on-thursday-9-april-2009 (accessed 22 Dec. 2022).

[21] Woo, *Singapore as an International Financial Centre: History, Policy and Politics*, p. 38.

[22] Hoe Ee Khor, Diwa C. Guinigundo and Masahiro Kawai, eds., *Trauma to Triumph: Rising from the Ashes of the Asian Financial Crisis* (Singapore: World Scientific, 2022), pp. 155–6.

independence, Singapore is internationally recognised as a leading global financial centre. This "state-led and development-driven approach" continues and is not expected to change.[23]

Manu Bhaskaran recalled that Lee "set the overall direction and framework within which the breakthrough economic policies were crafted". He was "prescient in encouraging the growth of the Singapore economy's second wing in the late-1980s, when he realised that as the economy matured, it would need to look beyond the confines of its territorial limits to find growth opportunities". Bhaskaran also noted Lee's "signal achievement" which was "the push for financial liberalisation in the late-1990s" which led to the creation of Singapore as a global financial centre.[24]

In 1987, "the world", Lee noted, "was becoming less bipolar and the great powers less ideologically motivated": "In short, we are already [in] a very changed world", he claimed, where there were "no historical precedents on how to maintain peace and stability and to ensure cooperation in a world of 160 nation states. And the age of instant communications and swift transportation, with technology growing exponentially" made "the situation even more complex". Lee adopted the idea of multilateral cooperation: "In one inter-dependent inter-related world, the decline in the relative dominance of the leaders of the two blocs increases the likelihood of a multi-polar world, and with it the difficulties of multilateral cooperation". Multilateral cooperation was the "key to development": "Hopes for a better life for our peoples depend on peace, stability and economic development in the world. We need to avoid or resolve regional wars and conflicts and to have international and regional economic cooperation... Of course, each can survive without the other [i.e. the developed and developing countries]. But to grow, to thrive, and to flourish, we need to work with each other".[25]

---

[23] Woo Jun Jie, "Singapore's Transformation into a Global Financial Hub" (2017), at https://lkyspp.nus.edu.sg/docs/default-source/case-studies/entry-1516-singapores_transformation_into_a_global_financial_hub.pdf?sfvrsn=a8c9960b_2https://lkyspp.nus.edu.sg/docs/default-source/case-studies/entry-1516-singapores_transformation_into_a_global_financial_hub.pdf?sfvrsn=a8c9960b_2 (accessed 4 July 2022); for an account of Singapore during the 1997 Asian Financial Crisis, which occurred during Goh Chok Tong's tenure, see Khor, Guinigundo and Kawai, eds., *Trauma to Triumph: Rising from the Ashes of the Asian Financial Crisis*, Chapter 9.
[24] Manu Bhaskaran, "An Architect of the Singapore Miracle", *The Business Times*, 25 March 2015.
[25] "Speech by Mr Lee Kuan Yew, Prime Minister of Singapore, Opening the Discussion on 'World Political Scene: Global Trends and Prospects'", Commonwealth Heads of Government Meeting, Vancouver, Canada, 13 Oct. 1987.

Lee repeated the above two ideas/themes two years later, in 1989, when it was much clearer that the confrontation between the communist and non-communist blocs as it had been experienced since World War Two was over. Yet he warned that "the competition between big powers for influence and power in the world will go on, in a multi-polar world. It has always been thus, whether it was the Three Kingdoms in China or the Warring States in Japan. The Big wants to assure its supremacy by growing bigger, and the Small tries to prevent this by alliances between themselves to block the Big, and to make him smaller". The competition between nations was likely to concentrate on economics.[26] In his October 1989 CHOGM (Commonwealth Heads of Government Meeting) speech, a few weeks before the fall of the Berlin Wall, he observed that "as the balance between the major powers changes, other states in the world have little choice but to adjust. But not all these developments are adverse. There is a strong desire in the East and West, in the North and South, to concentrate energies and resources on economic development, and to restrain expenditure on arms. This could usher in an era of worldwide international cooperation through multilateral institutions".[27]

Goh Chok Tong's economic policies and initiatives must be understood as a continuation of the Lee–Rajaratnam–Goh worldview and grand strategy. In December 1989, Goh Chok Tong (then first Deputy Prime Minister) mooted the idea of the Singapore–Johor–Riau (SIJORI) Growth Triangle with the aim of strengthening "the regional links and to optimise the complementarity" of the three adjacent areas by combining "Singapore's management expertise, capital, technology and infrastructure with the abundant labour, land and natural resources of Johore and the Riau province".[28] The Riau Islands form the closest Indonesian province to Singapore. Singapore and Johor have, in the words of historian Kwa Chong Guan, a "deeply connected history".[29] With more Malaysian and Indonesian states joining, SIJORI was renamed and formalised as the Indonesia–Malaysia–Singapore Growth Triangle (IMS-GT) in December 1994.[30] Manu Bhaskaran recalled that in the late-1980s, Lee Kuan Yew spearheaded

---

[26] Lecture by the Prime Minister of Singapore to the Thai National Defence College, Bangkok, 19 Sept. 1989.
[27] Toast by the Prime Minister at a Dinner for Commonwealth Heads of Government, Singapore, 25 Oct. 1989.
[28] Nor-Afidah Abd Rahman, "Growth Triangle", at https://eresources.nlb.gov.sg/infopedia/articles/SIP_58_2005-01-06.html (accessed 28 June 2021).
[29] I wish to thank Mr Kwa Chong Guan for sharing his draft essay "Singapore and Johor: A Connected History".
[30] Nor-Afidah Abd Rahman. See also Ooi Giok Ling, "The Indonesia–Malaysia–Singapore Growth Triangle: Sub-Regional Economic Cooperation and Integration", *GeoJournal* 36, no. 4 (Aug. 1995): 337–44.

economic integration with Indonesia's Riau Islands but was not so successful with Malaysia because of the lingering legacy of separation.[31] According to Kwa Chong Guan, Singapore's function as a gateway harbour to the Johor River realm of the Johore sultans declined when the sultans decided to move their capital to Bintan in the eighteenth century. A cycle of Singapore's connected history with Johor thus closed until a new cycle was launched by Raffles and Tengku Husain in 1819. Singapore again became the preferred trading port of the Johor–Riau Malay world until the 1960s. Goh Chok Tong's proposal of a Singapore–Johor–Riau Growth Triangle in a way renewed connections not only between Singapore and Johor, but also with the Riau Islands, recreating, in effect, the economic world of the old Johore Sultans.[32]

The establishment of the APEC (Asia-Pacific Economic Cooperation) forum, first broached by Australian Prime Minister Bob Hawke in January 1989, initially as an informal ministerial-level dialogue group of twelve countries in November that year, was a major expression of the increasing interdependence of regional economies at the end of the Cold War. APEC as an institution was formalised in 1993. Singapore was "Australia's strongest backer within ASEAN".[33] Michael Intal Magcamit has noted that "the linking of security and trade under the purview of APEC underscores the healthy and dynamic relations among member states in reducing the likelihood of regional conflicts. The constructivist vision of the APEC community is primarily rooted in the belief in harmony of interests that is made by possible interdependence".[34]

In a speech on 8 January 1993, Lee Kuan Yew (at that time Senior Minister) spoke about Singapore's need to develop an external economy—a "second wing" to give its economy an "external boost" just like other successful mature economies.[35] Since the speech, Arun Mahizhnan noted the year after, "the development of the external economy [had] become a major preoccupation in Singapore".[36] Lee's speech echoed and gave his imprimatur to the report entitled *The Strategic Economic Plan: Towards a Developed Nation* issued by the Singapore Government

---

[31] Bhaskaran, "An Architect of the Singapore Miracle".
[32] Email correspondence with Kwa Chong Guan on 5 June 2021.
[33] Graeme Dobell, "Lee Kuan Yew and Oz", *The Strategist*, 24 March 2015, at https://www.aspistrategist.org.au/lee-kuan-yew-and-oz/ (accessed 10 Jan. 2023).
[34] Michael Intal Magcamit, *Small Powers and Trading Security: Contexts, Motives and Outcomes* (London: Palgrave Macmillan, 2016), p. 50.
[35] Lee Kuan Yew, "Efforts to Overcome the Dearth of Entrepreneurs in Singapore", Speech at the Business Awards Ceremony at the Shangri-La Hotel, Singapore, 8 Jan. 1993. See also Arun Mahizhnan, "Developing Singapore's External Economy", in *Southeast Asian Affairs 1994* (Singapore: ISEAS, 1994) pp. 285–301.
[36] Mahizhnan, "Developing Singapore's External Economy", p. 285.

in 1991 which called upon "Singaporeans, who lacked a hinterland, to think of the whole world as their hinterland... Singapore needed to go global". The report envisaged going global as a series of concentric circles: "Singapore as a country, the region, the outer world, and finally the global economy in the outer ring".[37]

The Goh administration thus oversaw the development of Singapore's "second wing" (aka the "external economy"). Singapore became "a leader in negotiating free trade agreements to the rest of the world".[38] In the wake of the Asian Financial Crisis (1997), Singapore saw free trade agreements as the antidote to such crises and the solution to ensure Singapore's economic survival. Its first bilateral free trade agreement was with New Zealand, and this came into effect on 1 January 2001. As Manu Bhaskaran explained, "the web of bilateral agreements" would "enhance Singapore's regional hub status by expanding the country's connectivity and access to many large economies". Given that Singapore is one of the most trade-dependent countries in the world, such agreements would also offer "some insurance" against a possible collapse of the multilateral trade order.[39] It is worth noting that the World Trade Organisation (WTO) has not been able to achieve any major trade pact since its establishment in 1995: The WTO, after fourteen years of negotiations, had effectively ended the Doha Talks which began in 2001.[40] In Michael Intal Magcamit's analysis, for "a small and pragmatic state like Singapore, the means to survival is through sustained economic growth and progress via free trade". This would explain the Singapore government's persistent emphasis on "robust trade performance as a key of national security". Trade therefore "serves as a defence-upgrading mechanism that enhances and preserves Singapore's long-term viability in international politics".[41]

Tommy Koh described Goh Chok Tong as the "architect" of Singapore's FTA policy which helped "transcend the limitations of Singapore's small size".[42] By the end of Goh's tenure as prime minister in August 2004, Singapore had signed Free Trade Agreements with Japan, Australia, the European Free Trade Area (EFTA),[43] Jordan (the first with a Middle Eastern country) and most importantly,

---

[37] Ibid., pp. 285–6. An earlier 1986 report, produced in the wake of Singapore's first post-independence recession in 1985, entitled *The Singapore Economy: New Directions,* cited offshore activities as a key factor for future growth.
[38] Welsh et al., eds., *Impressions of the Goh Chok Tong Years in Singapore,* p. 211.
[39] Ibid., pp. 211–2.
[40] The Editorial Board, "Global Trade After the Failure of the Doha Round", *The New York Times,* 1 Jan. 2016.
[41] Magcamit, *Small Powers and Trading Security: Contexts, Motives and Outcomes,* p. 213.
[42] Welsh et al., eds., *Impressions of the Goh Chok Tong Years in Singapore,* p. 127.
[43] EFTA is an association of four European countries (Iceland, Liechtenstein, Norway and Switzerland), and is to be distinguished from the European Union (EU; EUSFTA 2019).

the United States. One of the most repeated stories was how Goh overcame the bureaucratic obstacles posed by American officials in the wake of the 1994 Michael Fay caning incident (discussed later in this chapter). Through "golf diplomacy" during the APEC meeting in Vancouver in November 1997, he managed to meet President Clinton for the first time—on the exclusive Shaughnessy Golf Course. This paved the way for the United States–Singapore Free Trade Agreement signed in May 2003. Although the Agreement was eventually signed by President George W. Bush, the idea was broached by Goh and agreed to by Clinton towards the end of his two-term presidency. As Peh Shing Huei, in his authorised biography of Goh Chok Tong noted, "the partner Singapore wanted to bed most was the United States. It would have a major signalling effect to other countries and greatly boost Singapore's chances to secure more FTAs".[44]

There is another aspect of FTAs besides business and economics, as an FTA implies more than just "economic integration that eliminates tariffs (and quantitative restrictions) between participating countries".[45] An FTA can also serve as "a tool for addressing security issues, namely: cooperative diplomacy, security alliance, competitive bilateralism and isolation avoidance".[46] Although here we are running ahead of our narrative, it is worth noting that it is for this reason that Singapore tried very hard but unsuccessfully to persuade Washington to ratify the Trans-Pacific Partnership (TPP) Agreement which it signed in 2016. As Lee Hsien Loong said in an interview with the US newsmagazine *Time* that year, the "TPP is more than just a trade deal".[47] But President Donald Trump in January 2017 withdrew the US from the TPP.

In Singapore's case, the leadership has "grafted the country's security requirements into its FTA agendas in the hope of effectively containing potential threats to its survival as a sovereign nation-state".[48] One example is that signed with the United States which is "the product of crisscrossing interests between the two states attempting to implant security elements within their trade

---

[44] For the full account, see Peh Shing Huei, *Standing Tall: The Goh Chok Tong Years, Volume 2* (Singapore: World Scientific, 2021), Chapter 13. It was extracted in Peh Shing Huei, "Ichigo Ichie—One Encounter, One Chance—in Ending US Blockage", *The Straits Times*, 29 May 2021; Welsh et al., *Impressions of the Goh Chok Tong Years in Singapore*, p. 125.
[45] Ishikawa, "The ASEAN Economic Community and ASEAN Economic Integration", p. 32.
[46] Magcamit, *Small Powers and Trading Security: Contexts, Motives and Outcomes*, pp. 49–50.
[47] "TPP is More than just a Trade Deal or Jobs Issue for Americans", *The Straits Times*, 27 Oct. 2016.
[48] Michael Intal Magcamit, "Trading in Paranoia: Exploring Singapore's Security-Trade Linkages in the Twenty-first Century", *Asian Journal of Political Science* 23, no. 2 (2015): 186.

relations".[49] Singapore's "linkage attempts" to overcome its multidimensional security complex brought about by geographical constraints, Magcamit warned, could for example result in "its failure to strategically balance conflicting American, Chinese and Japanese interests in the region". Linkages can be a "double-edged sword" as "for every additional security that a linkage provides a specific referent, corresponding insecurity is reflected in other referents". Magcamit argued that states, such as Singapore, which adopt and implement the Security-Trade Linking Strategy, "are virtually trading security given that for every security enhancement that a linkage creates, a consequent insecurity is generated". Thus, he concluded that "Singapore's objective of securing its defence space can result in its failure to effectively balance and reconcile the conflicting interests of its super power partners".[50] This is certainly food for thought and we return to it in the next chapter.

But for the present context, as Goh Chok Tong's biographer, Peh Shing Huei noted, Goh (during his tenure as Prime Minister from 1990 to 2004) "not only expanded Singapore's international space with his 'second wing' strategy through free trade agreements and investments abroad, but also cemented the city-state's status as a relevant global player with his multiple multilateral creations such as the Asia–Europe Meeting and the Asia–Middle East Dialogue. If Lee had drawn the attention of the world, Goh made sure Singapore was not going to be forgotten or ignored anytime soon".[51] Alan Chong has noted that the Asia-Europe Meeting (ASEM), the Forum for East Asia–Latin America Cooperation (FEALAC) and the Asia–Middle Eastern Dialogue (AMED) were "the most ambitious extensions of Goh's strategy of building presence through diplomatic bonhomie".[52] This echoes Rajaratnam's advice that Singapore should always make the maximum number of friends, and if possible not have any enemies. According to Chong, Goh's initiatives could on the one hand be interpreted as the "predictable extensions of the road map laid out by the Lee–Rajaratnam foreign policy Team in 1965, namely the resource-barren republic could only survive by being outward-oriented". At the same time, these initiatives also reflect Goh's "joining his ardent nationalism to a passionate idealism for an open and

---

[49] See discussion of the United States-Singapore Free Trade Agreement in Magcamit, "Trading in Paranoia: Exploring Singapore's Security-Trade Linkages in the Twenty-first Century", pp. 194–7.
[50] Magcamit, *Small Powers and Trading Security: Contexts, Motives and Outcomes*, p. 223.
[51] Peh, *Standing Tall: The Goh Chok Tong Years, Volume 2*, p. 265.
[52] Welsh et al., eds., *Impressions of the Goh Chok Tong Years in Singapore*, p. 133. For a full discussion see Chapter 11.

pacific social contract with the fledging notion of being global" which cannot be simply categorised as "power politics".[53]

III

Multilateral cooperation/Multilateralism, which Singapore strongly advocated and continues to advocate, is not confined to the economic realm. Towards the end of the Cold War, Lee Kuan Yew also advocated the strengthening of multilateral institutions, starting with the UN and its agencies. Lee however knew that it was beyond the capacity of Singapore to change the UN. In the late 1980s, he felt that Singapore needed a "friendly constituency within the UN that shared our concerns". This led to the formation of the Forum of Small States (FOSS) in the UN in 1992. As Chew Tai Soo noted, "FOSS came about from a simple observation that small states, which formed the majority of the membership in the UN, tended to be disadvantaged because they lack 'strategic weight'". [54] According to S. Jayakumar, FOSS had over the years developed into a "useful forum for discussing issues of common concern from the perspectives of small states" and has become so well-known and regarded in the UN that candidates running for key posts had requested the Singapore Permanent Representative (who leads FOSS) to convene FOSS meetings for them to canvass support. A Singapore initiative, the country has remained the Chair of FOSS since its inception. Noeleen Heyzer (former UN under-secretary general) noted that Singapore understands "the importance of multilateralism given its size as a small city-state"; "international bodies such as the UN have protected Singapore by providing a platform for small countries to build a network of friends and enlarge their diplomatic geopolitical space".[55] Lee Hsien Loong believed that small states such as Singapore, while it can do little to influence

---

[53] Ibid.

[54] Chew Tai Soo was Singapore Permanent Representative to the UN who oversaw the establishment of FOSS with 16 members. In 2017 (its 25th anniversary), FOSS comprised 107 member-countries, comprising more than half of the UN membership. See Tai Soo Chew, "A History of the Forum of Small States", in *50 Years of Singapore and the United Nations*, ed. Tommy Koh, Liling Chang and Joanna Koh (Singapore: World Scientific, 2015), pp. 35–8; Vanu Gopala Menon, "Singapore and the United Nations", in *The Little Nation that Can: Singapore's Foreign Relations and Diplomacy*, ed. Gillian Koh, Commentary, Volume 26 (2017), Chapter 18; S. Jayakumar, "Reflections on Diplomacy of a Small State", S. Rajaratnam Lecture, 2010, 19 May 2010, and Lee Hsien Loong, "Transcript of Video Message by PM Lee Hsien Loong at the United Nations General Assembly High Level Forum of Small States' (FOSS) Reception on 22 September 2022" (New York), at https://www.pmo.gov.sg/Newsroom/PM-Lee-Hsien-Loong-at-the-30th-Anniversary-of-the-Forum-of-Small-States (accessed 6 Jan. 2023).

[55] Goh Yan Huan, "Lifting Millions out of Poverty Still a Challenge for Asia: Ex-UN official", *The Straits Times*, 17 Nov. 2021.

big powers, are not entirely devoid of agency as "there are many opportunities for smaller countries to work together to deepen economic cooperation, strengthen regional integration, and build up multilateral institutions".[56]

In speeches during the period before and after he relinquished his position as Prime Minister, Lee Kuan Yew appraised the strategic problems that confronted the world after the end of the Cold War and the dissolution of the Soviet Union in 1991. He viewed the 1990s in the context of a new geopolitical configuration which posed new challenges and hazards for Asian countries. He highlighted the need for a new balance of power, but one that was founded on economic strength rather than military power. He also foresaw the shift in the global balance to the Asia-Pacific with the inevitable rise of China economically, followed by that of India. Lee believed that never had there been a moment "so propitious in history" for the industrial democracies to shape a system—along with the necessary institutions—to allow all countries to develop in cooperation and in competition.[57] Last but not least, he underlined the need for the United States to maintain a presence in the region as a countervailing power.

One early example is the formation of the ASEAN Regional Forum (ARF). The ARF was inaugurated in Singapore in 1993. It was formally launched in Bangkok in July 1994. Although the Forum was a Japanese idea, ASEAN was the driving force from the outset. ASEAN played a leading role in establishing the ARF with the objective of fostering "multilateral dialogue on security matters".[58] Singapore played a "quietly nudging" role by providing the first drafts of two key papers on the structure, role and membership of the ARF that were later adopted at the Forum's meetings in 1995 and 1996.[59]

Peter Ho (then Permanent Secretary at the Singapore Ministry of Foreign Affairs) recalled that the creation of the ARF "was not pre-ordained" and "it would have been unimaginable during the Cold War".[60] The end of the Cold War brought about a transformation in the security landscape. With the collapse of the

---

[56] PM Lee Hsien Loong at the IISS Shangri-La Dialogue 2019, at https://www.pmo.gov.sg/Newsroom/PM-Lee-Hsien-Loong-at-the-IISS-Shangri-La-Dialogue-2019 (accessed 25 Jan. 2022).
[57] "Never Has There Been a Moment so Propitious in History: PM" in *The Straits Times Weekly Overseas Edition*, 10 Feb. 1990.
[58] Carlyle A. Thayer, *Multilateral Institutions in Asia: The ASEAN Regional Forum* (Hawaii: The Asia–Pacific Center for Security Studies, December 2000), p. 5.
[59] Presentation by Kishore Mahbubani, Permanent Secretary (Singapore Ministry of Foreign Affairs) at the Policy Forum organised by the Institute of Policy Development, 20 Sept. 1996.
[60] Peter Ho, "The ASEAN Regional Forum: The Way Forward?", in *ASEAN–UN Cooperation in Preventive Diplomacy*, ed. Sarasin Viraphol and Werner Pfenning (Bangkok: Ministry of Foreign Affairs, Thailand, 1995), p. 251.

Soviet Union, the United States emerged as the sole superpower. For the ASEAN states, there was uncertainty whether Washington would remain engaged in the region. Washington's interest had been waning since the end of the Vietnam War. By the early 1990s, US forces had already vacated Clark Air Base and Subic Bay in the Philippines. Meanwhile, China was gradually rising and emerging as a global economic player.

"This sense of uncertainty", according to Ho, "inspired some serious thinking about a political and security framework in the Asia–Pacific". Ho revealed that ideas mooted in the early post-Cold War years by countries such as Australia, Canada and Japan however met with resistance because the major powers—the United States and China—were uncomfortable with any framework created by the other or their allies. ASEAN too felt that external parties were not sufficiently neutral to lead this project. Thus, almost by default, ASEAN (whose members also felt the "need to strengthen the network of linkages within the Asia–Pacific and in forging a predictable and constructive pattern of relationships") was perceived to be neutral, so as to assume a leading role. As he put it, "the ASEAN Regional Forum could be described as the culmination of almost two decades of steady ASEAN diplomacy" beginning in the 1970s with the introduction of "dialogue partnerships" with external powers.[61] In 1993, China and Russia had become regular guests at the annual ASEAN Ministerial meetings and Laos and Cambodia became Observers of ASEAN coinciding with the establishment of the ARF.

Singapore also played a key role in upgrading India's status as a full dialogue partner of ASEAN in 1995 as well as India's becoming a member of the ARF in 1996. During the later Cold War years of the 1970s and 1980s, Singapore and India were on different sides of the divide. ASEAN's relations with India were strained because of New Delhi's support for the Soviet Union and Vietnam's occupation of Cambodia. In 1987, however, New Delhi's position towards the Cambodian issue began to tilt towards supporting ASEAN's informal initiatives to resolve the almost-decade long Cambodia issue. Relations between Singapore and India, both members of the Commonwealth, also slowly improved beginning first with Lee Kuan Yew reaching out to Indira Gandhi's son and successor, Rajiv Gandhi, in March 1988. The bilateral relations intensified under Goh Chok Tong and India's Prime Minister Narasimha Rao when they met at the Non-Aligned Movement Summit in September 1992. In September 1994, Narasimha Rao visited Singapore where, for the first time, he articulated India's Look East Policy, which his successors followed. Singapore had "consistently advocated and actively

---

[61] Ibid.

supported India's engagement of the region" and had played a key role in helping India re-engage with it. In 2002, Singapore and India agreed to work towards a comprehensive economic partnership. The India–Singapore Comprehensive Economic Cooperation Agreement (CECA), a free trade agreement (FTA), was eventually signed by Goh's successor Lee Hsien Loong in June 2005. Singapore and India have also close defence relations. Both countries signed a Defence Cooperation Agreement (DCA) in October 2003. Singapore diplomat Gopinath Pillai noted that over the years, both countries "have shown reciprocity in enhancing their defence mechanism through joint exercises".[62]

It is common knowledge that ASEAN's twin objective for the ASEAN Regional Forum (though not mentioned so explicitly) was to "envelop" a rising China in this multilateral organisation[63] and to keep the unipolar power, the United States (absorbed by developments in Eastern Europe and elsewhere), engaged in the region within a multilateral framework. As the former Singapore diplomat Kishore Mahbubani observed: "the task of both restraining" the United States and China "while preserving at the same time their enthusiasm for the ARF is an inherently difficult task" even during the "propitious and relatively benign security environment" in the Asia–Pacific of the early 1990s. Then-Singapore Prime Minister Goh Chok Tong cautioned that if Sino–US relations failed to stabilise, it would start a second Cold War, affecting the whole region.[64] Singapore's support for the objectives of the ARF is consistent with Singapore/Lee Kuan Yew's views.

IV

It is to Singapore's relations with the US and China that we now turn. In keeping with the strategy of ensuring that Singapore is relevant and useful to these two countries at critical times, while remaining non-aligned, Singapore in turn has been a beneficiary not only of security cooperation with the US but also of China's economic success.

Singapore has kept faith with the United States from the time the countries established diplomatic relations. Commenting on the refocus to Southeast Asia—the "pivot to Asia" by the Obama Administration in 2009—Lee Kuan

---

[62] For a concise account of Singapore–India relations, see Koh, ed., *The Little Nation That Can: Singapore's Foreign Relations and Diplomacy*, Chapter 9.

[63] See Rosemary Foot, "China in the ASEAN Regional Forum: Organisational Processes and Domestic Modes of Thought", *Asian Survey* XXXVIII [38], no. 5 (May 1998): 425–40.

[64] Presentation by Kishore Mahbubani, Permanent Secretary (Singapore Ministry of Foreign Affairs) at the Policy Forum organised by the Institute of Policy Development, 20 Sept. 1996.

Yew noted that the US had left East Asia "fallow" over the last eight years, "preoccupied with [the US'] own wars". In fact, Washington, while it never really abandoned the region, had shifted its attention away from Southeast Asia since 1975 when the Vietnam War ended. Not long before he stepped down as prime minister, Lee Kuan Yew and US Vice President Dan Quayle signed an MOU in 1990 which facilitated the US presence in the region, which Singapore believed would provide the "security umbrella" under which emerging economies, such as Singapore, in Asia could thrive.[65] When the Philippine Congress in 1991 voted to shut down the American bases there, Singapore offered to upgrade its naval base to service the US fleet and to serve as a transit point for US naval operations in the region, thus providing the US with a forward operating facility in Singapore.[66] More than any other Southeast Asian country, Singapore has consistently believed in the need for an American presence to remain in Asia. Lee expressed his rationale: "Nature does not like a vacuum. And if there is a vacuum, we can be sure that somebody will fill it. I don't see Japan particularly wanting to fill that space unless it feels that its trade routes and access to Gulf oil are threatened. If the Americans are not around, they [the Japanese] cannot be sure who will protect their oil tankers. So they have to do something themselves. That will trigger the Koreans, who fear the Japanese, then the Chinese. Will India then come down to our seas with two aircraft carriers? It could be a disastrously unstable state of affairs. So why not stick with what has worked so far? The US presence has maintained peace on the high seas of the Pacific since 1945. The American presence, in my view, is essential for the continuation of international law and order in East Asia".[67] However, when President George W. Bush reportedly invited Singapore to become a non-NATO ally, Singapore demurred "owing to the political sensitivities with its Muslim neighbours Indonesia and Malaysia that any such acceptance might have provoked".[68]

Singapore and China established formal diplomatic relations in October 1990, shortly before Goh Chok Tong assumed the premiership in November 1990. Goh recalled that in the early 1990s, China had only just begun to open up but "it was still shrouded by a bamboo curtain". Few countries had direct links to the Chinese leadership or had much understanding of developments in China.

---
[65] "S'pore Interests Come First—Whatever the Global Shifts", *The Straits Times*, 11 Nov. 2016.
[66] See Daniel Chua, "Singapore's Relations with the United States of America" in Koh, ed., *The Little Nation that Can: Singapore's Foreign Relations and Diplomacy, Commentary*, Chapter 3.
[67] "Why American Economic and Security Presence [is] Vital for Asia", *The Straits Times*, 17 Dec. 1991.
[68] Tan See Seng, "(Still) Supporting the Indispensable Power: Singapore's Relations with the United States from Trump to Biden", *Asia Policy* 16, no. 4 (Oct. 2021): 80.

Singapore was thus "well-placed to play this role" of connecting western/European countries with China given that Singapore "had established strong links with the Chinese leadership and was well-regarded as a reliable interlocutor".[69] Singapore had played a positive role in assisting China's economic development when Deng Xiaoping was embarking on his open door and economic modernisation policy in the 1980s, and even into the 1990s when China was ostracised by the West in the immediate years after the Tiananmen Square incident. Goh Keng Swee, after he retired from politics, served for a period as an economic adviser to the coastal areas of China and was tasked to make recommendations on the development of China's coastal economic zones.[70] As John Wong noted, "the political and economic networks built over the years have proved most invaluable" and the China–Singapore Suzhou Industrial Park (SIP), established in February 1994, is "a concrete symbol of the substantive relationship between China and Singapore".[71] The Industrial Park therefore is a physical manifestation in the real world of Yuen Foong Khong's observation: "Singapore's preferred response is to engage China" and not "to contain it".[72] Finally, a clear indication of more than good relations between the two countries during this period was the choice of Singapore as the venue of the cross-strait dialogue, more commonly referred to as the Wang–Koo talks in 1993. Wang Daohan was chairman of China's Association for Relations Across the Taiwan Straits, and Koo Chen-fu was chief of Taiwan Straits Exchange Foundation. Twenty-two years later, in November 2015, Singapore would again be the venue of a cross-strait meeting between Chinese President Xi Jinping and Taiwanese President Ma Ying-jeou.

While the political leadership works towards ensuring that a small country like Singapore is always relevant and useful, the leadership is also very protective of its capacity to act independently and to make its own choices. Two episodes, one involving the United States and the other China, which happened during Goh Chok Tong's tenure illustrate this. In 1994, an American teenager, Michael Fay, was sentenced to six strokes of the cane for vandalism and theft. This created a

---

[69] Goh Chok Tong, "The Practice of Foreign Policy for Sustained Growth—the Singapore Experience", S. Rajaratnam Lecture, 17 Oct. 2014 (Singapore: MFA Academy, 2014).
[70] See Zheng Yongnian and John Wong, eds., *Goh Keng Swee on China* (Singapore: World Scientific, 2012).
[71] John Wong and Lye Liang Fook, "Introduction: Singapore–Suzhou Industrial Park 20 Years On: Development and Changes", in *Suzhou Industrial Park: Achievements, Challenges and Prospects*, ed. John Wong and Liang Fook Lye (Singapore: World Scientific, 2020), at https://www.worldscientific.com/doi/pdf/10.1142/9789811200045_0001 (accessed 19 Oct. 2021).
[72] See Yuen Foong Khong, "Singapore: A Time for Economic and Political Engagement", in *Engaging China: The Management of an Emerging Power*, ed. Alastair Iain Johnston and Robert S. Ross (London: Routledge, 1999), Chapter 5.

furor in the United States and pressure (from the highest level in the United States–President Clinton himself) was exerted on the Singapore government to grant clemency from caning. Despite the pressure, the caning went ahead although it was reduced from six to four strokes "out of consideration for Clinton's appeal".[73] The reduction was however not received with appreciation. S.R. Nathan recalled, "Singapore could not be seen to be practising double standards. We had previously caned many of our own criminal offenders and nationals from neighbouring countries. Our own public and these governments were watching closely to see if an American would get special treatment".[74]

The next episode occurred towards the end of Goh's tenure as prime minister. Lee Hsien Loong, who was scheduled to succeed Goh as prime minister in December 2004, paid a "private and unofficial" visit to Taiwan from 11–13 July 2004 "to get a first-hand feel of the current situation there". July was apparently the only "window" to go there before he became prime minister. Beijing created a ruckus over the visit. The Chinese had been informed in advance of the visit "as a courtesy" and they wanted the trip to be called off. As Lee explained, "Singapore's relations with China are based on equality and mutual respect. Singapore is a good friend of China. But to call off the trip at China's request would have undermined our right to make independent decisions and damaged our international standing".[75] Singapore at the time was hoping/planning to negotiate a bilateral free trade agreement with China. It was reported that the FTA "could suffer setbacks" because of the Taiwan trip. Responding to the report, Singapore Trade and Industry Minister George Yeo said that "if one wishes to delay, then it cannot be helped". "But", he quipped, "not too long, I hope".[76]

V

Readers may recall from the previous chapter that Singapore's relations with its two most important neighbours, Malaysia and Indonesia, had improved considerably from the low of the 1960s. We have mentioned the Singapore–Johor–Riau (SIJORI) Growth Triangle above, an example of cooperation among the three countries, which could only have come about because of improved relations.[77]

---

[73] For a first-person account, see S.R. Nathan, *An Unexpected Journey: Path to the Presidency* (Singapore: Editions Didier Millet, 2011), pp. 589–95.
[74] Ibid.
[75] "DPM Lee Responds to China's Protests", *The Straits Times*, 17 July 2004.
[76] "China Signals FTA Talks May Face Setbacks", *The Straits Times*, 5 Aug. 2004.
[77] For a brief discussion of SIJORI, see Bilveer Singh, *The Vulnerability of Small States Revisited: A Study of Singapore's Post-Cold War Foreign Policy* (Yogyakarta: Gadjah Mada University Press, 1999), p. 1845.

Goh's foreign policy towards Malaysia was inevitably shaped by his predecessor's experience with Malaysia (which we have described in the earlier chapters). Towards the end of his tenure, Lee (as well as his Malaysian counterpart Mahathir Mohamad) made efforts to resolve some of the outstanding issues, particularly water, in the hope of giving Goh a clean slate to shape the course of the bilateral relationship. In his National Day Rally speech in August 1986, Lee highlighted the importance of Malaysia to Singapore: Singapore "cannot exist independently without Malaysia. There should be the best of relations with our neighbours because we are interdependent... Malaysia is our guarantor for the economic and political stability of Singapore. We cannot deny this".[78] Reflecting on the Memorandum of Understanding on water and gas signed on 28 June 1988, after six years of negotiations, Lee described it as a "landmark towards a new cooperative relationship", a "framework so that those who follow us will be led into the paths of cooperation and not conflict". He however cautioned that it would take time but "if we stay on this course, we can reverse some of the mindsets of suspicion and wariness which befogged us".[79] The relationship culminated with the signing of the Point of Agreement (POA) in November 1990, just as Lee Kuan Yew handed the premiership to Goh Chok Tong, which aimed to resolve the issue of the railway land in Singapore owned by the Malaysian government. As Bilveer Singh noted, "in general, the Goh–Mahathir era has also been one of enhanced cooperation and collaboration, marking the period of most rapid bilateral ties between the two countries".[80] Unfortunately, the period was also tainted by problems during Goh's tenure. This is not the place to go through in detail all the bilateral problems which surfaced or to pass judgement on the rights and wrongs of either side. For this study, the focus is on explaining what lies behind Singapore's decision-making and approach.

Both countries had an ongoing territorial dispute over the ownership of Pedra Branca island. Lee Kuan Yew recalled that the first dispute surfaced in 1979 when Malaysia published a new map of its territorial waters and continental shelf boundaries, which included for the first time Pedra Branca. Singapore formally protested the 1979 map in February 1980. Both sides then agreed to search for

---

[78] Singh, *The Vulnerability of Small States Revisited: A Study of Singapore's Post-Cold War Foreign Policy*, pp. 192–3. For the Singapore–Malaysia 1988 memorandum of understanding on water, gas and ferry service, see *Singapore–Malaysia 1988 Memorandum of Understanding on Water, Gas and Ferry Service*, at https://eresources.nlb.gov.sg/infopedia/articles/SIP_2014-10-14_153754.html# (accessed 26 Oct. 2021).

[79] Singh, *The Vulnerability of Small States Revisited: A Study of Singapore's Post-Cold War Foreign Policy*, p. 192.

[80] Ibid.

documents to prove ownership. Kuala Lumpur put the issue on the back burner for several years because of other priorities. Lee proposed to Mahathir (who had since become prime minister) that if the matter could not be resolved by an exchange of documents, the dispute should be referred to the International Court of Justice (ICJ). The issue resurfaced not long after Goh became prime minister. In 1994, Kuala Lumpur agreed to refer it to the ICJ. As Lee said, "Singapore must remain committed to upholding the rule of law in relations between States. If a dispute cannot be resolved by negotiations, it is better to refer to a third-party dispute settlement mechanism, than to allow it to fester and sour bilateral relations. This was my approach and subsequent Singapore Prime Ministers have continued to subscribe to it".[81]

A plethora of other disputes includes the rental dispute over the Royal Malaysian naval base at Woodlands, Singapore, which had been operating in Singapore since 1952. In July 1991, the Singapore government further revised and raised the rental because property prices in Singapore had skyrocketed over the years. Both sides could not agree on either the new rates or alternative locations offered by Singapore. Kuala Lumpur eventually decided to relocate the naval base back to Malaysia. But the episode left a sour taste in the relationship. Mahathir believed that Singapore raised the rent to take back the land from Malaysia. This episode could also have contributed to the issue of the Malayan Railway (KTM) land, about which, as noted above, an Agreement was signed in November 1990 just before Lee Kuan Yew stepped down. Following the 1990 agreement, Kuala Lumpur wanted to make amendments and in 1994, Goh Chok Tong revealed that the interpretation of the 1990 Agreement was in dispute. Mahathir's view was that the POA was not yet a valid document as it had not been endorsed by his cabinet, whereas Singapore held the view that it was a legal document negotiated in good faith. K. Kesavapany (Singapore High Commissioner to Malaysia, 1997–2002) recalled that Singapore, in accordance with the terms of the POA, moved its Customs and Immigration facilities to Woodlands in July 1998. Incensed by what he perceived as Singapore's unilateral action, Mahathir, amongst other retaliatory actions, stopped the sale of sand to Singapore and denied Singapore military aircraft access to Johor's airspace. This issue dragged on unresolved. In September 2003, Singapore proposed to settle it amicably before the ICJ or through international arbitration.[82]

The water issue also re-emerged despite the June 1988 agreement which was then described as a "high point in the two countries' relations in the post-

---

[81] S. Jayakumar and Tommy Koh, *Pedra Branca: The Road to the World Court* (Singapore: NUS Press, 2009), see Foreword by Minister Mentor Lee Kuan Yew, pp. xi–xiii.
[82] "Railway Land: S'pore Wants Third Party Help", *The Straits Times*, 17 Oct. 2003.

separation era". Singapore was accused of grossly underpaying for Malaysian water and overcharging for selling treated water to Malaysia.[83] Kuala Lumpur wanted to renegotiate the pricing in the water agreement, but Singapore was concerned that it would set "an extremely harmful precedent, not only in bilateral relations, but in its general conduct of foreign relations with other countries".[84] Since independence, Singapore had strategically planned to diversify its water resources to reduce its reliance on Malaysian water supply.[85] Lee Kuan Yew, according to Asit Biswas, was "the only leader in the world...interested in water". Lee became so because first, "when he was a young man during the Japanese Occupation, the British blew up the Causeway to stop the Japanese from coming into Singapore. And below the Causeway was the pipe that was bringing water in" so that Singapore had only a week's supply of water. Second, soon after Singapore became independent, the British High Commissioner told him that if Singapore did not "do exactly what Malaysia wanted", the Tunku "would turn off the tap".[86] As W. H. Auden said, "thousands have lived without love, not one without water".

Writing in 2002, Joey Long argued that "the likelihood of the water issue becoming a proximate cause of war" between Singapore and Malaysia "has lost much of its credibility in light of...the robustness of Singapore's water schemes and the viability of its reserves to satisfy domestic water needs". Once the "sword of Damocles" hanging over the bilateral relations, the water issue has shifted from "a security to a pecuniary consideration" which could be "handled as a contractual matter in an international court of law and opinion" rather than

---

[83] Singh, *The Vulnerability of Small States Revisited: A Study of Singapore's Post-Cold War Foreign Policy*, p. 207. For details of the above issues and more, see Singh and N. Ganesan, "Malaysia–Singapore Relations: Some Recent Developments", *Asian Affairs* 25, no. 1 (Spring 1998): 21–36; Chang Li Lin, "Singapore's Troubled Relations with Malaysia: A Singapore Perspective", *Southeast Asian Affairs* (2003): 259–74; K. Kesavapany, "Singapore's Foreign Relations with Malaysia", in *The Little Nation that Can: Singapore's Foreign Relations and Diplomacy*, ed. Koh, Chapter 5; Kwa Chong Guan, ed., *Beyond Vulnerability: Water in Singapore-Malaysia Relations*, IDSS Monograph, Number 3 (Singapore: IDSS, 2002).

[84] Chang, "Singapore's Troubled Relations with Malaysia: A Singapore Perspective": 264.

[85] See Cecilia Tortajada, Yugal Kishore Joshi and Asit K. Biswas, *The Singapore Water Story: Sustainable Development in an Urban City State* (London: Routledge, 2013). For a short overview in comics format, see [Singapore] Public Utilities Board, "The Quest for Water Security", 24 Nov. 2017, at https://www.pub.gov.sg/PublishingImages/Quest_for_Water_Security_Hi-Res.jpg (accessed 27 Oct. 2021).

[86] Qtd. from Cheong Suk-Wai, "Plumbing Singapore's Water Story", *The Straits Times*, 26 June 2011; see also Feng Zengkun, "Singapore: Increasing the Flow of Water from National Taps", *The Straits Times*, 16 March 2013; Asit K. Biswas and Ng Joo Hee, "Singapore's Two-front Battle with Water Security and Climate Change", *The Straits Times*, 5 June 2021.

"necessitating a military response".[87] (See Lee Kuan Yew's statements on the water issue in earlier chapters.[88])

It is perhaps useful to highlight Rusdi Omar's observation by way of concluding this section. In his view, from the perspective of Malaysia, Singapore "opts for a rather over-legalistic approach that conveys the impression that the city state is insensitive to the cultural milieu in which it finds itself". Malaysia however views such an approach as "antagonistic and confrontational, and not in keeping with the general consensual approach based on musyawarah [consultation] and muafakat [consensus]" whereas Singapore "prefers to hold steadfastly to formal commitments that have issued from negotiations".[89] As S. Jayakumar said, "we should not be put off by such criticisms of being legalistic. It would be extremely difficult for a small country to conduct relations with other countries on the basis of mutual trust and respect if the sanctity of international agreements is not recognised. This is why we insist that agreements entered into in good faith should be honoured. On our part, we should always seek to meet our obligations under agreements to which we have become parties".[90] And, as Goh Chok Tong advised, "we should defend our interests stoutly, sometimes even at the expense of short-term tensions in bilateral relations".[91]

K. Kesavapany has recalled that the years from 1997 to 2003 were "filled with high tension drama, with bilateral relations descending to one of the lowest ebbs" because of the failure to reach agreements on a number of issues.[92] In contrast to Singapore–Malaysia relations, relations with Indonesia, as described in the previous chapter, significantly improved in the 1980s and remained generally trouble-free—almost uneventful one could say[93]—till the ouster of Suharto

---

[87] Kwa, ed., *Beyond Vulnerability: Water in Singapore–Malaysia Relations*, pp. 61, 135–8.

[88] Prime Minister Goh Chok Tong in 2001 said that while there were benefits of maintaining the water ties with Malaysia, if Kuala Lumpur were to use water as "a leverage", "Singapore had recourse to alternative water sources". See Kwa, *Beyond Vulnerability: Water in Singapore–Malaysia Relations*, p. 128.

[89] Rusdi Omar, "An Analysis of the Underlying Factors that Affected Malaysia–Singapore Relations During the Mahathir Era: Discords and Continuity", Unpublished PhD dissertation, University of Adelaide, May 2014, pp. 265–6.

[90] S. Jayakumar, "Reflections on Diplomacy of a Small State", S. Rajaratnam Lecture 2010, 19 May 2010.

[91] Goh Chok Tong, "The Practice of Foreign Policy for Sustained Growth—the Singapore Experience", S. Rajaratnam Lecture 17 Oct. 2014 (Singapore: MFA Academy, 2014).

[92] K.P. Menon, ed., *Footprints on Foreign Shores: Tales Told by Foreign Service Officers* (Singapore: Graceworks, 2021), pp. 98–9.

[93] Singh, *The Vulnerability of Small States Revisited: A Study of Singapore's Post-Cold War Foreign Policy*, pp. 235–47. Singh describes the years 1988 to 1997 as the "honeymoon" phase of Singapore–Indonesia relations. See p. 269.

because of the Asian Financial Crisis in 1997, and especially during the tenure of Suharto's successor, B.J. Habibie from 1998 to 1999. Leaders come and go but Habibie's infamous remark is a stark reminder of Singapore's vulnerability: "Look at that map. All the green [area] is Indonesia. And the red dot is Singapore. Look at that"[94]. Abdurrahman Wahid, who succeeded Habibie as President from 1999 to 2001, also had a lukewarm relationship with Singapore. Wahid had criticised Singapore "for not caring about countries to its South and for being profit-oriented". Nevertheless, Senior Minister Lee Kuan Yew accepted Wahid's invitation to attend a meeting of the International Advisory Panel in Jakarta saying he took a "long-term view of ties with Jakarta".[95] Singapore–Indonesia relations improved during the Megawati presidency (2001–04). As deputy prime minister Lee Hsien Loong said during his visit to Jakarta, "the more we can cooperate, the better for us both".[96]

VI

From Singapore's experiences with its immediate neighbours, described above, readers might be reminded of what Goh Keng Swee advised in the early 1970s (see Chapter 1). Firstly, while there was not "any realistic danger of war" between Singapore and her neighbours unless a "madcap regime" were established in either or both countries, Singapore could not be certain that this could not happen; therefore "it is necessary for us to continue to develop our military strength".[97] Second, when it comes down to brass tacks, "this really means getting on better terms with our two neighbours, Malaysia and Indonesia".

---

[94] Richard Borsuk and Reginald Chua, "Singapore Strains Relations with Indonesia's President", *The Wall Street Journal*, 4 Aug. 1998, at https://www.wsj.com/articles/SB902170180588248000 (accessed 10 Jan. 2023).
[95] Chua Lee Hoong, "SM: I Take Long-term View of Ties with Jakarta", *The Straits Times*, 16 Feb. 2001.
[96] Lee Hsien Loong, "Mutual Respect is Key to Ties Between Sovereign States", *The Straits Times*, 2 Feb. 2004.
[97] See "Barred Preacher's Supporters Stage Protests in Indonesia against Singapore", *The Straits Times*, 22 May 2022 and Ram Anand, "Mahathir's Remark on Reclaiming S'pore Aimed at Johor Sultan: Analysts", *The Straits Times*, 26 June 2022. The Indonesian preacher Abdul Somad Batubara said that Singapore is part of Riau and thus belongs to Indonesia. Mahathir on 19 June 2022 was reported to have said that Malaysia should reclaim Singapore (as well as the Riau Islands) as "they are Tanah Melayu". Former Malaysian Prime Minister Mahathir Mohamad, who is known to be antagonistic towards Singapore, said that his remarks were misinterpreted/misconstrued.

In relation to defence, we recall that by the mid-1980s, the "poisonous shrimp" deterrence strategy was replaced by that of the "porcupine". From 1982 to June 1991, Goh Chok Tong was the Minister of Defence and oversaw the transformation of the Singapore military. By the time he became prime minister in 1990, the Singapore Armed Forces (SAF) had indeed made a quantum leap from what it was like in the early years after independence (as described in the previous chapters) to become "arguably...the region's strongest force" and the Singapore Air Force had been described variously as "undoubtedly the most powerful in Southeast Asia" and "the largest and most potent in Southeast Asia".[98] The development of the Singapore Armed Forces has kept closely to the dictum of Goh Keng Swee elaborated in his 1971 speech (described in the previous chapter): to focus on technology. As the cover article on the Singapore Armed Forces in an issue of the *Asian Defence Journal* noted, "no issue is more relevant to the strategic planner or to the defence corporation than the direction of a military's technological acquisition".[99] Quoting then-Chief of Army, Brigadier General Han Eng Juan, "in the future high-tech digital battlefield, information may be even more critical than ammunition". Hardware is just one aspect. According to Peter Ho (Permanent Secretary of Defence, 2000–04), "the SAF was working towards the creation of a new generation of technology-aware and capable personnel with a clear understanding of their sophisticated systems and equipment to better exploit them in the field".[100] Tim Huxley, whose book, *Defending the Lion City: The Armed Forces of Singapore*, published in early 2000 based on 20 years of research and the first book which lifted the veil from the Singapore Armed Forces and the Ministry of Defence (which was very coy about releasing information), acknowledged that the SAF was the most impressive in the region. Indeed, he argued that Singapore could defeat Malaysia in a military conflict within hours. But he also emphasised that the SAF was a deterrent force and not there "to commit aggression against any of her neighbours".[101]

That the SAF was (and still is) a deterrent force was highlighted by then *Business Times* correspondent David Boey in a 2003 commentary on the Huxley book, which came into the spotlight during the tense period of Singapore–Malaysia

---

[98] "Singapore Puts Force Integration into Place", *Jane's Defence Weekly*, 30 April 1997, p. 25; "The RSAF: Procurement Programmes and Future Requirements", *Asian Defence Journal*, Feb. 1996, p. 23; Michael Richardson, "RSAF's Space Crunch", *The Straits Times*, 27 Dec. 2004.
[99] Qtd. in *Asian Defence Journal*, February 1996, p. 21.
[100] "Singapore-Deconstruction Forges Ahead", *Jane's Defence Weekly*, 27 June 2001.
[101] Tim Huxley, *Defending the Lion City: The Armed Forces of Singapore* (Sydney: Allen & Unwin, 2000). Boey's review appeared in *The Sunday Times* [Singapore], 18 March 2001; see also "Why a Book on S'pore's Military Might is Upsetting M'sia", *Today*, 6 Jan. 2003.

relations. Boey noted that when the book was first published, it "attracted hardly any attention in the Malaysian media or academic community". The content of the book was also not new, since it had undergone five print runs of 2,000 copies each since its initial publication. Furthermore, Huxley's scenario that Singapore had the capability to invade Johor and defeat the Malaysian Armed Forces in a matter of hours had already been published in his 1991 article. The "critical point" of the book "concerns the SAF's strategy of deterrence. At no point in the book did Dr Huxley conclude that the SAF would be used as an occupation force of conquest". Thus, to suggest otherwise was "mischievous and intellectually dishonest".[102] As Lee Kuan Yew said, "the SAF is an insurance in an uncertain world".[103]

Finally, beyond traditional/conventional security, it was in 1999, during Goh's administration, that Singapore set up a National Security Secretariat (NSS), a coordinating body to oversee security-related issues that were expected to be long-drawn. Peter Ho recalled that the genesis of setting up the NSS was in 1997. He was coy in revealing the exact context of the decision but alluded to the "climate of the region" in 1997 and 1998 (which readers may remember was the period of the Asian Financial Crisis).[104] In Ho's words, "it wasn't exactly a threat, but it was certainly non-traditional and we assessed that this would be a large security challenge for our agencies... But because the contingency for which it was set up did not happen, nobody took it that seriously" until 11 September 2001, the 9/11 attacks, followed by the discovering of the Jemaah Islamiyah network in Singapore, "which started another round of more serious thinking because this time it was more a real threat; it was a clear and present danger". The NSS morphed into the National Security Coordination Secretariat, with the Joint Counter-Terrorism Centre (JCTC) and the National Coordination Centre (NSCC) in the Prime Minister's Office.[105] Through the coordination of these agencies, the concept of security became more comprehensive, as a whole-of-society approach was seen as necessary. As related to the concept of Total Defence, the establishment of a National Coordination Centre would bring together the various pieces into a coherent defence strategy.

---

[102] David Boey, "Motive Behind Misreading of Book on SAF", *The Straits Times*, 14 Feb. 2003. See also Tim Huxley, "Singapore and Malaysia: A Precarious Balance?", *The Pacific Review* 4, no. 3 (1991): 204–13.

[103] Lee Kuan Yew, "The Fundamentals of Singapore's Foreign Policy: Then & Now", S. Rajaratnam Lecture, 9 April 2009 (Singapore: MFA Academy, 2009).

[104] For an account of the 1997 Asian Financial Crisis and its political and security impact on the region, see Ang, *Southeast Asia after the Cold War: A Contemporary History*, Chapter 2.

[105] Shashi Jayakumar, ed., *State, Society and National Security: Challenges and Opportunities in the 21st Century* (Singapore: World Scientific, 2016), pp. 7–8.

CHAPTER 5

The Lee Hsien Loong Years (since 2004): Singapore and Globalisation

I

This chapter examines Singapore's Grand Strategy under the premiership of Lee Hsien Loong, who succeeded Goh Chok Tong in 2004 and who is the PM at the point of writing. This chapter focuses on change and continuity from the previous administration. It will continue the discussion of Singapore's response to the ups and downs in its relations with its two most important sets of relationships: the US and China; and Malaysia and Indonesia. It will further examine Singapore's policy on multiracialism, which is a key pillar of the grand strategy.

Lee Hsien Loong succeeded Goh Chok Tong and became Singapore's third prime minister in August 2004. Goh became Senior Minister while Lee Kuan Yew assumed the title of Minister Mentor. In his assessment of the 14 years of the Goh administration, Tommy Koh noted that Goh "consolidated Lee Kuan Yew's legacy and expanded upon it...by delivering solid economic growth, by maintaining domestic peace and harmony, by launching new foreign policy initiatives, and by enlarging Singapore's economic and political space".[1] The younger Lee also acknowledged Goh's achievements and pledged "to continue to build on the foundations laid by" his predecessors.[2] Indeed, a number of initiatives planned and executed during the Goh administration came into fruition under Lee Hsien

---

[1] See Bridget Welsh et al., eds., *Impressions of the Goh Chok Tong Years in Singapore* (Singapore: NUS Press, 2009), pp. xi, 119.
[2] Ibid., p. 21.

Loong who was himself deputy prime minister through Goh's tenure as prime minister. As described in the previous chapter and as noted by Tommy Koh, Goh was the "architect" of Singapore's FTA policy. He also made "a major contribution to inter-regional cooperation and understanding".[3] The Goh administration, as Bernard Loo noted, "remains the most important period" in the transformation of the Singapore Armed Forces into "the most modern and most well-trained armed forces in Southeast Asia".[4]

Singapore's grand strategy during the younger Lee administration can be distilled from many of his speeches and interviews. It is perhaps helpful to begin this discussion by re-visiting a speech aptly titled "Singapore's Tomorrow, Tomorrow's Singapore", which he delivered in September 2002.[5] Although he was then still deputy prime minister, the speech is important for setting the external context/backdrop for understanding the strategic challenges that faced Singapore a decade after the Cold War ended as well as highlighting Singapore's future trajectory. Lee assumed leadership in the aftermath of two events. The first, the Asian Financial Crisis in 1997 (although it had occurred much earlier, it had a long tail), saw "a prospering Asia suddenly" go "into spasm". While the immediate trauma of the crisis had past, and even while Singapore had been less affected by the crisis than others, Lee's view was that "the picture" had changed "drastically". While he was optimistic that Singapore would continue "to grow and make progress", "the climate" however would be "less predictable", and "the competition" would be "much fiercer". The second event was the 11 September 2001 (9/11) terrorist attacks on the United States by Islamic extremists, which, according to Lee, "changed the world we live in" because "we live in a globalised world, and terrorism is a global problem". The discovery of the Jemaah Islamiyah terrorist group in Singapore testified to that.

In the speech, the younger Lee highlighted three issues which would affect Singapore in the years ahead. The first was globalisation which, Lee anticipated, would "progress faster than ever" over the next decade, particularly fuelled by the advancement of technology. Singapore is "totally dependent on the global economy... Without the global economy, we would not survive". But while globalisation would create opportunities, "shocks and crises" would also be transmitted and felt faster than ever, and this could make reacting and responding challenging: "The more plugged [in] we are, the less insulated we can be". Second was the importance of Southeast Asia. While Singapore is well-connected to

---

[3] Ibid., p. 127. See also Chapter 10.
[4] Ibid., pp. 19–20. See also Chapter 16.
[5] Speech by Deputy Prime Minister Lee Hsien Loong at the Kent Ridge Ministerial Forum 2002, 30 Sept. 2002, at https://www.nas.gov.sg/archivesonline/data/pdfdoc/2002093001.htm (accessed 7 Jan. 2023).

the US, Europe and Northeast Asia, "we are still located in Southeast Asia. The stability and prosperity of our neighbours are important to us". Lee specifically mentioned Malaysia and Indonesia in his speech. According to Lee, whether Malaysia develops along UMNO's secular, modern approach or in PAS's religious and conservative direction would have an impact on Singapore. As for Indonesia, "a stable Indonesia is even more important to Southeast Asia". A divided, politically unstable and economically weak Indonesia "would have deep and broad repercussions for Singapore and the region". The third issue was "the war against terrorism", which, Lee anticipated, would be "a long-drawn-out struggle". Singapore's approach towards Islamic fundamentalism and the terrorist threat is to go beyond fighting and killing the terrorists as "the more you kill, the more people will be agitated, radicalised and come forward, and volunteer for the next suicide mission". So, as Lee mentioned in later interviews, Singapore's counter-terrorism strategy is to "go deeper",[6] "at a strategic and philosophical level", thereby "getting people not to want to become terrorists or think like them".[7]

Looking ahead in his 30 September 2002 speech to the next decade, Lee said that "certain fundamental realities" would not change. Singapore's location meant that it would "inevitably be affected by what happens to its neighbours". Since it is "a small city-state", the country would remain "vulnerable to external threats...largely beyond our control". What is within Singapore's control is strengthening social cohesion to deal with the external problems "as one people".

Lee said in his 2005 IISS Asia Security Conference (Shangri-La Dialogue) speech that because Singapore is "a small country, vulnerable to the vagaries of global forces beyond our control" and "too small to shape the major events in Asia", the country assumes the world to be a "dangerous place" and does what it can "to make it less dangerous for ourselves" by helping "to foster peace and security in the region".[8] Singapore thus strongly supports the post-Cold War

---

[6] "Trying Times for America" (excerpts of Prime Minister Lee Hsien Loong's interview with Charlie Rose on 13 July 2005), *The Straits Times*, 5 Aug. 2005.
[7] "What Must Change in Singapore" (edited excerpt of interview with Prime Minister Lee Hsien Loong by Tom Plate on 22 Feb. 2007), *The Straits Times*, 3 March 2007. For Lee's views on globalisation which he described as "driving the changes in Asia, and [which] appears to be an unstoppable megatrend", see "Asia and America: Our Shared Future" ("Prime Minister Lee Hsien Loong's speech at the Asia Society/US–ASEAN Business Council Joint Gala Dinner, Washington DC, 4 May 2007"), *The Straits Times*, 5 May 2007; also available at https://asiasociety.org/america-and-asia-our-shared-future (accessed 26 Nov. 2022).
[8] Lee Hsien Loong, Keynote Address at the 4th IISS Asia Security Conference, Singapore, 3 June 2005, at https://www.nas.gov.sg/archivesonline/data/pdfdoc/2005060302.htm (accessed 26 Nov. 2022); see also "Securing Asia's Future" (excerpt from a speech by Prime Minister Lee Hsien Loong at the 4th International Institute of Strategic Studies Asia Security Conference in Singapore, 3 June 2005), *The Straits Times*, 6 June 2005.

efforts to "foster regional cooperation". In Lee's view, "there is a grand political project to integrate Asia as a whole into a peaceful world. This is in the natural interest of a small country".[9] Echoing the words of Singapore's first Foreign Minister S. Rajaratnam in 1965, Lee said 50 years later at the IISS Asia Security Conference: "we seek to be friends with all countries, while upholding our rights and interests internationally".[10] Closer to home, Singapore wanted to see a "more cohesive ASEAN". In a 2007 interview, Lee envisioned that the Association would have "two wings, China and India" which would help the region "take off". But "to have two wings without a body...we'll fall apart". Thus, ASEAN needed "to take the political decisions to cooperate on economics, on security, on politics, on many issues".[11]

II

We now turn to the US and China, which Lee Hsien Loong described in 2004 as "the most important bilateral relationship in Asia, and soon, perhaps in the world";[12] by 2012, the bilateral relationship could be "the most important...for both parties, and for the entire world".[13] More recently in 2021, Lee described Sino–US relations as "the most important bilateral relationship for the world in years to come".[14] Singapore had been able to adhere to its strategy of maintaining a balance in its relationship with both superpowers (as described in the previous chapter). In a 2013 Tokyo speech, Lee said that Singapore wanted both countries to have "constructive and stable relations". Then "we don't have to choose sides".[15] Lee urged nations not to view international relations through an "us versus them" lens: "I would be very careful about saying, 'Let's make a friendship amongst all countries which are frightened of China'. I don't think that is a constructive and helpful approach". Rather, Lee advocated making friends and developing

---

[9] "Germans Discover PM Lee", *The Straits Times Interactive*, 7 Dec. 2005.
[10] "Securing Asia's Future".
[11] "What Must Change in Singapore".
[12] "Strategic Issues that Confront a Rising Asia" (excerpted from the Deputy Prime Minister's speech at the Conference Board symposium on Asian Economies and Financial Markets, 27 May 2004), *The Straits Times*, 31 May 2004.
[13] "China and the World: Prospering and Progressing Together" (Prime Minister Lee Hsien Loong's speech at the Central Party School in Beijing, 6 Sept. 2012), *Today*, 7 Sept. 2012.
[14] Qtd. in Grace Ho, "Not Too Late for US, China to Reset Ties and Avert Clash: PM at WEF Event", *The Straits Times*, 30 Jan. 2021.
[15] Prime Minister Lee Hsien Loong's interview with *Washington Post* associate editor, Lally Weymouth, *The Straits Times*, 17 March 2013.

"constructive relations with one another in a multi-dimensional way".[16] Lee's viewpoint has however become increasingly challenging to execute from 2017. More of this later.

When Lee became prime minister in 2004, the international political dynamics in Asia, as seen in Singapore's eyes, was underpinned by a "pre-eminent" and indispensable US. As Lee noted, countries which were "uncomfortable with the scope of US pre-eminence and some of its policies" still want to have "the best possible relationship" with the US because "they know they cannot challenge US pre-eminence and that no issue in the region can be resolved without America's cooperation". That included China, whose "fundamental preoccupations" until the mid-2010s at least, were internal. Except for its core interests, most notably Taiwan, Beijing "knows that it is also in China's interest to have good relations with the US". Washington too needed Chinese cooperation to deal with many post-Cold War challenges.[17] It was not that the bilateral relationship had no problems but, as Lee noted in 2005, "we should not overstate the problems in the relationship" as "both sides have strong reasons to cooperate and manage the relationship for mutual advantage".[18] The George W. Bush administration (2001–09) already saw China as a challenge but took a low-key approach towards managing US relations with the country. The Obama administration (2009–17) signalled Washington's intent to challenge the rising influence of China in the region but was not able to give it its full attention.[19] China, in the new millennium, was still adhering to Deng Xiaoping's dictum of "hiding your light under a bushel and going quietly into the world".

Singapore's attitude towards the US is well-known. Lee said in his 2012 interview with Greg Sheridan (foreign editor of *The Australian*): "We are happy that the Americans are present in the region". Lee elaborated: "For our part, we have facilitated the visits by American air force and navy units to Singapore. They don't have bases here but they visit frequently and there's a logistic support unit here for their navy ships. We will be helping to keep their ships supplied while they are operating in the region. We think it is good that the US presence remains in the region, including the security presence and the Seventh fleet. We are such a tiny area that there are a lot of constraints, but what we can do to help the American

---

[16] Qtd. in Elgin Toh, "PM Lee Positive about Asia's Prospects", *The Straits Times*, 2 May 2013.
[17] Lee Hsien Loong, "Strategic Issues that Confront a Rising Asia", *The Straits Times*, 31 May 2004.
[18] Lee Hsien Loong, "A Historic and Beneficial Rise" (summary of his speech at the Central Party School, Beijing, 25 October 2005), *The Straits Times*, 26 Oct. 2005.
[19] See Ang Cheng Guan, *Southeast Asia after the Cold War* (Singapore: NUS Press, 2019), pp. 165–70.

presence we will do".[20] The following year, asked for his views on the Obama administration's "pivot" towards Asia, Lee said that "we are all in favour of the US taking an active and constructive interest in Asia. I'm not sure I would describe it as a pivot... you really want a long-term implacable, inexorable presence, and I'm not sure if the pivot conveys that nuance".[21]

Lee Hsien Loong acknowledged that "Singapore has been outspoken in encouraging America to engage ASEAN".[22] Singapore also expressed support for the policy of rotating 2,500 US marines through Darwin, Australia, each year. Under Lee's watch, Singapore and the US in 2005 updated the 1990 MOU signed between then-prime minister Lee Kuan Yew and the George H. W. Bush administration to a Strategic Framework Agreement which recognised Singapore as a Major Security Cooperation Partner of the US. In 2015, both countries signed an enhanced Defence Cooperation Agreement[23] and in 2019, PM Lee and President Donald Trump renewed the defence pact which would allow American forces to use Singapore's air and naval bases till 2035. Singapore's Ministry of Defence said that the renewal "underscores" Singapore's "support for the US presence in the region, which remains vital for regional peace, stability and prosperity".[24] In 2022, Singapore Defence Minister Ng Eng Hen's opinion, as reported in *The Straits Times*, was that "Singapore believe[d]" that the United States would "remain the world's largest economy and global military power", even if China was a larger trading partner for all Asian countries.[25]

---

[20] "From Istana to Canberra", *The Straits Times*, 11 Oct. 2012.

[21] Lee Hsien Loong, Interview with *Washington Post* associate editor, Lally Weymouth, *The Straits Times*, 17 March 2013.

[22] "Asia and America: Our Shared Future", *The Straits Times*, 5 May 2007; available also at https://asiasociety.org/america-and-asia-our-shared-future (accessed 26 Nov. 2022).

[23] "Singapore–US Pact to Enhance Military Ties", *The Straits Times*, 9 Dec. 2015; "P-8 Deployment Reinforces US Presence in Asia–Pacific", *The Straits Times*, 11 Dec. 2015; "Defence Pact's Renewal Shows Support for US Presence in Region: Mindef", *The Straits Times*, 25 Sept. 2015.

[24] "Key Pact on US Use of Air, Naval Bases in S'pore Renewed till 2035", *The Straits Times*, 25 Sept. 2019. See also Remarks by Minister for Defence, Dr Ng Eng Hen, at the 7th Reagan National Defense Forum Panel Session, "Advancing US National Defence: Working with Allies and Partners", 8 Dec. 2019. US Secretary of Defence Mark T. Esper and Ng Eng Hen signed a non-binding MOU establishing a Singapore Air Force permanent fighter training detachment in Guam from 2029.

[25] Linette Lai, "Small States are Primarily Concerned with Stability and International Rules: Ng Eng Hen", *The Straits Times*, 15 May 2022, at https://www.straitstimes.com/singapore/politics/small-states-are-primarily-concerned-with-stability-and-international-rules-ng-eng-hen (accessed 26 Nov. 2022)

As Lee said in a 2005 Beijing speech, Singapore anticipated that China's rise and growth would eventually "change the relative strengths of different countries and alter the global strategic balance". Singapore however took a positive view of China's rise, believing that it was "a major plus for Asia, and for the world". Singapore, like other Asian countries, would benefit from China's growth.[26] For Singapore, it is good for China "to continue to prosper". "Anything else", in Lee's words, "would create big problems".

Readers may recall from the previous chapter that Singapore leaders had the foresight to forge early friendships with Chinese leaders as they understood that such connections "are very important for the sustained growth of bilateral relations", although it must be said that "given the unpredictability and opacity of politics" in China, it is not easy to identify the right politicians.[27] The modern historical origins of Sino–Singapore relations meant that the trajectory has been very much in the economic realm. In 2014, the two countries were contemplating a third government-to-government project after the Suzhou Industrial Park and the Tianjin Eco-City. As Lye Liang Fook (then assistant director of the East Asian Institute) noted, "one of Singapore's overriding objectives is to stay relevant to China's growth…it is in Singapore's interests to constantly find opportunities to collaborate with China to derive win-win benefits".[28] Chongqing was eventually chosen as the site for the third project. Lee Hsien Loong and other Singapore leaders regularly promoted Singapore as "a good springboard" for Chinese firms looking to explore markets in ASEAN.[29]

Also in 2014, Singapore and China took the step to broaden their relationship, which had been largely economic and cultural in nature, to step up the military dimension. Both sides signed a four-point consensus "to deepen mutual understanding and trust through practical face-to-face interactions"—"increasing the scope and frequency of joint war drills and widening training scenarios as part of a new move to put in place concrete measures to expand military links".[30] The four-point consensus built on the agreement that the Singapore Armed Forces (SAF) and the People's Liberation Army (PLA) had signed in 2008, which formalised their bilateral defence activities.

---

[26] Lee, "A Historic and Beneficial Rise".
[27] "Singapore's Foresight in Forging Early Friendship", *The Straits Times*, 7 Feb. 2012.
[28] Rachel Chang and Kor Kian Beng, "3 Possible Locations for Third Sino–S'pore Project", *The Straits Times*, 8 Aug. 2014.
[29] "PM: Don't Let Rows Overshadow Good ASEAN–China Ties", *Today*, 17 Sept. 2014.
[30] Jermyn Chow, "Concrete Moves to Make Sino–S'pore Defence Ties Stronger", *The Straits Times*, 15 Nov. 2014.

Having himself experienced how the Chinese reacted to his Taiwan trip in 2004 (recounted in the previous chapter), Lee knew that Singapore could not simply rely on the goodwill of Beijing.[31] Lee Kuan Yew, now Minister Mentor, told his audience at the S. Rajaratnam Lecture in 2009 that the Chinese always say that all countries, big and small are equal. But when you displease them, they never fail to remind you that you have displeased 1,300 million.[32] In November 2016, the Hong Kong Port Authority seized nine SAF Terrex infantry carrier vehicles (ICVs), which were being shipped back to Singapore after training exercises in Taiwan. The military exercises in Taiwan (which started in 1975) and the shipping of military equipment transiting through the port of Hong Kong were not new. Beijing had until that time not made a public issue of it, but the Chinese government now said that it "had always firmly opposed countries that have diplomatic ties with China to have any form of official exchanges with Taiwan, including military exchanges and cooperation". The SAF vehicles were eventually returned to Singapore in late January 2017 after the Hong Kong authorities had supposedly completed their investigations.

In November 2015, just a year before the Terrex incident, in commemorating 25 years of diplomatic relations between Singapore and China, President Xi Jinping and Prime Minister Lee signed an agreement on an "All-Round Cooperative Partnership Progressing with the Times" in Singapore. Singapore was also the venue for the meeting between Xi Jinping and Taiwanese President Ma Ying-jeou in the same month. The Singapore Foreign Ministry described Singapore as a "good friend of both sides" and stated that Singapore has been a "consistent supporter of relations between China and Taiwan".[33]

Political and security analysts have speculated about the reason for China's actions in the November 2016 Terrex incident. Views include Beijing's unhappiness with Singapore which the Chinese perceived had moved too close to the US and Singapore's support for the ruling of the Permanent Court of Arbitration tribunal regarding Chinese claims in the South China Sea.[34] Indeed, despite the strong relationship culminating with Xi's visit, analysts such as Hoo Tiang Boon have highlighted that Singapore faced the challenge of striking a

---

[31] "Germans Discover PM Lee".

[32] See Ang Cheng Guan, *Lee Kuan Yew's Strategic Thought* (London: Routledge, 2013), pp. 96–7.

[33] "Singapore 'Glad to Facilitate Meeting'", *The Straits Times*, 9 Nov. 2015.

[34] See for example, Alan Chong and David Han, "Foreign Policy Lessons from the Terrex Episode", *RSIS Commentary*, Number 022, 2 Feb. 2017. In January 2013, Manila decided to bring its dispute with China over the South China Sea territories to an international tribunal, in accordance with the 1982 UNCLOS. Beijing rejected the approach. The ruling was announced on 12 July 2016. Singapore's position was to respect the rule of law.

delicate balance between China and the United States. As Hoo noted, while "this is not a new factor...Singapore must constantly be alert to 'new' dynamics that point to the development of a serious rivalry between the US and China".[35] Regardless of the true reason(s), what is important here is that if indeed China was using the impounding of the Terrex to pressure Singapore, the view of analysts, including Chinese scholars, was that China would find Singapore "harder to crack than other countries in its orbit...as it is less beholden to Chinese security and economic pressure".[36] In 2015, commenting on the Chinese response to the signing of the enhanced Defence Cooperation Agreement between Singapore and the US, which would see Singapore hosting the deployment of the P-9 Poseidon surveillance aircraft, Sino–Southeast Asia expert Xu Liping noted that "China [also] knows criticising Singapore would not stop the deployment and might create problems by hurting bilateral ties".[37]

III

This is perhaps the appropriate place to introduce Japan, India and Australia into our discussion of Singapore's grand strategy. In Singapore's view, Japan was (and still is) seen as "another key player in Asia" which together with the US and China "forms the strategic triangle that anchors the stability of the region". As early as the 1980s, Singapore's hope was for Japan to "increase her defence budget and become rather more active in her own territorial and naval defence in order to release US resources for use elsewhere". Lee Kuan Yew had publicly stated on several occasions that Singapore would welcome "a greater Japanese naval presence in the region" but not the stationing of Japanese troops in Southeast Asia.[38] In 2005, when Lee Hsien Loong made his assessment, Japan was still the biggest and most advanced economy in Asia. Lee noted that a new generation of Japanese wanted their country to be "normal again and play a bigger role in world affairs".[39] Singapore's position is that "we cannot forget history" but at the same time, "we should not be imprisoned by it". As Lee said, "we should move forward and not keep reopening old issues. Because if we keep re-opening old issues it becomes more difficult to develop the relationships and the cooperation which you need in

---

[35] "Entering New Phase in Unique Relationship", *The Straits Times*, 6 Nov. 2015.
[36] Greg Torode and Marius Zaharia, "Singapore May Prove a Tough Nut for China to Crack over Regional Security", Reuters, 1 Dec. 2016, at https://www.reuters.com/article/us-hongkong-singapore-taiwan-analysis-idUSKBN13R0N3 (accessed 30 Nov. 2022).
[37] "China Gives Restrained Response to S'pore", *The Straits Times*, 9 Dec. 2015.
[38] From the British High Commission in Singapore to the FCO, "Japan", 29 April 1981, FCO 15/2906.
[39] Lee Hsien Loong, "A Historic and Beneficial Rise".

order to thrive in the twenty-first century".[40] In response to media queries about Singapore's view regarding Japanese prime minister Shinzo Abe's visit to the Yasukuni Shrine, a MFA spokesperson stated that Singapore's consistent position had been that "such visits reopen old grievances and are unhelpful to building trust and confidence in the region".[41] In 2014, Lee painted two scenarios in which the three countries could interact to produce a "new strategic landscape". The positive scenario was one where the US remained engaged in Asia, China adhered to "international forms and maintain[-ed] constructive relations with other powers" and Japan "recover[-ed] its confidence". The negative scenario would be one in which the region was "fraught with tensions and trade disputes". In this scenario, Southeast Asia (including Singapore) would be forced to take sides and the region would once again revert to "a proxy battleground".[42]

Next is India, "the other huge economy besides China". Lee was of the view that if India's economic reforms, which started, belatedly, only in the 1990s, succeeded, and Sino–Indian relations stayed cordial, both countries would "transform the Asian landscape".[43] In 2005, Lee described India as a "very important player in a future Asia". Lee Kuan Yew when he was prime minister had said that foreign affairs for Singapore involved "find[-ing] a strategic balance for the area and special relationship with those who will be able to help us in our economy and our security". In Singapore's estimation, India was one such country/power. It is for this reason that Singapore has "consistently advocated and actively supported India's engagement of the region", although it also noted that the process of opening its economy "is not going as smoothly as elsewhere" because of its "confusing democratic order".[44]

And then there is Australia. The country, like the United States, has provided training facilities for the Singapore Armed Forces: the Shoalwater Bay Training Area in Queensland, which will be expanded by 2024, and a new Greenvale (Qld.) Training Area by 2028. Together these training areas will be ten times the size

---

[40] *Singapore Tonight*, 22 May 2013, transcriptions of relevant sections of the newsclip that deal with Singapore's view of Japan's actions regarding its wartime past (2013–14).

[41] *Singapore Tonight*, 29 Dec. 2013, transcriptions of relevant sections of the newsclip that deal with Singapore's view of Japan's actions regarding its wartime past (2013–14).

[42] "Next Two Decades an Historic Opportunity for Asia: PM", *Today*, 23 May 2014: PM Lee Hsien Loong's keynote address at the 20th Nikkei International conference on 'The Future of Asia', Tokyo, 22 May 2014.

[43] Lee Hsien Loong, "A Historic and Beneficial Rise".

[44] For details, see See Chak Mun, "Singapore–India Strategic Relations – Singapore's Perspective", in *The Merlion and the Ashoka: Singapore–India Strategic Ties*, ed. Anit Mukherjee (Singapore: World Scientific, 2016), Chapter 3; "Germans Discover PM Lee".

of Singapore.[45] As Lee Hsien Loong said, Singapore and Australia "share very compatible strategic perspectives on the region and on America's role" in it.[46] Both countries signed a joint Declaration on a Comprehensive Strategic Partnership in June 2015.[47]

Singapore's Defence Minister Ng Eng Hen explained that Singapore's relations with other countries, for example the US or China, are "premised on mutual benefit" and Singapore is "not dependent on any one country". Singapore's defence and foreign policy "as an independent, sovereign nation will continue to be based on positioning itself in the best possible position to survive and progress, whatever the calculations or policies of other countries may be...we will work with like-minded partners who pursue peace and stability in our region".[48]

We pause here and turn to Singapore's relations with Malaysia and Indonesia, before returning to the issue of US–China strategic rivalry.

IV

Whereas Singapore's relations with the major powers, and in particular the United States and China, had been generally smooth in the first decade of Lee Hsien Loong's administration, this cannot be said for its relations with its two most important neighbours—Malaysia and Indonesia. We recall from the last chapter that despite the positive re-start in Singapore–Malaysia relations at the beginning of Goh Chok Tong's administration, the relationship had turned acrimonious long before the end of his term in office. As Saw Swee Hock and K. Kesavapany recounted, the level of acrimony reached a point that the Singapore leadership concluded that relations would remain tense so long as Mahathir was prime minister. Singapore thus decided to "sit things out".[49] As with the previous chapter, we will not be recounting in detail all the issues, old and new that

---

[45] Lim Min Zhang, "New Treaty Allows SAF to Train in Vastly Expanded Area in Australia", *The Straits Times*, 23 March 2020, at https://www.straitstimes.com/singapore/new-treaty-allows-saf-to-train-in-vastly-expanded-area-in-australia (accessed 30 Nov. 2022).
[46] "From Istana to Canberra".
[47] "Joint Announcement: Australia–Singapore Comprehensive Strategic Partnership", at https://www.dfat.gov.au/geo/singapore/Pages/joint-announcement-australia-singapore-comprehensive-strategic-partnership (accessed 11 Jan. 2021).
[48] Kenneth Cheng, "S'pore–US Defence Ties 'Can Strengthen' under Trump", *Today*, 13 Nov. 2016; see also Danson Cheong, "S'pore Interests Come First—Whatever the Global Shifts", *The Straits Times*, 11 Nov. 2016.
[49] Saw Swee Hock and K. Kesavapany, *Singapore–Malaysia Relations under Abdullah Badawi* (Singapore: ISEAS, 2006); Yang Razali Kassim, "Cautious Optimism" [review of the book], *The Straits Times*, 27 July 2006.

have emerged or re-emerged since 2004—replacing the causeway, airspace, land reclamation etc.—or be following the twists and turns in the negotiations, but will highlight Singapore's approach in its attempts, to borrow Foreign Minister S. Jayakumar's words, "to leave the acrimony of the 'old era' behind and move the relationship with Malaysia forward".[50]

Singapore was supportive of the approach suggested by the Abdullah Badawi administration which took over from prime minister Mahathir in 2003: to target the "low hanging fruits" that "could be plucked and settled quickly". As Malaysia's Foreign Minister Syed Hamid Albar said, "we want to avoid dead knots that could harm efforts by the Prime Minister to renew ties with Singapore. From now on, negotiations...will be done behind closed doors to avoid the issues from becoming points of public contention both sides of the causeway" and "if no agreements are reached, we will seek third-party help". In short, Malaysia would adopt a "quiet diplomacy" approach to settling disagreements.[51] As K. Kesavapany (former Singapore High Commissioner to Malaysia) wrote, Singapore "is in favour of a similar process of adjudication/arbitration in respect of other outstanding issues, if a return to the negotiating table doesn't yield results".[52] Abdullah Badawi's first official visit to Singapore in January 2004 in his capacity as Prime Minister and Lee Hsien Loong's visit in August in his capacity as Singapore's prime minister were seen as a good and fruitful re-start in Singapore–KL relations.

During the premiership of Badawi from 2003 to 2009, while not all disagreements were resolved, the water supply issue would stay a "low-key affair" as Singapore indicated that it would not seek to renew the 1961 Water Agreement expiring in 2010; Badawi also decided to abandon the crooked bridge project. Disagreement over land reclamation was resolved in April 2005 after the verdict by the International Tribunal for the Law of the Sea (ITLOS) to which Kuala Lumpur had in 2003 referred for arbitration.[53] The resolution of the land reclamation issue "reinforced the merit of Singapore's long-standing policy of adhering to international law" and the belief in the peaceful resolution of disputes, which is another pillar of Singapore's foreign policy.[54] Both Singapore and KL also

---

[50] Lydia Lim, "Replacing Causeway 'Does not Make Sense'", *The Straits Times*, 6 Jan. 2004.
[51] "Bilateral Issues: KL Goes for 'Quiet Diplomacy'", *The Straits Times*, 25 Jan. 2004.
[52] "Let Us not be Captives of the Past", *Today*, 27 Jan. 2004.
[53] For details, see Cheong Koon Hean, Tommy Koh and Lionel Yee, *Malaysia & Singapore: The Land Reclamation Case* (Singapore: Straits Times Press, 2013); K. Kesavapany, "Economic Concerns Override Political Differences", *The Straits Times*, 28 Dec. 2006.
[54] Cheong, Koh and Yee, *Malaysia & Singapore: The Land Reclamation Case*, p. 120. See also Lynn Lee, "PM: Bilateral Issues Best Settled by International Law", *The Sunday Times*, 12 Aug. 2007.

agreed to refer their long-standing territorial dispute over Pedra Branca island (consisting of Pedra Branca, Middle Rocks and South Ledge) to the International Court of Justice (ICJ). Lee Hsien Loong said that he hoped Malaysia would accept the court's decision if it was in Singapore's favour. He was sure Singapore would accept one in Malaysia's favour.[55] The ICJ in May 2008 awarded Pedra Branca to Singapore and Middle Rocks to Malaysia. It ruled that South Ledge belonged to whoever owns the territorial waters in which it is located. Both parties agreed "to honour and abide by the ICJ's judgement and fully implement its decision".[56]

In the assessment of K. Kesavapany writing in 2006, "with the possibility of a crooked bridge forever symbolising ties between the two countries now out of the way, despite objections from former Malaysian premier Mahathir Mohamad, the atmosphere is now more conducive to continued and accelerated economic cooperation between the two sides. The larger and more successful economic cooperation between the two becomes, the less room there will be for political squabbles".[57] One example was the government-to-government cooperation on the Iskandar Development Region in Johor, with which, Lee said, Singapore would proceed "at the pace Malaysia is comfortable with".[58]

Najib Razak succeeded Badawi as Malaysian prime minister in April 2009. Reviewing Singapore–Malaysia relations at the point when Najib became premier, Balan Moses noted that despite the "valiant effort to take bilateral relations out of the rut that [they] had been since the 1990s, little has changed since then. It has been a case…of one neighbour tolerating the other, there being no other option, given the physical, emotional and historical proximity of the two nations". Balan Moses was of the view that under Najib things "may be set to change". The "point of convergence could be the Iskandar Malaysia Project as both the Malaysian and Singapore premiers had agreed to "pursue 'one or two' iconic projects to symbolise the bilateral relations".[59] As Prime Minister Najib said during his visit to Singapore in May 2009, "legacy issues should not be in the way of" both countries "moving ahead" as there was "much, much more to gain from productive and cooperative arrangements…The basic principle is to make sure that it is a classic win-win mode in terms of a relationship",[60] a view with which Singapore would no doubt

---

[55] Lee, "PM: Bilateral Issues Best Settled by International Law".
[56] "Third S'pore–Malaysia Joint Panel Meeting on Pedra Branca", *The Straits Times*, 9 Jan. 2010.
[57] Kesavapany, "Economic Concerns Override Political Differences".
[58] Lee, "PM: Bilateral Issues Best Settled by International Law".
[59] Balan Moses, "Chance to Write New, Positive Chapter", *The Straits Times*, 22 April 2009. See also K. Kesavapany, "KL–S'pore Ties: Turning of the Tide", *The Straits Times*, 22 July 2009.
[60] "Najib Seeks a Win-win Relationship with S'pore", *The Straits Times*, 23 May 2009.

concur. It was under Najib's watch, in May 2010, that a resolution to the basket of outstanding issues between the two countries—the Points of Agreement signed on 27 November 1990, the day before then Prime Minister Lee Kuan Yew stepped down—was agreed.[61] Tommy Koh, in his assessment of Lee Hsien Loong's achievements at the ten-year mark of his administration, highlighted Singapore–Malaysia relations as Lee's "most important foreign policy achievement".[62] When Mahathir Mohamad became prime minister again in 2018 (10 May 2018–1 March 2020) relations briefly turned sour once more.

Turning to Indonesia, we recall that the fall of Suharto brought about by the 1997 Asian Financial Crisis led to a deterioration of Singapore–Indonesia relations, particularly during the Habibie and Wahib presidencies (1998–99 and 1999–2001 respectively). Singapore's immediate assistance after the December 2004 Indian Ocean earthquake-cum-tsunami—the Singapore Armed Forces were the first contingent to arrive in Aceh Province and Meulaboh (a town devastated by the tsunami)—gave bilateral relations a lift. Both countries also cooperated very well in the area of counterterrorism, as then Director of the Indonesia State Intelligence Agency, Hendropriyono, acknowledged in a 2004 article. Referring to Habibie's infamous remark that Singapore was "smaller than the island in the middle of Lake Toba", Hendropriyono said that "a decent interval has passed since those caustic comments, and Indonesia–Singapore ties have rebounded strongly in many areas. Perhaps nowhere is this more true than in the war on terrorism".[63]

Under Indonesian President Susilo Bambang Yudhoyono who assumed the leadership of Indonesia in the same year as Lee Hsien Loong became prime minister in Singapore, relations further improved. As in the case of Malaysia, the strategy is to use "economic ties to bind Singapore and Jakarta". At the start of both administrations, as Paul Jacob noted, Singapore and Indonesia agreed to "move forward bilateral relations with trade, investment and other economic

---

[61] "Full Text of the Joint Statement Issued Yesterday after the Meeting between Singapore Prime Minister Lee Hsien Loong and Malaysian Prime Minister Najib Razak", *The Straits Times*, 25 May 2010; see also Prime Minister's Office, Singapore, Joint Statement for the Meeting between Prime Minister Lee Hsien Loong and Prime Minister Dato' Sri Mohd Najib Tun Abdul Razak on the Implementation of the Points of Agreement on Malayan Railway Land in Singapore (POA), 20 September 2010, Singapore, at https://www.pmo.gov.sg/Newsroom/joint-statement-meeting-between-prime-minister-lee-hsien-loong-and-prime-minister-dato (accessed 30 Nov. 2022).
[62] Tommy Koh, "Ten Years, Over 100 Trips and Millions of Miles", *The Straits Times*, 13 Aug. 2014, at https://www.straitstimes.com/opinion/ten-years-over-100-trips-and-millions-of-miles (accessed 30 Nov. 2022).
[63] Hendropriyono, "Jakarta–S'pore Ties: Time Right for a Fresh Start", *The Straits Times*, 26 Aug. 2004.

issues set to be the glue that cements ties further".[64] In Singapore's view, a "strong, united and confident Indonesia" is good for both Singapore and the region.[65]

Not that there were no more problems, but as then-deputy prime minister Lee Hsien Loong said during his February 2004 visit to Jakarta, "there are some bilateral issues which we are tackling. But it will take some time to solve them because these are complicated issues. We should put them in the context of our overall bilateral relations and enable the broadest range of cooperation to proceed".[66] There is no need to go into the details of all the issues that cropped up, particularly from 2007, including the ban on sand exports to Singapore, the failure to resolve the extradition treaty and the Indonesian Parliament's (DPR-RI) refusal to ratify the bilateral defence cooperation agreement signed by both countries. In Minister Mentor Lee Kuan Yew's view, these were the consequence of Indonesian domestic politics: "the new political changes mapped out by recent changes to its constitution",[67] which essentially meant that Indonesia's "political process has become more complicated".[68] Singapore would have to be patient and let the Indonesians work it out for themselves. But there were positives in the relationship as well, for example, the settlement of the Singapore–Indonesia western sea boundary in early 2009 (talks about which began in 2005). This settlement made it possible to begin talks on the eastern sea boundary, an issue which was eventually settled in 2014.[69] The conclusion of this treaty, the third,[70] which both sides stated was "a significant milestone in bilateral relations", "affirms the mutual commitment of both countries to resolve complex bilateral

---

[64] Paul Jacob, "Economic Ties to Bind Singapore and Jakarta", *The Straits Times*, 9 Nov. 2004.
[65] Salim Osman, "S'pore 'Sets Great Store by Jakarta Ties'", *The Straits Times*, 25 Aug. 2006.
[66] "Mutual Respect is Key to Ties between Sovereign States", *The Straits Times*, 2 Feb. 2004.
[67] Azhar Ghani, "Jakarta's Bind a Result of Charter Changes: MM", *The Straits Times*, 28 July 2007. There was also the haze problem, with one of the worst haze years in 2013. In 2014, Indonesia named a warship after two of its soldiers who had bombed MacDonald House in Singapore during Konfrontasi.
[68] See Leonard C. Sebastian, "When Relationships Change: Singapore–Indonesia Ties after Suharto and the Importance of Growing Together", in *The Little Nation that Can: Singapore's Foreign Relations and Diplomacy*, ed. Gillian Koh (Singapore: NUSS *Commentary*, 2017), Chapter 6, p. 55.
[69] "Singapore, Indonesia Submit Final Sea Border Treaty to UN as They Celebrate 50th Anniversary of Ties", *The Straits Times*, 26 Sept. 2017, at https://www.straitstimes.com/asia/se-asia/singapore-indonesia-submit-final-sea-border-treaty-to-un-as-they-celebrate-50th (accessed 15 Dec. 2022).
[70] The first agreement was the maritime boundary along the central part of the Singapore Straits signed in 1973, the second was the western section signed in 2009 (and which came into force in 2010), the third is the eastern boundary signed in 2014 (and which came into force in 2017).

issues, including maritime delimitation, in an amicable manner on the basis of international law".[71]

Singapore–Indonesia relations have remained good under President Joko Widodo. In October 2019, both leaders agreed on a framework acknowledging the core interests and rights of both countries, particularly in airspace management and military training.[72] A Singapore–Indonesia Bilateral Investment Treaty was also signed in 2018 and ratified in 2021. In January 2022, both countries finally signed a package of agreements: the management of airspace (which according to Prime Minister Lee Hsien Loong has taken fifty years to settle); an extradition treaty and a defence agreement. A former Singapore ambassador to Indonesia, Barry Desker, has said that both countries had "discussed these complex issues for several decades", including the years when he was ambassador from 1986 to 1993.[73] Almost all analysts hailed the agreements, but always with a caveat that "the road ahead may not be so straightforward".[74] The next stage would be the ratification of the agreements.[75] We recall the 2007 experience described earlier.

Finally, to bring this discussion of Singapore's two most important relationships to a close, it is worth quoting then Foreign Minister K. Shanmugam who in 2014 said that "underlying its relationship with Indonesia and Malaysia are strong links in trade, investment and people-to people flows… Day to day things may happen, there could be arguments, there could be kerfuffles, there could be some fights but… there are sensible people on all sides". Singapore would ride it out each time "because we know underlying it is a far more important relationship".[76]

---

[71] "Singapore, Indonesia Submit Final Sea Border Treaty to UN as They Celebrate 50th Anniversary of Ties".
[72] Arlina Arshad, "Leaders' Retreat: PM Lee Hsien Loong, President Joko Widodo Hope Singapore-Indonesia Ties Will Grow even Stronger", *The Straits Times*, 8 Oct. 2019, at https://www.straitstimes.com/singapore/leaders-retreat-pm-lee-jokowi-hope-deep-singapore-indonesia-ties-will-grow-even-stronger (accessed 15 Dec. 2022); Timothy Goh, "Singapore and Indonesia have Made Good Progress on Key Bilateral Issues: MFA", *The Straits Times*, 4 Jan. 2022, at https://www.straitstimes.com/singapore/singapore-and-indonesia-have-made-good-progress-on-key-bilateral-issues-mfa (accessed 15 Dec. 2022); Aristyo Darmawan, "Resolving Indonesia and Singapore's UNCLOS dispute", *East Asia Forum*, 7 April 2021.
[73] Barry Desker, "'Renewed' Deal for New Age: View of a Former Envoy", *RSIS Commentary*, Number 007/2022, 26 Jan. 2022.
[74] See for example Leonard C. Sebastian and Dedi Dinarto, "Indonesia–Singapore Ties: Timely Breakthrough", *RSIS Commentary*, Number 006/2022, 26 Jan. 2022; "Singapore–Indonesia Pacts Draw Critics, and a Staunch Defence", *The Straits Times*, 12 Feb. 2022.
[75] For an update on this from the end of 2022, see Arlina Arshad, "Indonesia Ratifies Longstanding Extradition, Defence Deal with S'pore", *The Straits Times*, 16 Dec. 2022.
[76] Qtd. in Leonard Lim, "Small Tiffs but Deep Ties", *The Straits Times*, 29 March 2014.

V

Vivian Balakrishnan (then-Singapore's Minister for the Environment and Water Resources) made the following remarks in Parliament during the Haze problem in 2013, and these are worth repeating here. He said, "Let me be frank with this House...the Indonesian ministers, sometimes in their unguarded moments...they just tell us, look...Indonesia has 240 million people, our GDP [gross domestic product] is multiples of yours. So that comment...if it's only a few dollars, keep it, we don't need it - it's not very diplomatic, but Singaporeans should draw the correct lessons from this episode. We are small, we are open, we are vulnerable. We're surrounded by much bigger countries who have their own political agendas and their own priorities".[77] Balakrishnan was not suggesting Singapore go to war to resolve the haze issue. But both his remarks and Shanmugam's above recall Goh Keng Swee's advice in the early years (see previous chapter) regarding Singapore's needful strategy to overcome its size and vulnerability.

Putting aside economic cooperation as a strategy, we now turn to defence. In a 2014 speech marking 30 Years of Total Defence, PM Lee counselled: "If we are small and unsuccessful, small and weak, I think people may be polite with you, people may say the right thing to you. But you can be sure people will also be able to take advantage of you".[78] Singapore continued to keep ahead of the curve in defence and security with its continued focus on technology and arms modernisation; as Defence Minister Ng Eng Hen said in his 2019 Total Defence Day speech, cyber security should be increased and "the price of freedom is constant vigilance against threats old and new"[79]. An example is the 2015 introduction of drones/unmanned aerial vehicles (UAVs). The goal of the SAF is "to integrate all of its weapons into one network to multiply its firepower and give it a deadlier punch".[80] "Without a strong SAF, there is no economic future, there is no security", said Minister Mentor Lee Kuan Yew.[81] When Lee

---

[77] "Lessons from Haze Talks", *Today*, 9 July 2013.
[78] Qtd. in Andrea Ong, "S'pore Must Remain a 'Shining Red Dot', says PM", *The Sunday Times* [Singapore], 16 Feb. 2014.
[79] Mark Johnston, "Cyber Security Added to Singapore's Total Defence Framework", Channel Asia, 18 Feb. 2019 at https://www.channelasia.tech/article/657810/cyber-security-added-singapore-total-defence-framework/ (accessed 9 Jan. 2023). See also "Digital Defence Pillar Added to Singapore's Total Defence Framework to Strengthen Cybersecurity", *Channel News Asia*, 14 Feb. 2019 and "3G Soldier has Whole SAF in his Backpack" (Interview with Deputy Prime Minister and Defence Minister Teo Chee Hean), *The Straits Times*, 1 July 2009.
[80] Jermyn Chow, "War Games Debut of Drones Marks Evolution of SAF", *The Straits Times*, 11 Dec. 2015.
[81] "SAF has Done Better than I Hoped', says Lee Kuan Yew", 21 May 2012, *AsiaOne*, at www.asiaone.com.sg (accessed 24 Jan. 2022).

died in 2015, Singapore had "one of the most formidable armies in the world... with more fighter jets than Spain, Poland or Sweden. Its army has as many tanks as Italy...Its navy boasts the only stealth ships in the region. IHS [Information Handling Services] Jane's described the SAF as 'the best-equipped military in Southeast Asia'".[82]

But as Defence Minister Ng Eng Hen explained in 2015, "Technology had lowered the barriers to wage war via such means. Weapons are now drawn from political, economic, information and even humanitarian domains". Ng drew attention to the concept of "hybrid warfare"—"the integration of conventional and unconventional tools of warfare by both states and non-state actors"—which he believed highlighted the "timeliness and timelessness of Total Defence". Going forward, Ng said that "equal investments in all five pillars of Total Defence will have to be made".[83] Three years later, in 2018, Ng noted that while Singapore was well-prepared to handle physical threats, it was less prepared as a society against threats from the digital domain even though "the impact of some of these threats from the cyber area can be as devastating, if not more".[84] In 2019, Digital Defence became the sixth pillar of Singapore's Total Defence strategy. As Shashi Jayakumar had noted a few years earlier, "most national security strategies now place cyber security high on the list of priorities".[85] Indeed, Technology is now the buzzword in a tech-driven world. Technology is all-pervasive, and certainly not confined to the defence sector.[86] In late-October 2022, the SAF's Digital and Intelligence Service, described as "a significant milestone for the next generation SAF", was formed.[87] This would "better coordinate and improve Singapore's cyber defence and intelligence gathering".[88]

---

[82] Alberto Riva, "Lee Kuan Yew's Other Legacy: Why Singapore has One of the World's Toughest Militaries", *International Business Times,* 24 March 2015, at https://www.ibtimes.com/lee-kuan-yews-other-legacy-why-singapore-has-one-worlds-toughest-militaries-1857454 (accessed 24 Jan. 2022).

[83] Ng, qtd. in Ho Shu Huang, "Total Defence Against Threat of Hybrid Warfare", *The Straits Times*, 12 May 2015.

[84] Lim Min Zhang, "Total Defence Could Include Sixth Pillar to Tackle Cyber Threats", *The Straits Times*, 5 Oct. 2018.

[85] Shashi Jayakumar, ed., *State, Society and National Security: Challenges and Opportunities in the 21st Century* (Singapore: World Scientific, 2016), pp. 30–1.

[86] See "Staying Relevant in a Tech-driven Global Economy", *The Straits Times*, 27 Jan. 2022.

[87] Mindef Singapore, "Establishment of the Digital and Intelligence Service: A Significant Milestone for the Next Generation SAF", at https://www.mindef.gov.sg/web/portal/mindef/news-and-events/latest-releases/article-detail/2022/October/28oct22_nr2 (accessed 30 Dec. 2022).

[88] Clement Yong, "Hiring for SAF's New Cyber Service to Start this Month", *The Straits Times*, 1 July 2022.

As recounted in the previous chapter, 9/11 reinforced the urgency and importance of dealing with the terrorist threat. Under Lee's administration, efforts continued to strengthen coordination between agencies to deal with non-conventional warfare and transnational terrorism. Given that we are now in the digital age, cybersecurity is a concern of the Ministries of both Defence and Home Affairs, and of the SAF.[89] At the same time, Singapore is also "aware that the long-term ideological nature of the war on global terrorism requires a strategy to win hearts and minds".[90] In sum, Singapore adopts a whole-of-government approach to security and an SAF which has become much more integrated, reflecting the multi-service as well as multi-agency nature of its operations.[91]

VI

In March 2015, Singapore's founding prime minister, Lee Kuan Yew, passed away. Lee was officially Minister Mentor from 2004 (when Lee Hsien Loong became prime minister). A "mentor", as the Oxford dictionary defines it, is an "experienced and trusted adviser". Although he retired from that position in 2011, there was no doubt that his advice was still sought and seriously considered till his death four years later. As portrayed by Graham Allison and Robert Blackwell, Lee Kuan Yew was the "grand master".[92] Lee Hsien Loong recalled in 2015: "my father stepped down as prime minister in 1990, so it's 25 years ago and I'm not his successor but his successor's successor. He had a long shadow, and he gave us sage advice, even till old age, but he prepared very well for his gradual fading away. One great tribute to him was that on the day he died, the stock market didn't move. People had confidence; they knew that Singapore would carry on".[93]

Since Lee's passing, particularly from 2017, US–China relations have deteriorated considerably. At the end of 2019, the coronavirus pandemic struck the world. Today, at the time of writing, there would be common agreement with Maleeha Lodhi's description of the world today: "there is no doubt that the world

---

[89] See Wong Yu Han, "Singapore's Approach to Cybersecurity", in *State, Society and National Security: Challenges and Opportunities in the 21st Century*, ed. Shashi Jayakumar, Chapter 15.
[90] Andrew T. H. Tan, "Singapore's Approach to Homeland Security", in *Southeast Asian Affairs 2005* (Singapore: ISEAS, 2005), p. 360. See also *The Fight Against Terror: Singapore's National Security Strategy* (Singapore: National Security Coordination Centre, 2004).
[91] See for example Michael Raska, "Modern War - How to Win without Fighting", *The Straits Times*, 2 Dec. 2021; "3G Soldier has Whole SAF in his Backpack".
[92] See Graham Allison and Robert D. Blackwell, with Ali Wyne, *Lee Kuan Yew: The Grand Master's Insights on China, the United States, and the World* (Cambridge, MA: MIT, 2012).
[93] Lim Yan Liang, "Growth in Region, Skills, Key to Economic Future" (Dialogue with PM Lee Hsien Loong at the Singapore Summit, 19 Sept. 2015), *The Straits Times*, 20 Sept. 2015.

is in the throes of one of its most unsettled periods". The pandemic "only added to uncertainty when the world is in flux—with global power shifting" and challenges to multilateralism.[94] Han Fook Kwang, who had worked with Lee Kuan Yew on his final book, recalled that Lee "did not foresee" all that occurred after 2015 but "though he did not predict the subsequent earthshaking events, he was mostly right about the larger forces that shape the world".[95] One example will suffice to illustrate his prescience.

In a 2010 interview with the editor-in-chief of *Asahi Shimbun*, Yoichi Funabashi, Lee Kuan Yew said: "Without America, you can take Japan, you can put North and South Korea together, you can put the whole of Asean together, you can even get India together - you can't balance China. India is too far away and they can't project the forces into the Pacific. But the Americans can".[96] This echoes his views 10 years earlier in a Sydney speech that South Korea, Japan, Australia, New Zealand, the Philippines, Singapore and Indonesia saw the need for the US as a "balancer". Malaysia, he said took a "contrary view". The mainland Southeast Asian countries also had "different views".[97]

Indeed, Lee believed that the importance of the US presence in the region would only increase rather than recede in the future when China became a formidable economic power. As he said, "a country such as the US which had risen to the pinnacle of the world, would not easily give up its super-power position". The US would want to remain "the world's top player for as long as possible".[98] At the same time, the Chinese know that the US would yield to "any extension of Chinese influence reluctantly, and only when they have to".[99] On another occasion, he put it more starkly: "As a rising power, China cannot be expected to acquiesce in the status quo if it is against its interests. As the pre-eminent global power, US interest is the preservation of the status quo. The fundamental

---

[94] Maleeha Lodhi, "Geopolitics in Unsettled Times", *Dawn*, 19 Jan. 2022, at https://www.dawn.com/news/1658194 (accessed 24 March 2022).
[95] Han Fook Kwang, "In Post-Lee Kuan Yew World, is his Strategic Vision still Relevant?", *The Straits Times*, 10 April 2019.
[96] "On Power and Stabilising Forces", *The Straits Times*, 17 May 2010.
[97] Address by Senior Minister Lee Kuan Yew to the Asia Society Australasia Centre Annual Dinner, 20 Nov. 2000, Sydney, at https://www.nas.gov.sg/archivesonline/data/pdfdoc/2000112004.htm (accessed 28 Nov. 2022).
[98] "US Presence in E. Asia will Become more Vital, says SM", *The Straits Times*, 23 Jan. 2001.
[99] "Senior Minister Lee Kuan Yew's Interview with Arnaud de Borchgrave, UPI International's Editor-at-large, on 11 May 2001", *The Business Times*, 19 May 2001 and *The Sunday Times* [Singapore], 20 May 2001.

difference of interests cannot be wished away".[100] China is very conscious of being circumscribed by the United States and its allies. But Lee did not believe that China had intentions to challenge the US militarily as they are aware of the wide technology gap between them and the US. Chinese strategy in the near term is to "build up the military capability to make it expensive for America to intervene if they [China] decide they have to use force on Taiwan... not to win, but to deter the Americans... What will happen in 50 years, I don't know".[101] It is expected that China and America will be rivals but "not necessarily enemies"[102] as "the world's monetary and political problems require both countries to take parallel paths". Cooperation and competition between the two countries will continue, relations will move forward, regardless of occasional conflicts.[103]

Recent (post-2000) actions, comments and speeches by the Singapore leaders, of both the current so-called "third generation" and the "fourth generation" (who have yet to inherit the full mantle of the present leadership) show that Singapore's grand strategy has remained unchanged since Lee Kuan Yew's passing in 2015. Singapore retains a dogged focus on and pursuit of globalisation. As Lee Hsien Loong has said, "there is still a lot going for globalisation though it may be under pressure, and the imperative for countries to cooperate is not going away".[104] Singapore's belief is that it is not possible for the republic to choose between the US and China "given the extensive ties the Republic has with both superpowers... Generally, it is that we [Singapore] want to be friends with both, but we have to find our own way forward".[105] Teo Chee Hean (Senior Minister and Coordinating Minister for National Security) in a 2022 article shared his belief that the lessons of the previous few years are that "countries need to work together out of enlightened—and not narrow—self-interest for the world to be a less dysfunctional place" and that while countries, including Singapore, hope to see the US and China manage their issues, "small countries have agency to step up and do something for ourselves through partnerships...to help to shape the global

---

[100] Address by Senior Minister Lee Kuan Yew at the 1st International Institute for Strategic Studies Asia Security Conference, 31 May 2002, Singapore.
[101] "Will Japan Fall behind China?", *The Straits Times*, 13 Aug. 2005.
[102] "'I Saw it Coming...'", *The Straits Times*, 12 Aug. 2005.
[103] "China and the US Need Each Other", *The Straits Times*, 8 April 2010.
[104] Hariz Baharudin, "Globalisation has Benefited Everyone in S'pore, says PM", *The Straits Times*, 15 March 2021, at https://www.straitstimes.com/singapore/politics/globalisation-has-benefited-everyone-in-spore-says-pm (accessed 15 Dec. 2022).
[105] Tham Yuen-C, "'Not Possible for S'pore, Many Countries, to Choose between US and China' PM Lee Tells BBC", *The Straits Times*, 15 March 2021, at https://www.straitstimes.com/singapore/not-possible-for-spore-many-countries-to-choose-between-us-and-china-pm-lee-tells-bbc (accessed 15 Dec. 2022).

order…to uphold and update the global security architecture or trading system, even if the major countries are unable to do so in the short-term".[106]

The "fourth generation" leaders have expressed comparable sentiments in their remarks. For example, Chan Chun Sing (Minister of Education) in 2021 noted that it has been Singapore's "inclination to consider each issue carefully and take principled positions" based on its "long-term interests to uphold the rule of international law in the global order, so that might does not equal right".[107] In an article published a few days after Teo's, Ong Ye Kung (Minister of Health) echoed S. Rajaratnam's 1972 speech on Singapore as a "global city".[108] During the coronavirus pandemic, Singapore remained committed to maintaining its status as a major logistics, transportation and energy hub[109] even as it addressed the health ramifications of COVID-19. Lawrence Wong (co-chair of the multi-ministry task force handling the pandemic) explained that Singapore's size and lack of resources meant that the country "cannot close its borders for a prolonged period": "Being open, staying open…[are] existential to Singapore".[110] It is a fine balancing act, as Ong Ye Kung elaborated: "The fulcrum of the balance is different for each country… From day one, in fact, in our 700 years of history as an island… we have always depended on being connected with the world to survive and do well, and prosper as an entity".[111] Chan Chun Sing noted that Singapore's global

---

[106] Teo Chee Hean, "Whatever Happened to the Middle Way?", *Fulcrum*, 6 Jan. 2022, at https://fulcrum.sg/whatever-happened-to-the-middle-way/ (accessed 11 Jan. 2023).

[107] Chan, as reported in Justin Ong, "Singapore Takes Principled Positions not Sides in US–China Rivalry: Chan Chun Sing", *The Straits Times*, 10 Nov. 2021, at https://www.straitstimes.com/singapore/politics/singapore-takes-principled-positions-not-sides-in-us-china-rivalry-chan-chun-sing (accessed 15 Dec. 2022); see also Chan Chun Sing, "Singapore amid Great Power Rivalry", *The Straits Times*, 10 Nov. 2021, at https://www.straitstimes.com/opinion/singapore-amid-great-power-rivalry (accessed 15 Dec. 2022).

[108] Ong Ye Kung, "Singapore – Lessons from the Rise and Fall of Great Cities", *The Straits Times*, 14 Jan. 2022. One comparable point is seen in Ong's view that "what we lack in resources and strategic mass, we can make up with nimbleness, and unity of purpose and action".

[109] MFA Press Statement: Minister for Foreign Affairs Dr Vivian Balakrishnan's written reply to parliamentary question on Singapore's contributions to global efforts to combat COVID-19, 10 Jan. 2022.

[110] "Working at Keeping Economy Open amid Covid-19 Fight", *The Straits Times*, 8 May 2021.

[111] Ong, cited in Justin Ong, "4 Ways to Travel Safely with no Quarantine: Ong Ye Kung", *The Straits Times*, 7 May 2021, at https://www.straitstimes.com/singapore/transport/4-ways-to-travel-safely-with-no-quarantine-ong-ye-kung (accessed 22 Dec. 2022); see also Justin Ong, "S'pore's Reopening Balances Business, Health Needs: Wong", *The Straits Times*, 21 Aug. 2021; Linette Lai, "'S'pore Committed to Staying Open to World': Ong Ye Kung", *The Straits Times*, 21 Aug. 2021.

connections "have benefitted the country in times of crisis", enabling the country to keep its supply chains resilient.[112]

Readers may recall that we had earlier identified four speeches which are essential to understanding Singapore's grand strategy. To the four, we now in this chapter add a fifth, Prime Minister Lee Hsien Loong's speech "Choice and Conviction" for the 8th S. Rajaratnam Lecture (27 November 2015) in which he highlighted the realities of small states, how Singapore though small refused to accept its smalless "as our fate", and how the country does have agency and can transcend its inherent limitations by being an "active and constructive player" internationally, by always anticipating developments in order "to protect our interests, whichever way events may break". Last but not least, this strategy can ensure that Singapore stays relevant.[113] Together, these five speeches form the core ideas and thrusts of Singapore's grand strategy.

---

[112] "'S'pore's Global Ties have Benefitted it in Times of Crisis': Chan", *The Straits Times*, 10 July 2021.
[113] Lee Hsien Loong, "Choice and Conviction—The Foreign Policy of a Little Red Dot", S. Rajaratnam Lecture, 27 Nov. 2015 (Singapore: MFA Academy, 2015).

Conclusion

I

The preceding chapters have attempted to trace the evolution of Singapore's grand strategy from 1965 to the present. There are two objectives for writing this book. The first is to contribute to the scholarly debate and literature on "Grand Strategy", which have so far focused on that of great powers. This study has shown that small countries do have grand strategies too,[1] and Singapore, a small country lacking in natural resources, with a small population, and which has often been described as punching above its weight, makes a good case study. Related to this, the second purpose of writing this book is to fill a gap in the literature of the post-1965 diplomatic, defence, and security history of Singapore, which historians have yielded to political scientists.

The term "Grand Strategy" has not generally been used in the context of Singapore. It is more common to talk or read about Singapore's foreign policy or defence policy, or occasionally Singapore's National Strategy or National Security Strategy. Essentially, they refer to the same set of deliberations and concerns as those of "Grand Strategy".[2] Singapore is not exceptional in this respect. China, for example, also does not use the term officially although Chinese academics

---

[1] See Anders Wivel, "The Grand Strategies of Small States", in *The Oxford Handbook of Grand Strategy*, ed. Thierry Balzacq and Ronald R. Krebs (London: Oxford University Press, 2021), Chapter 30.

[2] See for example Andrew Preston, "National Security as Grand Strategy: Edward Mead Earle and the Burdens of World Power", in *Rethinking American Grand Strategy*, ed. Elizabeth Borgwardt, Christopher McKnight Nichols and Andrew Preston (Oxford: Oxford University Press, 2021), Chapter 11.

have been using it since the 1980s.[3] There are those who do not consider "Grand Strategy" a useful concept. Those who find the term useful, including this author, hold the view that leaders do "draw on some set of notions about how the world works as they respond to new situations",[4] even when on occasion they must react at short notice and with limited information. Without a grand strategy, "policymaking is reactive, often haphazard, and always dangerous".[5] Hal Brands, quoting Eisenhower, reminds us that "Grand Strategy" is not "some immutable blueprint from which policy must never deviate". It "requires purpose and a willingness to look ahead" and at the same time, it "demands significant tactical flexibility as well".[6]

As described in the introductory chapter, there is a multitude of useful definitions of "Grand Strategy". While there are differences in emphasis, focus and nomenclature, there are also considerable overlaps and a fair amount of consensus among scholars who study the concept. Christopher Layne defined grand strategy as "the meeting point where the international system's geopolitical constraints intersect with a state's domestic political culture and its sense of identity".[7] This book adopts a comparable simple, clear and concise description offered by Peter Feaver who defined "Grand Strategy" as "the collection of plans and policies that comprise the state's deliberate effort to harness political, military, diplomatic and economic tools together to advance that state's

---

[3] Wu Chunqiiu, "Dialectics and the Study of Grand Strategy: A Chinese View", Chinese Aerospace Studies Institute, 2002, at https://www.airuniversity.af.edu/Portals/10/CASI/documents/Translations/2021-12-09%20Dialectics%20and%20the%20Study%20of%20Grand%20Strategy-%20A%20Chinese%20Perspective.pdf?ver=6iCNZjxKfbGYulHZ7CpCaA%3d%3d (accessed 30 Jan. 2022). This article was released by the PLA's Academy of Military Sciences. See also David B.H. Denoon, ed., *China's Grand Strategy: A Roadmap to Global Power?* (New York, NY: New York University Press, 2021); Andrew Scobell et al., *China's Grand Strategy: Trends, Trajectories, and Long-Term Competition*, at https://www.rand.org/pubs/research_reports/RR2798.html (accessed 14 Feb. 2022); Kanti Bajpai, Saira Basit and V. Krishnappa, eds., *India's Grand Strategy: History, Theory, Cases* (London: Routledge, 2016) and Bernhard Beitelmair-Berini, *India's Grand Strategy and Foreign Policy: Strategic Pluralism and Subcultures* (London: Routledge, 2022).
[4] Paul C. Avery, Jonathan N. Markowitz and Robert J. Reardon, "Disentangling Grand Strategy: International Relations Theory and US Grand Strategy", *Texas National Security Review* 3, no.1 (Nov. 2018): 30.
[5] Robert Wilkie, "America Needs a Grand Strategy", *The Heritage Foundation*, 3 Nov. 2021, at https://www.heritage.org/defense/report/america-needs-grand-strategy (accessed 30 Jan. 2022).
[6] Hal Brands, "Getting Grand Strategy Right: Clearing Away Common Fallacies in the Grand Strategy Debate", in *Rethinking American Grand Strategy*, ed. Borgwardt, McKnight Nichols and Preston, pp. 32–4.
[7] Christopher Layne quoted in *Rethinking American Grand Strategy*, p. 220.

national interest".[8] This study also shares Avery Goldstein's view that strategy is not "simply a collection of preferred policies" but "a vision informed by the recognition that the state's policies must be implemented in an international context of interdependent choice". "Grand Strategy" must "refer to a carefully crafted, detailed government plan".[9] One can just substitute the word "state" in this case with "Singapore".

The study of grand strategy would require analysing principles, strategic planning and behaviour.[10] This book thus presents a chronological and interpretative analysis of the etiology of Singapore's grand strategy, ideology and praxis of three cabinets and two leadership transitions. The first three chapters cover Lee Kuan Yew (1965–90), Chapter 4 covers Goh Chok Tong (1990–2004) and Chapter 5, Lee Hsien Loong (2004–present); together then, the book spans the Cold War and post-Cold War periods.

To understand Singapore's grand strategy, it is essential to revisit its experience when it separated from Malaysia (of which it was a part from 1963) and became independent in August 1965. While it was a bloodless independence, it was swift if not sudden in the eyes of most people. The national narrative is that independence was "thrust" upon Singapore.[11] As an "unexpected nation",[12] to borrow the phrase of one historian, policies had to be made on the run and the fundamentals of a grand strategy were shaped, informed and forged during the aftermath of 9 August 1965. As this study shows, Singapore's grand strategy has been remarkably consistent since the country came into being in 1965.

---

[8] Peter Feaver, "What is Grand Strategy and Why Do We Need It?", *Foreign Policy*, 8 April 2009, at https://foreignpolicy.com/2009/04/08/what-is-grand-strategy-and-why-do-we-need-it/ (accessed 11 Jan. 2023).

[9] Avery Goldstein, "China's Grand Strategy under Xi Jinping", *International Security* 45, no. 1 (Summer 2020): 166.

[10] See Thierry Balzacq, Peter Dombrowski and Simon Reich, eds., *Comparative Grand Strategy: A Framework and Cases* (Oxford: Oxford University Press, 2019).

[11] See for example, S.R. Nathan, "Singapore's Foreign Policy: Beginnings and Future", The Inaugural S. Rajaratnam Lecture, 10 March 2008 (Singapore: MFA Diplomatic Academy, 2008); Lee Kuan Yew, "The Fundamentals of Singapore's Foreign Policy: Then & Now", S. Rajaratnam Lecture, 9 April 2009 (Singapore: MFA Academy, 2009), at https://www.pmo.gov.sg/Newsroom/speech-mr-lee-kuan-yew-minister-mentor-s-rajaratnam-lecture-09-april-2009-530-pm-shangri (accessed 9 Jan. 2023).

[12] Edwin Lee, *Singapore: The Unexpected Nation* (Singapore: ISEAS, 2008).

II

Singapore has had a singular and crystal-clear strategic priority or goal in place since 1965: to ensure its survival and independence as a nation-state. As its founding prime minister, Lee Kuan Yew said, Singapore "cannot be a satellite of any nation" for unless it is able "to retain its own point of view", "it would lose all effectiveness in the new world order".[13] The goal was rephrased in the form of a series of questions by Prime Minister Lee Hsien Loong in his 2015 "Choice and Conviction" lecture.[14] Among the questions were: "How can we ensure that we survive, and keep our place in the sun?" and "How can Singapore advance [its] national interests?".

This strategic priority is derived from the belief that small states cannot survive for long: as the senior Lee once said, "in the context of the second half of the 20th century Southeast Asian island nations are a political joke".[15] Over night, the narrative that an independent Singapore was not viable and therefore being part of Malaysia was an existential necessity (which was the main argument proffered in the late-1950s and early 1960s in support of merger to form Malaysia in 1963) had to be abruptly revised. The hope that Singapore would be the "New York" of Malaysia also evaporated.

On 8 August 1965, the new country was 581.5 square kilometers in area with a population of just 1.887 million people, a trading port without a hinterland and unable to defend itself. Everything that has been done in the domains of Foreign Policy, Defence and Economics in the last 56 years (at the point of writing this chapter) has been to address this strategic priority of ensuring that Singapore will/can survive and prosper. This is based on the premise that Singapore, unlike its larger neighbours, is "of no intrinsic interest to any developed country". Small states have little, if any, power to alter the region, not to mention the world. Thus, to survive, Singapore needs to be relevant, useful and successful: "Singapore has to continually reconstruct itself and keep its relevance to the world and create political and economic space".[16] Because

---

[13] Clarissa Oon, "MM Lee: We Cannot Be a Satellite of Any Nation", *The Straits Times*, 30 Dec. 2009.
[14] Lee Hsien Loong, "Choice and Conviction—The Foreign Policy of a Little Red Dot", S. Rajaratnam Lecture, 27 Nov. 2015 (Singapore: MFA Academy, 2015).
[15] Lee Kuan Yew speaking at the Singapore Legislative Assembly on 5 March 1957, quoted in Bilahari Kausikan, "A 'Happy Mistake': Bilahari Kausikan on Singapore's Biggest Foreign Policy Blunder", *The Straits Times*, 21 Jan. 2020.
[16] Lee Kuan Yew, "The Fundamentals of Singapore's Foreign Policy: Then & Now" (S. Rajaratnam Lecture, 2009); Lee Hsien Loong, "Choice and Conviction—The Foreign Policy of a Little Red Dot", S. Rajaratnam Lecture, 27 Nov. 2015.

Singapore is successful, the world pays attention to it, as nobody would take a failed state seriously.[17] This has remained the mantra ever since Independence, even though the physical size of Singapore has increased to 728.3 square kilometres and the population has grown to 5.69 million.[18] As S. Jayakumar quipped, "One day, a small state, The next day still a small state".[19]

Lee Kuan Yew (1923–2015), S. Rajaratnam (1915–2006) and Goh Keng Swee (1918–2010) are frequently mentioned in this book, especially Lee who remained influential up to his death (and some may say even after his death). An understanding of their beliefs and premises is imperative for anyone interested in understanding and analysing Singapore's grand strategy because these ideas serve as "a prism" which shapes their "perceptions and diagnoses" of international politics as well as "provide[s] norms, standards and guidelines" that influence Singapore's choice of "strategy and tactics, structuring and weighing of alternative courses of action".[20]

Studies of grand strategies are "inherently context heavy",[21] as this study shows. But this is a good place to briefly correlate the worldviews of the above three figures with International Relations theories and strategic thinkers which students of IR and Strategic Studies may well be familiar with. Heinrich von Treitschke and Friedrich von Bernhardi believed that the state needed an elite and a certain hierarchy to survive in a hostile environment, at home confronting an irrational mass of citizens and, abroad, hostile powers. Colin Gray and Herman Kahn argued that to survive, a state required a well-equipped armed force and a foreign policy focused on national security. Carl von Clausewitz noted that while statesmen do not actively seek war, they must regard it as a rational instrument and be willing and ready to use it when necessary. Robert Gilpin argued that politics and economics are inseparable as economics is one of the important foundations of state power and vice versa. According to Kenneth Waltz and Stephen Krasner,

---

[17] Lee Hsien Loong, "Choice and Conviction – The Foreign Policy of a Little Red Dot".

[18] These are 2020 figures. See also S. Jayakumar, "Reflections on Diplomacy of a Small State", S. Rajaratnam Lecture, 19 May 2010 (Singapore: MFA Diplomatic Academy, 2010); ST Graphics in *The Straits Times*, 9 Aug. 2015; Microfilm Reel NL 33598 and Lee Hsien Loong, "Choice and Conviction".

[19] Irene Ng, "How to Make Friends and Advance Interests of Singapore", *The Straits Times*, 28 Oct. 2000.

[20] Alexander L. George, "The 'Operational Code': A Neglected Approach to the Study of Political Leaders and Decision-Making", *International Studies Quarterly* 13, no. 2 (June 1969): 190–222.

[21] Paul van Hooft, "Grand Strategy", Oxford Bibliographies, at https://www.oxfordbibliographies.com/view/document/obo-9780199743292/obo-9780199743292-0218.xml (accessed 30 Jan. 2022).

international economic exchange is useful but fragile. Cooperation can be short-lived, and today's friend may become tomorrow's enemy.[22] In a recent commentary in the context of the Ukraine crisis, Stephen Walt wrote: "at the most basic level, realism begins with the recognition that war occurs because there is no agency or central authority that can protect states from one another and stop them from fighting if they choose to do so…There is no way states can know for certain what others may do in the future, which makes them reluctant to trust one another and encourages them to hedge against the possibility that another powerful state may try to harm them at some point down the road".[23]

The reader may well conclude from reading this book that the Singapore leaders, although they were never known to be "hung up" on theory, share the same views as the above realist thinkers. Indeed, after the Cold War, while many Western elites abandoned Realism and believed that liberal ideas should guide the conduct of foreign policy, Lee Kuan Yew did not share this view.

Rajaratnam and Goh retired from political office in 1986 and 1988, respectively. They gradually faded out in the 1990s due to poor health. After Lee stepped down as Prime Minister in 1990, he assumed the title of Senior Minister from 1990 till 2004,[24] and then Minister Mentor from 2004 to 2011. He remained a member of Parliament till his death in 2015. Thus unlike his other two colleagues, Lee was a key maker and shaper of Singapore's grand strategy during both the Cold War and the post-Cold War periods. Goh Chok Tong, Lee's successor and the second prime minister of Singapore, said that he "learnt to swim in the swirling ocean of foreign affairs from Rajaratnam, Mr Lee Kuan Yew…". He recalled that he "read their speeches", was "taken by them to many meetings, and observed how they engaged other leaders" and "benefited from their advice". Goh noted that "together, they laid down the fundamental tenets of Singapore's foreign policy—to safeguard our sovereignty and freedom of action, stay relevant, make [the] maximum number of friends and—if possible—no enemies, and respect international laws and norms in our dealings with other countries. These tenets continue to be salient today".[25]

---

[22] See Jürg Martin Gabriel, *Worldviews and Theories of International Relations* (London: St. Martin's Press, 1994).
[23] Stephen M. Walt, "Liberal Illusions Caused the Ukraine Crisis", *Foreign Policy*, 19 Jan. 2022, at https://foreignpolicy.com/2022/01/19/ukraine-russia-nato-crisis-liberal-illusions/ (accessed 30 Jan. 2022).
[24] S. Rajaratnam was Senior Minister from 1985 to 1988, the first time the title was introduced.
[25] Goh Chok Tong, "The Practice of Foreign Policy for Sustained Growth—the Singapore Experience", S. Rajaratnam Lecture, 17 Oct. 2014 (Singapore: MFA Academy, 2009).

Through a process of first-hand experience and osmosis, four generations of decision-makers in Singapore shared a common strategic culture "which influence[s] their strategic choices at the highest political level (in terms of relating means to political ends) and military options at the operational or tactical level".[26] In Jack L. Snyder's terms, "strategic culture" here arises from and within "the body of attitudes and beliefs that guides and circumscribes thought on strategic questions, influences the way strategic issues are formulated, and sets the vocabulary and perceptual parameters of strategic debate".[27] This "body of attitudes and beliefs" takes reference from "Singapore's traditions, values, attitudes, patterns of behaviour, habits, symbols, achievements and particular way of adapting to the environment and solving problems with respect to the threat and use of force".[28]

That Singapore had so far been able to maintain a cohesive multi-racial society, despite having an ethnic Chinese majority, helps. This and the fact that the ruling government has been in power since 1965 give Singapore's grand strategy coherence and continuity, which in turn have allowed for an effective all-of-government approach to operationalising its grand strategy. The need "to work effectively as a seamless whole" is, according to a 2010 lecture by then Senior Minister and Co-ordinating Minister for National Security, S. Jayakumar, "increasingly vital" in dealing with "multifaceted challenges to ensure Singapore's continued economic success and relevance on the international stage".[29] As Lee Hsien Loong noted, political stability is important "to maintain a clear understanding of our national interests, and to pursue that consistently over a long period". Political stability could "compensate" for Singapore's "lack of

---

[26] Chin Kin Wah, "Reflections on the Shaping of Strategic Cultures in Southeast Asia", in *Southeast Asian Perspectives on Security*, ed. Derek de Cunha (Singapore: ISEAS, 2000), Chapter 1, p. 5.

[27] Snyder, quoted in Borgwardt, McKnight Nichols and Preston, eds., "Introduction", *Rethinking American Grand Strategy* (Oxford: Oxford University Press, 2021), p.11. Snyder expands on this line of thought, and offers his definition of "strategic culture" ("the sum total of ideas, conditioned emotional responses, and patterns of behavior..." [p. 8]) in the context of the Soviet nuclear threat in his report for the USAF: *The Soviet Strategic Culture: Implications for Limited Nuclear Operations* (Santa Monica, CA: Rand Corp., Sept. 1977), pp. 8–9 (the quotation, cited here, from Borgwardt et al. appears on Snyder's p. 9). The report is available at https://www.rand.org/pubs/reports/R2154.html (accessed 15 Dec. 2022).

[28] Ken Booth, "The Concept of Strategic Cultures Affirmed", in *Strategic Power: USA/USSR*, ed. Carl G. Jacobsen (London: Macmillan, 1990), p. 121.

[29] S. Jayakumar, "Reflections on Diplomacy of a Small State"; see also Goh, "The Practice of Foreign Policy for Sustained Growth". For the "whole of society approach to cyber security", see Shashi Jayakumar, ed., *State, Society and National Security: Challenges and Opportunities in the 21st Century* (Singapore: World Scientific, 2016), Chapter 15.

heft".[30] The notion that politics should "stop at the water's edge" has remained an unwritten maxim of Singapore politics since 1965.

III

Security Studies scholars devote considerable attention to the development and content of strategy. While appropriate, such attention is incomplete without a thorough consideration of the equally important implementation of strategy: how the ends relate to the means, intentions to capabilities and objectives to resources.[31] As this book shows, Singapore's grand strategy is operationalised or manifested in the following ways. Firstly, through careful management of its relations with Malaysia and Indonesia, and, beyond the vicinity and region, its relations with the United States and China. Second, it is operationalised through the promotion and support for multilateralism, both for economics and security. As early as 1966 Lee Kuan Yew was calling for "multilateral cooperation" for the region (although the idea of multilateral security arrangements was well ahead of its time). To Lee, "the self-contained national unit, national self-sufficiency, is old-fashioned and out-of-date. It does not work unless you are a big land mass like the United States of America or the USSR". Thus, with regional cooperation, "you lump together 300 million people, and everybody stands to gain". He envisaged that Singapore "could be the catalyst that could speed up the course of economic development" and act as "a spark plug" for economic progress and development in the region. But first, all the countries had to agree that "nobody can swallow up the whole and we have to cooperate".[32] Geographical proximity is a necessary but not sufficient condition for this. Multilateral cooperation/Multilateralism, which Singapore strongly advocated and continues to advocate, is not confined to the economic realm. One early example is the formation of the ASEAN Regional Forum (ARF) in July 1993.

The next two demonstrations of Singapore's grand strategy are in the areas of defence and international law. Singapore takes the rule of law very seriously as it believes that "small states cannot survive if interaction is governed by relative

---

[30] Lee Hsien Loong, "Choice and Conviction—The Foreign Policy of a Little Red Dot".
[31] John Lewis Gaddis, *Strategies of Containment: A Critical Appraisal of Postwar American National Security Policy* (Oxford: Oxford University Press, 1982), p. viii.
[32] "Transcript of at Talk Given by the Prime Minister, Mr. Lee Kuan Yew, on the Subject 'Big and Small Fishes in Asian Waters' at a Meeting of the University of Singapore Democratic Socialist Club at the University Campus", 15 June 1966; "Interview (Hugh D.S. Greenway, *Time/Life* Bureau Chief, Southeast Asia) with the Prime Minister, Mr. Lee Kuan Yew", 10 June 1969.

power".[33] Singapore has on occasions been criticised for being too legalistic in its interactions but, as Professor S. Jayakumar (who had held various ministerial appointments, including Foreign Minister, Law Minister and Coordinating Minister for National Security) said, "we should not be put off by such criticism of being legalistic".[34] Singapore has always advocated for the settlement of disputes through international law, for example its territorial disputes with Malaysia and, similarly, the issue of the South China Sea. In the 2014 case of Russia's annexation of Crimea, the Singapore Foreign Ministry declared that "Singapore opposes the annexation of any country or territory as it contravenes international law. Singapore also objects to any unprovoked invasion of a sovereign country under any pretext".[35] This was the same attitude Singapore adopted with regards to the Vietnamese invasion of Kampuchea in December 1978. Singapore thus adopts a very consistent position. As Singapore's Chief Justice put it: "For Singapore, the rule of law for Singapore is not so much an aspirational ideal as it is an existential necessity".[36]

Lee Hsien Loong quoted a Finnish diplomat who said that "as a small country, our only weapons are words and treaties". While Singapore takes international norms and agreements seriously, "ultimately, words have to be carried out and realised in actions and outcomes, consequences. Therefore, it is important for us to have a strong defence, to be able to protect Singapore when all else fails".[37] The primary role of the SAF is therefore to be "the final guarantor of Singapore's sovereignty".[38] Singapore has certainly come a long way since 1965 when Yusof Ishak, the Yang Di-Pertuan Negara, in his address at the opening of the first Singapore Parliament acknowledged that at that time, Singapore had to "accept British bases for some time to come" because it was then unable to defend itself.[39]

---

[33] S. Jayakumar, "Reflections on Diplomacy of a Small State".
[34] Ibid.
[35] Singapore Ministry of Foreign Affairs, "MFA Spokesman's Comments in Response to Media Queries on the Russian Parliament's Ratification of a Treaty Joining Crimea to Russia on 21 March 2014", at https://www.mfa.gov.sg/Newsroom/Press-Statements-Transcripts-and-Photos/2014/03/MFA-Spokesmans-Comments-in-response-to-media-queries-on-the-Russian-Parliaments-ratification-of-a-tr (accessed 25 Nov. 2022).
[36] The Honorable Chief Justice Sundaresh Menon, "The Rule of Law, the International Legal Order, and the Foreign Policy of Small States", S. Rajaratnam Lecture, 15 Oct. 2019 (Singapore: MFA Diplomatic Academy, 2019).
[37] Lee, "Choice and Conviction".
[38] Teo Chee Hean, "New Challenges and Strategies for a More Secure World", S. Rajaratnam Lecture, 30 Nov. 2012 (Singapore: MFA Diplomatic Academy, 2012).
[39] "Yang Di-Pertuan Negara's Policy Speech on the Opening of Parliament on 14 December 1965", Singapore Parliament Reports (Hansard), at https://sprs.parl.gov.sg/search/email/link/?id=004_19651208_S0005_T0015&fullContentFlag=true (accessed 25 Nov. 2022).

IV

At the point of writing, Singapore expects a leadership transition within the next few years. The next general election is expected to be held some time before 23 November 2025. The crafting of grand strategy has and still is concentrated in the topmost ranks of government. This is unlikely to change in the foreseeable future even though it has been observed that in recent years "foreign policy features more prominently in Singapore's domestic discourse".[40] Asked why "defence" was not included in the Forward Singapore conversations initiated by the 4-G leadership in mid-2022, Defence Minister Ng Eng Hen replied that "Omission doesn't reflect a lack of importance. Also not included were home security and foreign affairs. This triumvirate [doesn't] always lend [itself] to public discourses".[41] Yet this book has identified five speeches from 1965 to the present which distil the essence of Singapore's Grand Strategy: Lee Kuan Yew's "Big and Small Fishes in Asian Waters" (15 June 1966); Goh Keng Swee's "What Kind of War?" (19 November 1971); S. Rajaratnam's "Singapore: Global City" (6 February 1972) and Lee Hsien Loong's "Security Options for Small States" (16 October 1984) and "Choice and Conviction—The Foreign Policy of a Little Red Dot" (30 November 2012).

There is so far no evidence of change or the emergence of any alternative strategy to that chronicled in the aforementioned line of speeches.[42] The public statements, speeches and interviews of the most prominent members of the fourth-generation leadership echelon—namely, Heng Swee Keat, Lawrence Wong, Chan Chun Seng and Ong Ye Kung—show that everyone continues to sing from the same song sheet. The second, third and fourth generation of leaders all echo Lee Kuan Yew.

That having been said, it is worth reflecting on the view that "grand strategy changes when the international system changes".[43] Yet in the last fifty-odd years, despite having straddled the Cold War period and after, Singapore has seen little need to change its grand strategy. Jennifer Mitzen notes that "no state's grand strategy

---

[40] Dr Tony Tan, "The Domestic Context of Singapore's Foreign Policy", S. Rajaratnam Lecture, 28 Nov. 2017 (Singapore: MFA Academy, 2017).
[41] "On Why Defence Was Not Included in the Forward Singapore Conversation", *The Straits Times*, 1 July 2022.
[42] See William D. James, "Grand Strategy and the Challenge of Change", in *The Oxford Handbook of Grand Strategy*, ed. Balzacq and Krebs, Chapter 32. According to James, short of a catastrophic shock, grand strategic change is rare although possible. See also Rebecca Lissner, "Re-thinking Grand-Strategic Change: Overhauls versus Adjustments in Grand Strategy", Chapter 33 in the same book.
[43] Michael Clarke, *American Grand Strategy and National Security* (London: Palgrave Macmillan, 2021), p. 27.

can succeed in isolation; each requires a supportive international environment".[44] So far, it would appear that the US, China, Malaysia and Indonesia with their mixed motives have implicitly been cooperative with Singapore.

Singapore's grand strategy has so far been successful. Whether the current strategic rivalry between the US and China will lead to or compel a change remains to be seen. As Singapore's prime minister Lee Hsien Loong said in 2017, "as a friend to both America and China, Singapore can be put in a difficult situation if there is...friction between the two giants".[45] This difficulty could be exacerbated if the present globalised world reverts to a "vertical world" where "nations will be walled off from one another" and the world divided into "new mini-empires and new blocs", as Abishur Prakash (geopolitical futurist and co-founder of the Center for Innovating the Future [Toronto, Canada]) predicts.[46]

It is perhaps both useful and appropriate to end with a 1981 statement by Lee Kuan Yew: "In an imperfect world, we have to seek the best accommodation possible. And no accommodation is permanent. If it lasts long enough for progress to be made until the next set of arrangements can be put in place, let us be grateful for it".[47]

---

[44] Jennifer Mitzen, "Illusion or Intention? Talking Grand Strategy into Existence", *Security Studies* 24, no. 1 (March 2015): 65. Jennifer Mitzen and Kyle Larson distinguish "ontological security"—"the specific intuition [of which] is that all social actors feel that they need a stable sense of self in order to get by and realize a sense of agency in the world"—from "material" or "physical" security, a more common focus of security studies ("Ontological Security and Foreign Policy", *Oxford Research Encyclopedia of Politics* [2017] at https://www.researchgate.net/publication/315117360_Ontological_Security_and_Foreign_Policy [accessed 9 Jan. 2023]). In relation to "ontological security", "non-traditional" security threats (e.g. the haze, SARS, Covid, rising sea levels) show the relevance of a whole-of-society approach to "total defence".
[45] Charissa Yong, "PM: S'pore's Position Will Become Tougher if US-China Tensions Rise", *The Straits Times*, 2 March 2017.
[46] Abishur Prakash, "New Mini-empires, New Blocs Will Divide the World", *Asia Times*, 20 Dec. 2021.
[47] Transcript of the extempore remarks made by Prime Minister Lee Kuan Yew at the Commonwealth Heads of Government meeting (CHOGM), Melbourne, Australia, 1 Oct. 1981.

Bibliography

"3G Soldier has Whole SAF in his Backpack" (Interview with Deputy Prime Minister and Defence Minister Teo Chee Hean), *The Straits Times*, 1 July 2009.

"A Close but Difficult Relationship", *Today*, 23 March 2015.

Acharya, Amitav. *Singapore's Foreign Policy: The Search for Regional Order*. Singapore: World Scientific, 2008.

Allison, Graham. "The Key to Henry Kissinger's Success", *The Atlantic*, 27 Nov. 2015. Available at https://www.theatlantic.com/international/archive/2015/11/kissinger-ferguson-applied-history/417846 (accessed 10 Jan. 2023).

Allison, Graham and Robert D. Blackwell with Ali Wyne. *Lee Kuan Yew: The Grand Master's Insights on China, the United States, and the World*. Cambridge, MA: MIT, 2012.

American Consul, Singapore. *From American Consul, Singapore to the Department of State*.

Ang Cheng Guan. *Southeast Asia after the Cold War: A Contemporary History*. Singapore: NUS Press, 2019.

_____. *Lee Kuan Yew's Strategic Thought*. London: Routledge, 2013.

_____. *Singapore, ASEAN and the Cambodian Conflict, 1978–1991*. Singapore: NUS Press, 2013.

_____. "Malaysia, Singapore, and the Road to the Five Power Defence Arrangements (FPDA), July 1970–November 1971", *War & Society* 30, no. 3 (Oct. 2011): 207–25.

_____. *Southeast Asia and the Vietnam War*. London: Routledge, 2010.

_____. "Singapore and the Vietnam War", *Journal of Southeast Asian Studies* 40, no. 2 (June 2009): 1–32.

_____. "United States-Indonesia Relations: The 1965 Coup and After", *War & Society* 21, no.1 (May 2003): 119–36. https://doi.org/10.1179/072924703791202023.

Arshad, Arlina. "Leaders' Retreat: PM Lee Hsien Loong, President Joko Widodo Hope Singapore-Indonesia Ties Will Grow even Stronger", *The Straits Times*, 8 Oct. 2019. Available at https://www.straitstimes.com/singapore/leaders-retreat-pm-lee-jokowi-hope-deep-singapore-indonesia-ties-will-grow-even-stronger (accessed 15 Dec. 2022).

_____. "Indonesia Ratifies Longstanding Extradition, Defence Deal with S'pore", *The Straits Times*, 16 Dec. 2022.

Ashton, S.R. and Wm Roger Louis, eds. *British Documents on the End of Empire, Series A, Volume 5, East of Suez and the Commonwealth, 1964–1971*. London: TSO, 2004.

"Asia and America: Our Shared Future" ("Prime Minister Lee Hsien Loong's speech at the Asia Society/US–ASEAN Business Council Joint Gala Dinner, Washington DC, 4 May 2007"), *The Straits Times*, 5 May 2007. Also available at https://asiasociety.org/america-and-asia-our-shared-future (accessed 26 Nov. 2022).

Australian National University. *Making Grand Strategy*. Available at https://programsandcourses.anu.edu.au/2019/course/stst8055 (accessed 9 Feb. 2023).

Avery, Paul C., Jonathan N. Markowitz and Robert J. Reardon. "Disentangling Grand Strategy: International Relations Theory and US Grand Strategy", *Texas National Security Review* 3, no. 1 (Nov. 2018): 28–51. http://dx.doi.org/10.26153/tsw/869.

Awang, Nabilah, Ng Jun Sen and S.M. Naheswari. "High Time to Talk about Racism, but Singapore Society Ill-equipped after Decades of Treating it as Taboo", *Channel News Asia*, 21 June 2021. Available at https://www.channelnewsasia.com/singapore/the-big-read-racism-singapore-society-race-interracial-1955501 (accessed 24 Nov. 2022).

Baharudin, Hariz. "Globalisation has Benefited Everyone in S'pore, says PM", *The Straits Times*, 15 March 2021. Available at https://www.straitstimes.com/singapore/politics/globalisation-has-benefited-everyone-in-spore-says-pm (accessed 15 Dec. 2022).

Bajpai, Kanti, Saira Basit and V. Krishnappa, eds. *India's Grand Strategy: History, Theory, Cases*. London: Routledge, 2016.

Baldwin, James. "The Blind Men and the Elephant". *American Literature*. Available at https://americanliterature.com/author/james-baldwin/short-story/the-blind-men-and-the-elephant (accessed 9 Feb. 2023).

Balzacq, Thierry, Peter Dombrowski and Simon Reich. "Is Grand Strategy a Research Program? A Review Essay", *Security Studies* 28, no. 1 (2019): 58–86. https://doi:10.1080/09636412.2018.1508631.

―――, eds. *Comparative Grand Strategy: A Framework and Cases*. Oxford: Oxford University Press, 2019.

Balzacq, Thierry and Ronald R. Krebs, eds. *The Oxford Handbook of Grand Strategy*. Oxford: Oxford University Press, 2021.

Barzilai, Amnon. "A Deep, Dark, Secret Love Affair", *Haaretz*, 16 July 2004. https://www.haaretz.com/1.4758973.

Barr, Michael D. *Singapore: A Modern History*. London: I.B. Tauris, 2019.

Beitelmair-Berini, Bernhard. *India's Grand Strategy and Foreign Policy: Strategic Pluralism and Subcultures*. London: Routledge, 2022.

Benvenuti, Andrea and Moreen Dee. "The Five Power Defence Arrangements and the Reappraisal of the British and Australian Policy Interests in Southeast Asia, 1970–1975", *Journal of Southeast Asian Studies* 41, no. 1 (2010): 101–23. https://doi:10.1017/S0022463409990270.

Bew, John. *Realpolitik: A History*. Oxford: Oxford University Press, 2015.
Bhaskaran, Manu. "An Architect of the Singapore Miracle", *The Business Times* [Singapore], 25 March 2015.
"Bilateral Issues: KL Goes for 'Quiet Diplomacy'", *The Straits Times*, 25 Jan. 2004.
Biswas, Asit K. and Ng Joo Hee. "Singapore's Two-front Battle with Water Security and Climate Change", *The Straits Times*, 5 June 2021.
Black, Eugene R. *Alternative in Southeast Asia*. New York: Frederick A. Praeger, 1969.
Boey, David. "Motive Behind Misreading of Book on SAF", *The Straits Times*, 14 Feb. 2003.
Booth, Ken. "The Concept of Strategic Cultures Affirmed", in *Strategic Power: USA/USSR*, ed. Carl G. Jacobsen. London: Macmillan, 1990, pp. 121–8.
Borsuk, Richard and Reginald Chua. "Singapore Strains Relations with Indonesia's President", *The Wall Street Journal*, 4 Aug. 1998. Available at https://www.wsj.com/articles/SB902170180588248000 (accessed 10 Jan. 2023).
Boyce, Peter. *Malaysia and Singapore in International Diplomacy: Documents and Commentaries*. Sydney: Sydney University Press, 1968.
Boys, James D. *Clinton's Grand Strategy: US Foreign Policy in a Post-Cold War World*. London: Bloomsbury, 2015.
Brands, Hal. "Getting Grand Strategy Right: Clearing Away Common Fallacies in the Grand Strategy Debate", in *Rethinking American Grand Strategy*, ed. Elizabeth Borgwardt, Christopher McKnight Nichols and Andrew Preston. Oxford: Oxford University Press, 2021, pp. 32–4.
―――. *The Promise and Pitfalls of Grand Strategy*. Strategic Studies Institute: US Army War College, 2012.
Bryant, Ralph C. "The Evolution of Singapore as a Financial Centre", in *Management of Success: The Moulding of Modern Singapore*, ed. Kernial Singh Sandhu and Paul Wheatley. Singapore: ISEAS, 1989, chapter 16.
Chan Chin Bock et al. *Heart Work: Stories of How EDB Steered the Singapore Economy from 1961 into the 21st Century*. Singapore: Singapore Economic Development Board and EDB Society, 2002.
Chan Chun Sing. "Singapore amid Great Power Rivalry", *The Straits Times*, 10 Nov. 2021. Available at https://www.straitstimes.com/opinion/singapore-amid-great-power-rivalry (accessed 15 Dec. 2022).
Chan Heng Chee. "Singapore's Foreign Policy, 1965–1968", *Journal of Southeast Asian History* 10, no. 1 (March 1969): 177–91. https://doi:10.1017/S0217781100004348.
Chan Heng Chee and Obaid ul Haq, eds. *The Prophetic and the Political: Selected Speeches and Writings of S. Rajaratnam*. Singapore: Graham Brash, 1987.
Chan, Samuel Ling Wei. *Aristocracy of Armed Talent: The Military Elite in Singapore*. Singapore: NUS Press, 2019.

Chan Sek Keong. "Multiculturalism in Singapore: The Way to a Harmonious Society", *Singapore Academy of Law Journal* 2013. Available at https://journalsonline.academypublishing.org.sg/Journals/Singapore-Academy-of-Law-Journal/e-Archive/ctl/eFirstSALPDFJournalView/mid/495/ArticleId/500/Citation/JournalsOnlinePDF (accessed 5 July 2022).

Chang, Jennifer I-wei. "Taiwan's Military Ties to Singapore Targeted by China", *The Global Taiwan Brief* 5, no. 9 (May 2020): 5–7. Available at https://globaltaiwan.org/2020/05/vol-5-issue-9 (accessed 10 Jan. 2023).

Chang Li Lin. "Singapore's Troubled Relations with Malaysia: A Singapore Perspective", *Southeast Asian Affairs 2003*, pp. 259–74.

Chang, Rachel and Kor Kian Beng. "3 Possible Locations for Third Sino–S'pore Project", *The Straits Times*, 8 Aug. 2014.

Cheng, Kenneth. "S'pore–US Defence Ties 'Can Strengthen' under Trump", *Today*, 13 Nov. 2016.

Cheong, Danson. "S'pore Interests Come First—Whatever the Global Shifts", *The Straits Times*, 11 Nov. 2016.

Cheong Koon Hean, Tommy Koh and Lionel Yee. *Malaysia and Singapore: The Land Reclamation Case*. Singapore: Straits Times Press, 2013.

Cheong Suk-Wai. "Plumbing Singapore's Water Story", *The Straits Times*, 26 June 2011.

Chew, Ernest C.T. and Edwin Lee, eds. *A History of Singapore*. Oxford: Oxford University Press, 1991.

Chew, Melanie. *Leaders of Singapore*. Singapore: Resource Press, 1996.

Chew Tai Soo. "A History of the Forum of Small States", in *50 Years of Singapore and the United Nations*, ed. Tommy Koh, Liling Chang and Joanna Koh. Singapore: World Scientific, 2015, pp. 35–8.

Chin Kin Wah. "Reflections on the Shaping of Strategic Cultures in Southeast Asia", in *Southeast Asian Perspectives on Security*, ed. Derek de Cunha. Singapore: ISEAS, 2000, Chapter 1.

⸺, ed. *Defence Spending in Southeast Asia*. Singapore: ISEAS, 1987.

"China and the US Need Each Other", *The Straits Times*, 8 April 2010.

"China and the World: Prospering and Progressing Together", *Today*, 7 Sept. 2012.

"China Gives Restrained Response to S'pore", *The Straits Times*, 9 Dec. 2015.

"China Signals FTA Talks May Face Setbacks", *The Straits Times*, 5 Aug. 2004.

Chong, Alan. "Singapore's Foreign Policy Beliefs as 'Abridged Realism': Pragmatic and Liberal Prefixes in the Foreign Policy Thought of Rajaratnam, Lee, Koh, and Mahbubani", *International Relations of the Asia-Pacific* 6, no. 2 (2006): 269–306. https://doi:10.1093/irap/lci137.

_____. "Singapore's Relations with Taiwan 1965–2005: From Cold War Coalition to Friendship under Beijing's Veto", in *Ensuring Interests: Dynamics of China-Taiwan Relations and Southeast Asia*, ed. Ho Khai Leong and Hou Kok Chun. Kuala Lumpur: Institute of China Studies, 2006.

Chong, Alan and David Han. "Foreign Policy Lessons from the Terrex Episode", *RSIS Commentary*, Number 022, 2 Feb. 2017.

Chong, Terence and Darinee Alagirisamy. "Chasing Ideals, Accepting Practicalities, Banishing Ghosts", *Intellectuals.SG*, 2 July 2021. Available at https://sgintellectuals.medium.com/chasing-ideals-accepting-practicalities-banishing-ghosts-f8840992aac1 (accessed 10 Jan. 2023).

Choo, Daryl. "Rooting Out Everyday Racism", *Today*, 29 June 2022. Available at https://www.todayonline.com/big-read/big-read-short-rooting-out-everyday-racism-1932656 (accessed 24 Nov. 2022).

Choo, Winston, with Chua Siew San and Judith D'Silva. *A Soldier at Heart: A Memoir*. Singapore: Landmark Books, 2021.

Chow, Jermyn. "War Games Debut of Drones Marks Evolution of SAF", *The Straits Times*, 11 Dec. 2015.

_____. "Concrete Moves to Make Sino–S'pore Defence Ties Stronger", *The Straits Times*, 15 Nov. 2014.

Christensen, Thomas. *Useful Adversaries: Grand Strategy, Domestic Mobilisation, and Sino–American Conflict, 1947–1958*. Princeton: Princeton University Press, 1996.

Chua, Daniel. "Singapore's Relations with the United States of America", in *The Little Nation That Can: Singapore's Foreign Relations and Diplomacy*, ed. Gillian Koh. Commentary vol. 26. Singapore: The National University of Singapore Society, 2017.

_____. *US–Singapore Relations, 1965–1975: Strategic Non-Alignment in the Cold War*. Singapore: NUS Press, 2017.

Chua, Daniel Wei Boon. "Konfrontasi: Why it Still Matters to Singapore", Nanyang Technological University, Singapore: RSIS Commentaries, No. 054 (2015).

Chua Lee Hoong. "SM: I Take Long-term View of Ties with Jakarta", *The Straits Times*, 16 Feb. 2001.

Clarke, Michael. *American Grand Strategy and National Security*. London: Palgrave Macmillan, 2021

Cohen, Eliot A. "The Return of Statecraft: Back to Basics in the Post-American World", *Foreign Affairs* 101, no. 3 (May/June 2022): 117–29.

Darmawan, Aristyo. "Resolving Indonesia and Singapore's UNCLOS dispute", *East Asia Forum*, 7 April 2021.

Dawson, Alan. "Implications of a Long-term Conflict on Thai–Vietnamese Relations", in *Confrontation or Coexistence: The Future of ASEAN–Vietnam Relations*, ed. William

S. Turley. Bangkok: Institute of Security and International Studies, Chulalongkorn University, 1985, pp. 154–5.

"Defence Pact's Renewal Shows Support for US Presence in Region: Mindef", *The Straits Times*, 25 Sept. 2015.

Denoon, David B.H., ed. *China's Grand Strategy: A Roadmap to Global Power?* New York: New York University Press, 2021.

Desker, Barry. "'Renewed' Deal for New Age: View of a Former Envoy", *RSIS Commentary*, Number 007/2022, 26 Jan. 2022.

⸻⸻⸻. "Lee Kuan Yew and Suharto: Friends till the End", *The Straits Times*, 8 April 2015.

Desker, Barry and Ang Cheng Guan, eds. *Perspectives on the Security of Singapore: The First Fifty Years*. Singapore: World Scientific & Imperial College Press, 2016.

"Digital Defence Pillar Added to Singapore's Total Defence Framework to Strengthen Cybersecurity", *Channel News Asia*, 14 Feb. 2019.

Dobell, Graeme. "Lee Kuan Yew and Oz", *The Strategist*, 24 March 2015. Available at https://www.aspistrategist.org.au/lee-kuan-yew-and-oz (accessed 10 Jan. 2023).

"DPM Lee responds to China's protests", *The Straits Times*, 17 July 2004.

Drezner, Daniel W., Ronald R. Krebs and Randall Schweller. "The End of Grand Strategy", *Foreign Affairs* (May/June 2020): 107–17.

Duara, Prasenjit. *The Crisis of Global Modernity: Asian Traditions and a Sustainable Future*. Cambridge: Cambridge University Press, 2015.

Dueck, Colin. *The Obama Doctrine: American Grand Strategy Today*. Oxford: Oxford University Press, 2015.

Ehrhardt, Andrew. "War and Adjustment: Military Campaigns and Grand Strategy", *War on the Rocks*, 2 May 2022. Available at https://warontherocks.com/2022/05/war-and-adjustment-military-campaigns-and-national-strategy/ (accessed 9 Feb. 2023).

Ehrhardt, Andrew and Maeve Ryan. "Grand Strategy is no Silver Bullet, But it is Indispensable", *War on the Rocks*, 19 May 2020. Available at https://warontherocks.com/2020/05/grand-strategy-is-no-silver-bullet-but-it-is-indispensable (accessed 10 Jan. 2023).

"Entering New Phase in Unique Relationship", *The Straits Times*, 6. Nov. 2015.

Erlanger, Steven. "Singapore Chief Fears for Cambodia", *The New York Times*, 25 Oct. 1989.

Feaver, Peter. "What is Grand Strategy and Why Do we Need it?", *Foreign Policy*, 8 April 2009. Available at https://foreignpolicy.com/2009/04/08/what-is-grand-strategy-and-why-do-we-need-it (accessed 11 Jan. 2023).

Feng Zengkun. "Singapore: Increasing the Flow of Water from National Taps", *The Straits Times*, 16 March 2013.

Fernandez, Warren. "Why Singapore Had to Take a Strong Stand against Russia's Attack on Ukraine", *The Straits Times*, 26 March 2022. Available at https://www.straitstimes.com/singapore/why-singapore-had-to-take-a-strong-stand-against-russias-attack-on-ukraine (accessed 24 Nov. 2022).

Foot, Rosemary. "China in the ASEAN Regional Forum: Organisational Processes and Domestic Modes of Thought", *Asian Survey* XXXVIII [38], no. 5 (May 1998): 425–40. https://doi:10.2307/2645501.

Foreign Relations of the United States (FRUS) Series. Office of the Historian. Washington, DC: Government Printing Office, 2006. Available at https://history.state.gov/historicaldocuments/frus1969-76v17 (accessed 9 Feb. 2023).

Freedman, Lawrence. *Ukraine and the Art of Strategy*. Oxford: Oxford University Press, 2019.

"From Istana to Canberra", *The Straits Times*, 11 Oct. 2012.

"Full Text of the Joint Statement Issued Yesterday after the Meeting between Singapore Prime Minister Lee Hsien Loong and Malaysian Prime Minister Najib Razak", *The Straits Times*, 25 May 2010.

Gabriel, Jürg Martin. *Worldviews and Theories of International Relations*. London: St. Martin's Press, 1994.

Gaddis, John Lewis. *On Grand Strategy*. New York: Penguin Books, 2018.

―――. *Strategies of Containment: A Critical Appraisal of Postwar American National Security Policy*. Oxford: Oxford University Press, 1982.

Ganesan, N. *Realism and Interdependence in Singapore's Foreign Policy*. London: Routledge, 2005.

―――. "Malaysia–Singapore Relations: Some Recent Developments", *Asian Affairs* 25, no. 1 (Spring 1998): 21–36.

―――. "Singapore's Foreign Policy Terrain", *Asian Affairs: An American Review* 19, no. 2 (Summer 1992): 67–79. https://doi:10.1080/00927678.1992.10553526.

George, Alexander L. "The 'Operational Code': A Neglected Approach to the Study of Political Leaders and Decision-Making", *International Studies Quarterly* 13, no. 2 (June 1969): 190–222. https://doi:10.2307/3013944.

"Geopolitics in Unsettled Times", *Dawn*, 19 Jan. 2022. Available at https://www.dawn.com/news/1658194 (accessed 9 Feb. 2023).

"Germans Discover PM Lee", *The Straits Times Interactive*, 7 Dec. 2005.

Ghani, Azhar. "Jakarta's Bind a Result of Charter Changes: MM", *The Straits Times*, 28 July 2007.

"Global Trade After the Failure of the Doha Round", *The New York Times*, 1 Jan. 2016.

"Globalisation Has Benefited Everyone in S'pore", *The Straits Times*, 15 March 2021.

Goh Chok Tong. "The Practice of Foreign Policy for Sustained Growth–the Singapore Experience", S. Rajaratnam Lecture, 17 Oct. 2014. Singapore: MFA Academy, 2009.

Goh, Daniel P.S. "Multiculturalism and the Problem of Solidarity", in *Management of Success: Singapore Revisited*, ed. Terence Chong. Singapore: ISEAS, 2010, Chapter 30.

Goh, Evelyn and Daniel Chua. *Singapore Chronicles: Diplomacy*. Singapore: Straits Times Press, 2015.

Goh Keng Swee. *The Practice of Economic Growth*. Singapore: Federal Publications, 1997.

———. *The Economics of Modernisation*. Singapore: Federal Publications, 1972.

Goh, Timothy. "Singapore and Indonesia Have Made Good Progress on Key Bilateral Issues: MFA", *The Straits Times*, 4 Jan. 2022. Available at https://www.straitstimes.com/singapore/singapore-and-indonesia-have-made-good-progress-on-key-bilateral-issues-mfa (accessed 15 Dec. 2022).

Goh Yan Huan. "Lifting Millions out of Poverty Still a Challenge for Asia: Ex-UN Official", *The Straits Times*, 17 Nov. 2021.

Goldstein, Avery. "China's Grand Strategy under Xi Jinping", *International Security* 45, no. 1 (Summer 2020) 164–201.

Guo, Yvonne and Woo Jun Jie. "The Secrets to Small State Survival", *The Straits Times*, 23 Sept. 2013. Available at https://www.straitstimes.com/singapore/the-secrets-to-small-state-survival (accessed 4 July 2022).

Han Fook Kwang. "In Post-Lee Kuan Yew World, is his Strategic Vision still Relevant?", *The Straits Times*, 10 April 2019.

———. "Is Lee Kuan Yew's Strategic Vision for Singapore Still Relevant?", *East Asia Forum*, 7 April 2019.

Hawkins, David. *The Defence of Malaysia and Singapore: From AMDA to ANZUK*. London: RUSI, 1972.

Hendropriyono. "Jakarta–S' pore Ties: Time Right for a Fresh Start", *The Straits Times*, 26 Aug. 2004.

Heng Yee-Kuang. "A Global City in an Age of Global Risks: Singapore's Evolving Discourse on Vulnerability", *Contemporary Southeast Asia* 35, no. 3 (Dec. 2013): 423–46. https://doi:10.1355/cs35-3e.

Hitchcock, William I., Melvyn P. Leffler and Jeffrey W. Legro, eds. *Shaper Nations: Strategies for a Changing World*. Cambridge, MA: Harvard University Press, 2016.

Ho, Grace. "Not Too Late for US, China to Reset Ties and Avert Clash: PM at WEF Event", *The Straits Times*, 30 Jan. 2021.

Ho Khai Leong. "Prime Ministerial Leadership and Policy-making Style in Singapore: Lee Kuan Yew and Goh Chok Tong Compared", *Asian Journal of Political Science* 8, no. 1 (2000): 91–123. https://doi:10.1080/02185370008434161.

Ho Khai Leong and Hou Kok Chung, eds. *Ensuring Interests: Dynamics of China-Taiwan Relations and Southeast Asia*. Kuala Lumpur: Institute of China Studies, 2006.

Ho, Peter. "The ASEAN Regional Forum: The Way Forward?", in *ASEAN–UN Cooperation in Preventive Diplomacy*, ed. Sarasin Viraphol and Werner Pfenning. Bangkok: Ministry of Foreign Affairs, Thailand, 1995.

Ho Shu Huang. "Total Defence Against Threat of Hybrid Warfare", *The Straits Times*, 12 May 2015.

Ho Shu Huang and Samuel Chan. *Singapore Chronicles: Defence*. Singapore: Straits Times Press, 2015.

Ho Shu Huang and Graham Ong-Webb, eds. *National Service in Singapore*. Singapore: World Scientific, 2019.

Hsieh, Pasha L. "The Quest for Recognition: Taiwan's Military and Trade Agreements with Singapore under the One-China Policy", *International Relations of the Asia-Pacific* 19, no. 1 (2019): 89–115.

Huxley, Tim. *Defending the Lion City: The Armed Forces of Singapore*. Sydney: Allen & Unwin, 2000.

⸺. "Singapore and Malaysia: A Precarious Balance?", *The Pacific Review* 4, no. 3 (1991): 204–13.

Hyder, Khurshid. "China's Representation in the United Nations", *Pakistan Horizon* 24, no. 4 (1971): 75–9.

"I Saw It Coming…" (Lee Kuan Yew interview with *Der Spiegel*), *The Straits Times*, 12 Aug. 2005.

Ishikawa, Koichi. "The ASEAN Economic Community and ASEAN Economic Integration", *Journal of Contemporary East Asian Studies* 10, no. 1 (March 2021): 24–41. https://doi:10.1080/24761028.2021.1891702.

Jacob, Paul. "Economic Ties to Bind Singapore and Jakarta", *The Straits Times*, 9 Nov. 2004.

James, William D. "Grand Strategy and the Challenge of Change", in *The Oxford Handbook of Grand Strategy*, ed. Thierry Balzacq and Ronald R. Krebs. London: Oxford University Press, 2021, Chapter 32.

Jayakumar, S. "Reflections on Diplomacy of a Small State", S. Rajaratnam Lecture, 19 May 2010. Singapore: MFA Diplomatic Academy, 2010.

Jayakumar, S. and Tommy Koh. *Pedra Branca: The Road to the World Court*. Singapore: NUS Press, 2009.

Jayakymar, Shashi, ed. *State, Society and National Security: Challenges and Opportunities in the 21st Century*. Singapore: World Scientific, 2016.

"Joint Announcement: Australia–Singapore Comprehensive Strategic Partnership", Australian Government: Department of Foreign Affairs and Trade, 6 May 2016.

Jones, Lee. *ASEAN, Sovereignty and Intervention in Southeast Asia*. London: Palgrave Macmillan, 2012.

Johnston, Mark. "Cyber Security Added to Singapore's Total Defence Framework", Channel Asia, 18 Feb. 2019. Available at https://www.channelasia.tech/article/657810/cyber-security-added-singapore-total-defence-framework/ (accessed 9 Jan. 2023).

Kausikan, Bilahari. *Dealing with an Ambiguous World*. Singapore: World Scientific Publishing, 2017.

_____. *Singapore is Not an Island: Views on Singapore Foreign Policy*. Singapore: Straits Times Press, 2017.

_____. "Pragmatic Adaptation, Not Grand Strategy, Shaped Singapore's Foreign Policy", in *Perspectives on the Security of Singapore: The First Fifty Years*, ed. Barry Desker and Ang Cheng Guan. Singapore: World Scientific and Imperial College Press, 2016, pp. 295–307.

_____. "Some Fundamentals of Singapore's Foreign Policy", in *The Little Red Dot: Reflections by Singapore's Diplomats*, ed. Tommy Koh and Chang Li Lin. Singapore: World Scientific, 2005.

Kelanic, Rosemary A. "Kelanic on Martel, 'Grand Strategy in Theory and Practice: The Need for an Effective American Foreign Policy'". Review of *Grand Strategy in Theory and Practice: The Need for an Effective American Foreign Policy* by William C. Martel. *H-Diplo* (Aug. 2015): 1–3. Available at https://networks.h-net.org/node/28443/reviews/79718/kelanic-martel-grand-strategy-theory-and-practice-need-effective. (accessed 11 Jan. 2023).

Kesavapany, K. "Singapore's Foreign Relations with Malaysia", in *The Little Nation That Can: Singapore's Foreign Relations and Diplomacy*, ed. Gillian Koh. *Commentary* vol. 26. Singapore: The National University of Singapore Society, 2017.

_____. "KL–S'pore Ties: Turning of the Tide", *The Straits Times*, 22 July 2009.

_____. "Economic Concerns Override Political Differences", *The Straits Times*, 28 Dec. 2006.

"Key Pact on US Use of Air, Naval Bases in S'pore Renewed till 2035", *The Straits Times*, 25 Sept. 2019.

Khor Hoe Ee, Diwa C. Guinigundo and Masahiro Kawai, eds. *Trauma to Triumph: Rising from the Ashes of the Asian Financial Crisis*. Singapore: World Scientific, 2022.

Kings College, London. *Centre for Grand Strategy*. Available at https://www.kcl.ac.uk/research/kcl-centre-for-grand-strategy (accessed 9 Feb. 2023).

Kirss, Alexander. "Review: Does Grand Strategy Matter?", *Strategic Studies Quarterly* 12, no. 4 (Winter 2018): 116–32.

Koh, Gillian, ed. *The Little Nation That Can: Singapore's Foreign Relations and Diplomacy*. *Commentary* vol. 26. Singapore: The National University of Singapore Society, 2017.

Koh, Tommy. "Ten Years, Over 100 Trips and Millions of Miles", *The Straits Times*, 13 Aug. 2014. Available at https://www.straitstimes.com/opinion/ten-years-over-100-trips-and-millions-of-miles (accessed 30 Nov. 2022).

Koh, Tommy and Chang Li Lin, eds. *The Little Red Dot: Reflections by Singapore's Diplomats*. Singapore: World Scientific, 2005.

Koh, Tommy, Li Lin Chang and Joanna Koh, eds. *50 Years of Singapore and the United Nations*. Singapore: World Scientific, 2015.

Kwa Chong Guan, ed. *Beyond Vulnerability: Water in Singapore-Malaysia Relations*. IDSS Monograph, Number 3. Singapore: IDSS, 2002.

Lai, Linette. "Small States are Primarily Concerned with Stability and International Rules: Ng Eng Hen", *The Straits Times*, 15 May 2022.

———. "S'pore Committed to Staying Open to World: Ong Ye Kung", *The Straits Times*, 21 Aug. 2021.

Lau, Albert. "Nation-Building and the Singapore Story: Some Issues in the Study of Contemporary Singapore History", in *Nation Building: Five Southeast Asian Histories*, ed. Wang Gungwu. Singapore: ISEAS, 2005, pp. 239–41.

Lau Teik Soon. "ASEAN and the Cambodian Problem", *Asian Survey* 22, no. 6 (June 1982): 548–60. https://doi:10.2307/2643686.

———. "Malaysia–Singapore Relations: Crisis of Adjustment, 1965–68", *Journal of Southeast Asian History* X [10], no. 1 (March 1969): 155–76.

Lee Boon Hiok. "Constraints on Singapore's Foreign Policy", *Asian Survey* 22, no. 6 (June 1982): 524–35. https://doi:10.2307/2643684.

Lee, Edwin. *Singapore: The Unexpected Nation*. Singapore: ISEAS, 2008.

Lee Hsien Loong. "Choice and Conviction—The Foreign Policy of a Little Red Dot", S. Rajaratnam Lecture, 27 Nov. 2015. Singapore: MFA Academy, 2015.

———. "A Historic and Beneficial Rise" (summary of his speech at the Central Party School, Beijing, 25 Oct. 2005), *The Straits Times*, 26 Oct. 2005.

———. "Securing Asia's Future" (excerpt from the above Keynote Address at the 4th IISS Asia Security Conference, Singapore, 3 June 2005), *The Straits Times*, 6 June 2005.

———. Keynote Address at the 4th International Institute of Strategic Studies Asia Security Conference in Singapore, 3 June 2005. Available at https://www.nas.gov.sg/archivesonline/data/pdfdoc/2005060302.htm (accessed 26 Nov. 2022).

———. "Mutual Respect is Key to Ties Between Sovereign States", *The Straits Times*, 2 Feb. 2004.

———. "Strategic Issues that Confront a Rising Asia", *The Straits Times*, 31 May 2004.

Lee Khoon Choy. *Diplomacy of a Tiny State*. Singapore World Scientific, 1993.

Lee Kuan Yew. *Hard Truths To Keep Singapore Going*. Singapore: Straits Times Press, 2011.

———. "The Fundamentals of Singapore's Foreign Policy: Then & Now" (S. Rajaratnam Lecture, 2009). Available at https://www.pmo.gov.sg/Newsroom/speech-mr-lee-kuan-yew-minister-mentor-s-rajaratnam-lecture-09-april-2009-530-pm-shangri (accessed 9 Jan. 2023).

———. *From Third World to First, The Singapore Story: 1965–2000*. Singapore: Times Editions, 2000.

———. *The Singapore Story: Memoirs of Lee Kuan Yew*. Singapore: Singapore Press Holdings, 1998.

Lee, Lynn. "PM: Bilateral Issues Best Settled by International Law", *The Sunday Times*, 12 Aug 2007.

Leifer, Michael. *Singapore's Foreign Policy: Coping with Vulnerability*. London: Routledge, 2000.

"Lessons from Haze Talks", *Today*, 9 July 2013.

"Let Us Not be Captives of the Past", *Today*, 27 Jan. 2004.

Lim, Edmund. "Secret Documents Reveal Extent of Negotiations for Separation", *The Straits Times*, 22 Dec. 2015.

Lim, Leonard. "Small Tiffs but Deep Ties", *The Straits Times*, 29 March 2014.

Lim, Lydia. "Replacing Causeway 'Does not Make Sense'", *The Straits Times*, 6 Jan. 2004.

Lim Min Zhang. "Total Defence Could Include Sixth Pillar to Tackle Cyber Threats", *The Straits Times*, 5 Oct. 2018. Available at https://www.straitstimes.com/singapore/total-defence-could-include-sixth-pillar-to-tackle-cyber-threats (accessed 11 Jan. 2023).

———. "New Treaty Allows SAF to Train in Vastly Expanded Area in Australia", *The Straits Times*, 23 March 2020. Available at https://www.straitstimes.com/singapore/new-treaty-allows-saf-to-train-in-vastly-expanded-area-in-australia (accessed 30 Nov. 2022).

Lim Yan Liang. "Growth in Region, Skills, Key to Economic Future", *The Straits Times*, 20 Sept. 2015.

Lissner, Rebecca. *Wars of Revelation: The Transformative Effects of Military Intervention on Grand Strategy*. Oxford: Oxford University Press, 2022.

———. "Re-thinking Grand-Strategic Change: Overhauls versus Adjustments in Grand Strategy", in *The Oxford Handbook of Grand Strategy*, ed. Thierry Balzacq and Ronald R. Krebs. Oxford: Oxford University Press, 2021, Chapter 33.

Lissner, Rebecca Friedman. "What is Grand Strategy? Sweeping a Conceptual Minefield", *Texas National Security Review* 2, no. 1 (Nov. 2018): 52–73.

Liu, Philip Hsiaopong. "Love the Tree, Love the Branch: Beijing's Friendship with Lee Kuan Yew, 1954–1965", *China Quarterly* 242 (June 2020): 550–72. https://doi:10.1017/S0305741019000900.

Lodhi, Maleeha. "Geopolitics in Unsettled Times", *Dawn*, 19 Jan. 2022. Available at https://www.dawn.com/news/1658194 (accessed 24 March 2022).

Loh Kah Seng and Liew Kai Khuin, eds. *The Makers & Keepers of Singapore History*. Singapore: Ethos Books, 2010.

Loke Hoe Yeong. "From Scepticism to Accepted Way of Life", *The Straits Times*, 24 Aug. 2013.

⎯⎯⎯⎯, ed. *Speaking Truth to Power: Singapore's Pioneer Public Servants*. Vol. 1. Singapore: World Scientific, 2020.

Low, Linda, ed. *Wealth of East Asian Nations: Speeches and Writings by Goh Keng Swee*. Singapore: Federal Publications, 1995.

Magcamit, Michael Intal. *Small Powers and Trading Security: Contexts, Motives and Outcomes*. London: Palgrave Macmillan, 2016.

⎯⎯⎯⎯. "Trading in Paranoia: Exploring Singapore's Security-Trade Linkages in the Twenty-first Century", *Asian Journal of Political Science* 23, no. 2 (Jan. 2015): 184–206. https:// doi:10.1080/02185377.2014.999248.

Mahbubani, Kishore. *Has China Won?* New York: Public Affairs, 2020.

⎯⎯⎯⎯. "The Kampuchean Problem: A Southeast Asian Perception", *Foreign Affairs* (Winter 1983/84): 401–25. https://doi:10.2307/20041824.

Mahizhnan, Arun. "Developing Singapore's External Economy", in *Southeast Asian Affairs 1994*, ed. Daljit Singh. Singapore: ISEAS, 1994, pp. 285–301.

Martel, William C. *Grand Strategy in Theory and Practice: The Need for an Effective American Foreign Policy*. Cambridge: Cambridge University Press, 2015.

Meany, Thomas and Stephen Wertheim. "Grand Flattery: The Yale Grand Strategy Seminar", *The Nation*, 28 May 2012. Available at https://www.thenation.com/article/archive/grand-flattery-yale-grand-strategy-seminar/ (accessed 11 Jan. 2023).

Menon, K.P., ed. *Footprints on Foreign Shores: Tales told by Foreign Service Officers*. Singapore: Graceworks, 2021.

Menon, Vanu Gopala. "Singapore and the United Nations", in *The Little Nation That Can: Singapore's Foreign Relations and Diplomacy*, ed. Gillian Koh. Commentary vol. 26. Singapore: The National University of Singapore Society, 2017.

MFA Press Statement. "Minister for Foreign Affairs Dr Vivian Balakrishnan's Written Reply to Parliamentary Question, 10 Jan. 2022", Ministry of Foreign Affairs: Singapore, 2022. Available at https://www.mfa.gov.sg/Newsroom/Press-Statements-Transcripts-and-Photos/2022/01/20220110-written-pq (accessed 9 Feb. 2023).

"MFA: S'pore, Jakarta Made Good Progress on Key Issues", *The Straits Times*, 4 Jan. 2022.

Milevski, Lukas. *The Evolution of Modern Grand Strategy*. Oxford: Oxford University Press, 2016.

Miller, Benjamin, with Ziv Rubinovitz. *Grand Strategy from Truman to Trump*. Chicago, IL: The University of Chicago Press, 2020.
Mindef Singapore. "Establishment of the Digital and Intelligence Service: A Significant Milestone for the Next Generation SAF". Available at https://www.mindef.gov.sg/web/portal/mindef/news-and-events/latest-releases/article-detail/2022/October/28oct22_nr2 (accessed 30 Dec. 2022).
Mitzen, Jennifer. "Illusion or Intention? Talking Grand Strategy into Existence", *Security Studies* 24, no. 1 (March 2015): 65.
Mitzen, Jennifer and Kyle Larson. "Ontological Security and Foreign Policy", *Oxford Research Encyclopedia of Politics* [2017]. Available at https://www.researchgate.net/publication/315117360_Ontological_Security_and_Foreign_Policy (accessed 9 Jan. 2023).
Mokhtar, Faris. "The Man Who Helped Create Singapore's Housing Boom is Getting Worried", *The Business Times*, 23 June 2022. Available at https://www.businesstimes.com.sg/real-estate/the-man-who-helped-create-singapores-housing-boom-is-getting-worried (accessed 1 July 2022).
Monaghan, Andrew. "Putin's Russia: Shaping a 'Grand Strategy'?", *International Affairs* 89, no. 5 (2013): 1221–36. https://doi:10.1111/1468-2346.12068.
Morgan-Owen, David Gethin. "History and the Perils of Grand Strategy", *The Journal of Modern History* 92 (June 2020): 351–85. https://doi:10.1086/708500.
Moses, Balan. "Chance to Write New, Positive Chapter", *The Straits Times*, 22 April 2009.
"Najib Seeks a Win-win Relationship with S'pore", *The Straits Times*, 23 May 2009.
Narizny, Kevin. *The Political Economy of Grand Strategy*. Ithaca, NY: Cornell University Press, 2007.
Nathan, S.R. *An Unexpected Journey: Path to the Presidency*. Singapore: Editions Didier Millet, 2011.
⸺. *Singapore's Foreign Policy: Beginnings and Future* (The Inaugural S. Rajaratnam Lecture, 10 March 2008, MFA Diplomatic Academy).
"Never Has There Been a Moment so Propitious in History: PM", *The Straits Times Weekly Overseas Edition*, 10 Feb. 1990.
Ng, Irene. "How to Make Friends and Advance Interests of Singapore", *The Straits Times*, 28 Oct. 2000.
Ng, Kelly. "The Policies that Shaped a Multiracial Nation", *Today*, 10 Aug. 2017. Available at https://www.todayonline.com/singapore/policies-shaped-multiracial-nation (accessed 24 Nov. 2022).
Ng Pak Shun. *From "Poisonous Shrimp" to "Porcupine": An Analysis of Singapore's Defence Posture Change in the Early 1980s*. Working Paper No. 397, Strategic and Defence Studies Centre, Canberra, Australia, April 2005.

Nor-Afidah Abd Rahman. "Growth Triangle". Singapore Infopedia. Available at https://eresources.nlb.gov.sg/infopedia/articles/SIP_58_2005-01-06.html (accessed 28 June 2021).

Omar, Rusdi. "An Analysis of the Underlying Factors that Affected Malaysia-Singapore Relations during the Mahathir Era: Discords and Continuity". Unpublished PhD dissertation, University of Adelaide, 2014.

"On Power and Stabilising Forces" [interview with Lee Kuan Yew by Yoichi Funabashi of the *Asahi Shimbun*], *The Straits Times*, 17 May 2010.

"On Why Defence Was Not Included in the Forward Singapore Conversation", *The Straits Times*, 1 July 2022.

Ong, Andrea. "S'pore Must Remain a 'Shining Red Dot', says PM", *The Sunday Times* [Singapore], 16 Feb. 2014.

Ong, Justin. "4 Ways to Travel Safely with No Quarantine: Ong Ye Kung", *The Straits Times*, 7 May 2021.

⎯⎯⎯⎯⎯⎯⎯. "Singapore Takes Principled Positions, not Sides in US–China Rivalry: Chan Chun Sing", *The Straits Times*, 10 Nov. 2021.

⎯⎯⎯⎯⎯⎯⎯. "S'pore's Reopening Balances Business, Health Needs: Wong", *The Straits Times*, 21 Aug. 2021.

Ong Ye Kung. "Singapore – Lessons from the Rise and Fall of Great Cities", *The Straits Times*, 14 Jan. 2022.

Ooi Giok Ling. "The Indonesia–Malaysia–Singapore Growth Triangle: Sub-Regional Economic Cooperation and Integration", *GeoJournal* 36, no. 4 (Aug. 1995): 337–44.

Oon, Clarissa. "MM Lee: We Cannot Be a Satellite of Any Nation", *The Straits Times*, 30 Dec. 2009.

Osman, Salim. "S'pore 'Sets Great Store by Jakarta Ties'", *The Straits Times*, 25 Aug. 2006.

"P-8 Deployment Reinforces US Presence in Asia-Pacific", *The Straits Times*, 11 Dec. 2015.

Pace, Barbara French. *Regional Cooperation in Southeast Asia: The First Two Years of ASEAN – 1967–1969, Study I in The Guam Doctrine: Elements of Implementation*, Report RAC-R-98-2, Oct. 1970. McLean, VA: Research Analysis Corporation.

"'Pawns' in Conflict", *Wellington Dominion*, 12 March 1965.

Peh Shing Huei. "Ichigo Ichie – One Encounter, One Chance – in Ending US Blockage", *The Straits Times*, 29 May 2021.

⎯⎯⎯⎯⎯⎯⎯. *Standing Tall: The Goh Chok Tong Years*. Vol. 2. Singapore: World Scientific, 2021.

"People's Republic of China In, Taiwan out, at U.N.", *The New York Times*, 25 Oct. 2011.

Périer, Miriam. "Interview with Thierry Balzacq Professor", *SciencesPo*, 19 Feb. 2019. Available at https://www.sciencespo.fr/ceri/en/content/interview-thierry-balzacq-professor (accessed 11 Jan. 2023).

Platias, Athanassios G. and Constantinos Koliopolis. *Thucydides on Strategy*. Oxford: Oxford University Press, 2017.

"PM: Don't Let Rows Overshadow Good ASEAN–China Ties", *Today*, 17 Sept. 2014.

"PM Lee, Jokowi Hope Bilateral Ties Will Strengthen Further", *The Straits Times*, 9 Oct. 2019.

Prakash, Abishur. "New Mini-empires, New Blocs Will Divide the World", *Asia Times*, 20 Dec. 2021.

Preston, Andrew. "National Security as Grand Strategy: Edward Mead Earle and the Burdens of World Power", in *Rethinking American Grand Strategy*, ed. Elizabeth Borgwardt, Christopher McKnight Nichols and Andrew Preston. Oxford: Oxford University Press, 2021, Chapter 11.

Prime Minister's Office, Singapore, Joint Statement for the Meeting between Prime Minister Lee Hsien Loong and Prime Minister Dato' Sri Mohd Najib Tun Abdul Razak on the Implementation of the Points of Agreement on Malayan Railway Land in Singapore (POA), 20 Sept. 2010, Singapore. Available at https://www.pmo.gov.sg/Newsroom/joint-statement-meeting-between-prime-minister-lee-hsien-loong-and-prime-minister-dato (accessed 30 Nov. 2022).

"Railway Land: S'pore Wants Third Party Help", *The Straits Times*, 17 Oct. 2003.

"Raja on Early Days of 'Do-it-yourself' Foreign Policy", *The Straits Times*, 2 April 1987.

Raska, Michael. "Modern War - How to Win without Fighting", *The Straits Times*, 2 Dec. 2021.

Régnier, Philippe. *Singapore: City-State in Southeast Asia*. Honolulu, HI: University of Hawaii Press, 1987.

Richardson, Michael. "RSAF's Space Crunch", *The Straits Times*, 27 Dec. 2004.

Riva, Alberto. "Lee Kuan Yew's Other Legacy: Why Singapore Has One of the World's Toughest Militaries", *International Business Times*, 24 March 2015. Available at https://www.ibtimes.com/lee-kuan-yews-other-legacy-why-singapore-has-one-worlds-toughest-militaries-1857454 (accessed 24 Jan. 2022).

Roberts, Alasdair. "Grand Strategy Isn't Grand Enough", *Foreign Policy*, 20 Feb. 2018. Available at https://foreignpolicy.com/2018/02/20/grand-strategy-isnt-grand-enough (accessed 11 Jan. 2023).

Rosecrance, Richard and Arthur A. Stein. *The Domestic Bases of Grand Strategy*. Ithaca, NY: Cornell University Press, 1993.

"SAF Has Done Better than I Hoped, says Lee Kuan Yew", *AsiaOne*, 21 May 2012.

Saint-Amour, Paul K. "On the Partiality of Total War", *Critical Inquiry* 40, no. 2 (Winter 2014): 420–49. https://doi:10.1086/674121.

Saw Swee Hock and K. Kesavapany. *Singapore-Malaysia Relations Under Abdullah Badawi*. Singapore: ISEAS, 2006.

Sayle, Timothy Andrews. "Defining and Teaching Grand Strategy", *The Telegram* 4 (Jan. 2011): 1–6. Available at https://www.fpri.org/docs/media/201101.sayle_.teachinggrandstrategy.pdf (accessed 11 Jan. 2023).

Scalice, Joseph. "A Region in Dispute: Racialized Anticommunism and Manila's Role in the Origins of Konfrontasi 1961–63", *Modern Asian Studies* 57, no. 3 (2023): 1004–26. doi:10.1017/S0026749X22000397.

Scobell, Andrew et al. *China's Grand Strategy: Trends, Trajectories, and Long-Term Competition*. RAND Corporation. Available at https://www.rand.org/pubs/research_reports/RR2798.html (accessed 14 Feb. 2022).

Sebastian, Leonard C. "When Relationships Change: Singapore–Indonesia Ties after Suharto and the Importance of Growing Together", in *The Little Nation That Can: Singapore's Foreign Relations and Diplomacy*, ed. Gillian Koh. *Commentary* vol. 26. Singapore: The National University of Singapore Society, 2017.

Sebastian, Leonard C. and Dedi Dinarto, "Indonesia–Singapore Ties: Timely Breakthrough", *RSIS Commentary*, Number 006/2022, 26 Jan. 2022.

See Chak Mun. "Singapore–India Strategic Relations – Singapore's Perspective", in *The Merlion and the Ashoka: Singapore–India Strategic Ties*, ed. Anit Mukherjee. Singapore: World Scientific, 2016, pp. 45–62.

"Senior Minister Lee Kuan Yew's Interview with Arnaud de Borchgrave, UPI International's Editor-at-large, on 11 May 2001", *The Business Times* [Singapore], 19 May 2001 and *The Sunday Times* [Singapore], 20 May 2001.

Silove, Nina. "Beyond the Buzzword: The Three Meanings of 'Grand Strategy'", *Security Studies* 27, no. 1 (2018): 27–57. Available at https://www.tandfonline.com/doi/pdf/10.1080/09636412.2017.1360073 (accessed 11 Jan. 2023).

Sim, Susan. "Drafting 'a Bloodless Coup'", *The Straits Times*, 4 Dec. 2016.

⸻. *E.W. Barker: The People's Minister*. Singapore: Straits Times Press, 2016

"Singapore's Foresight in Forging Early Friendship", *The Straits Times*, 7 Feb. 2012.

"Singapore 'Glad to Facilitate Meeting'", *The Straits Times*, 9 Nov. 2015.

"Singapore, Indonesia Submit Final Sea Border Treaty to UN as They Celebrate 50th Anniversary of Ties", *The Straits Times*, 26 Sept. 2017. Available at https://www.straitstimes.com/asia/se-asia/singapore-indonesia-submit-final-sea-border-treaty-to-un-as-they-celebrate-50th (accessed 15 Dec. 2022).

"Singapore Opposes Crimea Annexation: MFA", *The Straits Times*, 22 March 2014. Available at https://www.straitstimes.com/singapore/singapore-opposes-crimea-annexation-mfa (accessed 11 Jan. 2023).

Singapore, Parliamentary Debates: Official Report 24, 8 Dec. 1965. Available at https://sprs.parl.gov.sg/search/#/topic?reportid=004_19651208_S0005_T0015 (accessed 9 Feb. 2023).

"Singapore–US Pact to Enhance Military Ties", *The Straits Times*, 9 Dec. 2015.

Singh, Bilveer. *Singapore: Foreign Policy Imperatives of a Small State*. Singapore: Heinemann Asia, 1988.

──────. *The Vulnerability of Small States Revisited: A Study of Singapore's Post-Cold War Foreign Policy*. Yogyakarta: Gadjah Mada University Press, 1999.

Singh, Bilveer and N. Ganesan. "Malaysia–Singapore Relations: Some Recent Developments", *Asian Affairs* 25, no. 1 (Spring 1998): 21–36.

Southgate, Laura. *ASEAN Resistance to Sovereignty Violation: Interests, Balancing and the Role of the Vanguard State*. Bristol: Bristol University Press, 2019.

"'S'pore's Global Ties have Benefitted it in Times of Crisis': Chan", *The Straits Times*, 10 July 2021.

Strangio, Sebastian. "Why have Southeast Asian Governments Stayed Silent over Ukraine?", *The Diplomat*, 23 Feb. 2022.

Tai Soo Chew. "A History of the Forum of Small States", in *50 Years of Singapore and the United Nations*, ed. Tommy Koh, Liling Chang and Joanna Koh. Singapore: World Scientific, 2015, pp. 35–8.

Tan, Andrew T.H. "Singapore's Approach to Homeland Security", in *Southeast Asian Affairs 2005*, ed. Chin Kin Wah and Daljit Singh. Singapore: ISEAS, 2005

Tan Kok Chiang. *My Nantah Story: The Rise and Demise of the People's University*. Singapore: Ethos Books, 2017.

Tan See Seng. "(Still) Supporting the Indispensable Power: Singapore's Relations with the United States from Trump to Biden", *Asia Policy* 16, no. 4 (Oct. 2021): 80.

Tan, Tony. "The Domestic Context of Singapore's Foreign Policy", S. Rajaratnam Lecture, 28 Nov. 2017. Singapore: MFA Academy, 2017.

Tarling, Nicholas. *Southeast Asian Regionalism: New Perspectives*. Singapore: ISEAS, 2011.

Teo Chee Hean. "New Challenges and Strategies for a More Secure World", S. Rajaratnam Lecture, 30 Nov. 2012. Singapore: MFA Diplomatic Academy, 2012.

──────. "Whatever Happened to the Middle Way?" *Fulcrum*, 6 Jan. 2022. Available at https://fulcrum.sg/whatever-happened-to-the-middle-way (accessed 11 Jan. 2023).

Terhalle, Maximilian. "The 1970s and 2008: Theorizing Benchmark Dates for Today's Decentred Global Order", *International Studies* 56, no. 1 (March 2019): 1–27. https://doi:10.1177/0020881718825076.

Tham, Davina. "Ukraine's Sovereignty, Territorial Integrity 'Must be Respected', Says Singapore as Russia Recognises Breakaway Regions", *Channel News Asia*, 22 Feb. 2022.

Tham Yuen-C. "'Not Possible for S'pore, Many Countries, to Choose between US and China' PM Lee Tells BBC", *The Straits Times*, 15 March 2021, at https://www.

straitstimes.com/singapore/not-possible-for-spore-many-countries-to-choose-between-us-and-china-pm-lee-tells-bbc (accessed 15 Dec. 2022).

_____. "Would S'pore Have Avoided a Return to Phase 2 if it had Shut the Borders Early?", *The Straits Times*, 8 May 2021.

Thayer, Carlyle A. *Multilateral Institutions in Asia: The ASEAN Regional Forum*. Honolulu, HI: The Asia-Pacific Center for Security Studies, 2000.

The Fight Against Terror: Singapore's National Security Strategy. Singapore: National Security Coordination Centre, 2004.

"The Man with a Secret", *Today*, 5–6 Oct. 2002.

"The Quest for Water Security", [Singapore] Public Utilities Board, 24 Nov. 2017. Available at https://www.pub.gov.sg/Pages/TheQuestforWaterSecurity.aspx (accessed 11 Jan. 2023).

"Third S'pore–Malaysia Joint Panel Meeting on Pedra Branca", *The Straits Times*, 9 Jan. 2010.

Till, Geoffrey. "A Little Ray of Sunshine; Britain, and the Origins of the FPDA – A Retrospective on Objectives, Problems and Solutions", in *Five Power Defence Arrangements at Forty*, ed. Ian Storey, Ralf Emmers and Daljit Singh. Singapore: ISEAS, 2011.

Toh, Elgin. "PM Lee Positive about Asia's Prospects", *The Straits Times*, 2 May 2013.

Tomba, Mattia, ed. *Beating the Odds Together: 50 Years of Singapore-Israel Ties*. Singapore: World Scientific, 2020.

Torode, Greg and Marius Zaharia. "Singapore May Prove a Tough Nut for China to Crack over Regional Security", Reuters, 1 Dec. 2016. Available at https://www.reuters.com/article/us-hongkong-singapore-taiwan-analysis-idUSKBN13R0N3 (accessed 30 Nov. 2022).

Tortajada, Cecilia, Yugal Kishore Joshi and Asit K. Biswas. *The Singapore Water Story: Sustainable Development in an Urban City State*. London: Routledge, 2013.

"Trying Times for America" [selections from Lee Hsien Loong's interview with Charlie Rose], *The Straits Times*, 5 Aug. 2005.

Turnbull, C.M. *A History of Modern Singapore, 1891–2005*. Singapore: NUS Press, 2009.

Turnbull, Mary. *A History of Singapore 1819–1975*. Kuala Lumpur: Oxford University Press, 1977.

UK Parliament. "Who does UK Grand Strategy?". Available at https://publications.parliament.uk/pa/cm201011/cmselect/cmpubadm/memo/grandstrat/gs12.htm (accessed 9 Feb. 2023).

"US Presence in E. Asia will Become more Vital, says SM", *The Straits Times*, 23 Jan. 2001.

van Hooft, Paul. "Grand Strategy", Oxford Bibliographies. Available at https://www.oxfordbibliographies.com/view/document/obo-9780199743292/obo-9780199743292-0218.xml (accessed 30 Jan. 2022).

Vasu, Norman. "Locating S Rajaratnam's Multiculturalism", in *S. Rajaratnam on Singapore: From Ideas to Reality*, ed. Kwa Chong Guan (Singapore: World Scientific, 2006), pp. 125–58.

Vasu, Norman and Nur Diyanah Binte Anwar. "The Maligned Malays and National Service", in *National Service in Singapore*, ed. Ho Shu Huang and Graham Ong-Webb. Singapore: World Scientific, 2019, Chapter 9.

Viraphol, Sarasin and Werner Pfenning, eds. *ASEAN-UN Cooperation in Preventive Diplomacy*. Bangkok: Ministry of Foreign Affairs, Thailand, 1995.

Walt, Stephen M. "Liberal Illusions Caused the Ukraine Crisis", *Foreign Policy*, 19 Jan. 2022. Available at https://foreignpolicy.com/2022/01/19/ukraine-russia-nato-crisis-liberal-illusions/ (accessed 30 Jan. 2022).

Wang Gungwu, ed. *Nation-Building: Five Southeast Asian Histories*. Singapore: ISEAS, 2005.

"War Games Debut of Drones Marks Evolution of SAF", *The Straits Times*, 11 Dec. 2015.

Welsh, Bridget et al., eds. *Impressions of the Goh Chok Tong Years in Singapore*. Singapore: NUS Press, 2009.

"What Must Change in Singapore", *The Straits Times*, 3 March 2007.

"Why American Economic and Security Presence Vital for Asia", *The Straits Times*, 17 Dec. 1991.

Wilairat, Kawin. "Singapore's Foreign Policy: A Study of the Foreign Policy System of a City-State". Unpublished PhD diss., Georgetown University, 1975.

_____. *Singapore's Foreign Policy: The First Decade*. Singapore: ISEAS, 1975.

Wilkie, Robert. "America Needs a Grand Strategy", *The Heritage Foundation*, 3 Nov. 2021. Available at https://www.heritage.org/defense/report/america-needs-grand-strategy (accessed 30 Jan. 2022).

"Will Japan fall behind China?", *The Straits Times*, 13 Aug. 2005.

Wivel, Anders. "The Grand Strategies of Small States", in *The Oxford Handbook of Grand Strategy*, ed. Thierry Balzacq and Ronald R. Krebs. London: Oxford University Press, 2021, Chapter 30.

Wong, John and Liang Fook Lye, eds. *Suzhou Industrial Park: Achievements, Challenges and Prospects*. Singapore: World Scientific, 2020. https://www.worldscientific.com/doi/pdf/10.1142/9789811200045_0001.

Wong Kan Seng. *Lessons for Singapore's Foreign Policy: The Cambodian Conflict*. S Rajaratnam Lecture, 23 Nov. 2011. Singapore: MFA Diplomatic Academy.

Wong Yu Han. "Singapore's Approach to Cybersecurity", in *State, Society and National Security: Challenges and Opportunities in the 21st Century*, ed Shashi Jayakumar. Singapore: World Scientific, 2016. Chapter 15.

Woo, J.J. *Singapore as an International Financial Centre: History, Policy and Politics*. London: Macmillan Palgrave Pivot, 2016.
Woo Jun Jie. "Singapore's Transformation into a Global Financial Hub" (2017). Available at https://lkyspp.nus.edu.sg/docs/default-source/case-studies/entry-1516-singapores_transformation_into_a_global_financial_hub.pdf?sfvrsn=a8c9960b_2https://lkyspp.nus.edu.sg/docs/default-source/case-studies/entry-1516-singapores_transformation_into_a_global_financial_hub.pdf?sfvrsn=a8c9960b_2 (accessed 4 July 2022).
Wu Chunqiiu. "Dialectics and the Study of Grand Strategy: A Chinese View", Chinese Aerospace Studies Institute, 2002. Available at https://www.airuniversity.af.edu/Portals/10/CASI/documents/Translations/2021-12-09%20Dialectics%20and%20the%20Study%20of%20Grand%20Strategy-%20A%20Chinese%20Perspective.pdf?ver=6iCNZjxKfbGYulHZ7CpCaA%3d%3d (accessed 30 Jan. 2022).
Wu Yuan-li. *The Strategic Land Ridge: Peking's Relations with Thailand, Malaysia, Singapore, and Indonesia*. Stanford, CA: Hoover Institution Press, 1975.
Yaacob, Abdul Rahman. "Singapore's Threat Perception: The Barter Trade Crisis and Malaysia's Decision to Use Military Force against Singapore, October–December 1965", *Australian Journal of Politics and History* 68, no. 1 (2022): 72–89. Available at https://onlinelibrary.wiley.com/doi/abs/10.1111/ajph.12719 (accessed 1 July 2022).
Yale University. "The Brady-Johnson Program in Grand Strategy". Available at https://grandstrategy.yale.edu (accessed 9 Feb. 2023).
Yang Razali Kassim. "Cautious Optimism", *The Straits Times*, 27 July 2006.
Yearbook of the United Nations, 1971, Volume 25. New York: Office of Public Information, United Nations, 1974.
Yong, Charissa. "PM: S'pore's Position Will Become Tougher if US–China Tensions Rise", *The Straits Times*, 2 March 2017.
Yong, Clement. "Hiring for SAF's New Cyber Service to Start this Month", *The Straits Times*, 1 July 2022.
Yuen Foong Khong. "The Elusiveness of Regional Order: Leifer, the English School and Southeast Asia", *The Pacific Review* 18, no. 1 (March 2005): 23–41. https://doi:10.1080/09512740500047058.
―――. "Singapore: A Time for Economic and Political Engagement", in *Engaging China: The Management of an Emerging Power*, ed. Alastair Iain Johnston and Robert S. Ross. London: Routledge, 1999, Chapter 5.
Zhang Xiaoming. "Deng Xiaoping and China's Decision to go to War with Vietnam", *Journal of Cold War Studies* 12, no. 3 (Summer 2010): 3–29. https://doi:10.1162/JCWS_a_00001.

Zheng Yongnian and John Wong, eds. *Goh Keng Swee on China*. Singapore: World Scientific, 2012

Zhuo, Tee. "Parliament: Only 8% of 2 Million Public Government Records Searchable on National Archives Online Portal", *The Straits Times*, 4 Sept. 2019. Available at https://www.straitstimes.com/politics/parliament-only-160000-of-two-million-public-government-records-have-metadata-on-nas-web (accessed 11 Jan. 2023).

Index

Abe, Shinzo, 136
"Abu Bakar Takes Two-China Line" news report, 67
Afro-Asian countries, 33, 53, 54
Afro-Asian solidarity, concept of, 55
age of globalisation, 85
Age of Uncertainty, 79
Air Force Working Group, 42
Albar, Syed Hamid, 138
Alliance Government, 24
Allison, Graham, 145
"All-Round Cooperative Partnership Progressing with the Times" in Singapore, 134
Alternative in Southeast Asia (1969), 75
American Consulate General, in Singapore. *See also* US
Anglo-Malayan Defence Agreement (AMDA), 38, 49
anti-American barbs, 56
anti-Chinese alliance, 30
ANZUK brigade, in Singapore, 39, 43, 45
arms race, 79–80
Asahi Shimbun, 146
ASEAN Economic Community (AEC), 103
ASEAN Free Trade Area (AFTA), 103
ASEAN Regional Forum (ARF), 114–16, 157
ASEAN Way, 89
Asia Development Bank (ADB), 41, 75
Asia-Europe Meeting (ASEM), 112
Asia–Middle Eastern Dialogue (AMED), 112

Asian Defence Journal, 125
Asian Financial Crisis (1997), 106, 110, 124, 126, 128, 140
Asia-Pacific Economic Cooperation (APEC), 109
Association of Southeast Asia (ASA), 71–2
Association of Southeast Asian Nations (ASEAN), 14
  Common Market, 75, 103
  defence role for, 74
  diplomacy, 86
  effort to free Kampuchea from Vietnamese occupation, 93
  formation of, 71
  interlocutors for, 89
  management of the Cambodia problem, 93, 115
  Ministerial meetings, 115
  objective to humiliate Vietnam, 91
  Paris Conference on Cambodia, 88
  relations with India, 115
  role in establishing the ASEAN Regional Forum (ARF), 114
  Singapore's policy towards, 75
  solidarity from 1978 to 1991, 62, 89
  US backing for, 93
Auden, W.H., 122

Badawi, Abdullah, 138–9
Balakrishnan, Vivian, 143
balance of power, 14, 61, 62, 65, 85, 108, 114

INDEX

Bangkok Accords, 18, 29
Barker, E.W., 57, 59
Bell, James, 58–9
Bello, James D., 59
Bhaskaran, Manu, 107–8, 110
"Big fish eats small fish" analogy, 60–1, 98
Biswas, Asit, 122
Black, Eugene, 75
Blackwell, Robert, 145
Boey, David, 125–6
Bogaars, George, 26–7, 30–1, 58–9
Boyce, Peter, 54
Brands, Hal, 1, 6, 10, 151
British bases, in Singapore, 20–1, 54
British colonial administration, 100
British High Commissioner, 40–1, 43–4, 47, 76, 122
British territories, in the Far East, 38
Bundy, William, 56–7, 72
Bury, Leslie, 49
Bush, George W., 111, 117, 131, 132
Business Times, The, 125

Carrington, Lord, 39–40, 43, 45, 48
Carter administration (US, 1977–81), 60, 92
Centre for Grand Strategy (King's College, London), 2, 6
Chan Chun Sing, 148
Chan, Samuel, 82, 99
Chen Yi, 66
Chew, Melanie, 20
Chew Tai Soo, 113
Chiang Ching-kuo, 71
Chiang Kai Shek, 69
China Rock, 41–3
China–Singapore Suzhou Industrial Park (SIP), 118
Chinese Singaporeans, 85
Chin Kin Wah, 82
Choo, Winston, 33, 35, 97
Clark Air Base, Philippines, 115
Clinton, Bill, 111, 119

Coalition Government of Democratic Kampuchea (CGDK), 92
Cold War, 11, 52, 155
  end of, 113–14
  Singapore–PRC relations during, 70
  Singapore's grand strategy during, 22
Commonwealth Jungle Warfare Centre (CJWC), 42
Communalists, 18, 36
communism, spread of, 50
Communist China, 54, 63
  actions in the November 2016 Terrex incident, 134
  admission to the UN, 66
  Association for Relations Across the Taiwan Straits, 118
  attack on Vietnam, 91
  backing of Khmer Rouge, 91
  claims in the South China Sea, 134
  coastal economic zones, 118
  economic development, 118
  establishment of diplomatic relations with Singapore, 65
  Nixon visit to, 69
  People's Liberation Army, 74
  predatory expansionist policy, 74
  relations with
    Singapore, 70, 133
    Taiwan, 134
    United States, 116, 145
  response to the signing of the enhanced Defence Cooperation Agreement between Singapore and the US, 135
  rise of, 114
  Three Kingdoms, 108
  Tiananmen Square incident, 118
communist ideology, 65
Communist Party of Indonesia (PKI), 28–9
Communist Party of Thailand, 87
Communists, 18, 92, 94
competition between big powers, 108
Confrontation (*Konfrontasi*), policy of, 18, 25, 27–9, 31, 60, 71, 102, 108, 123

coronavirus (Covid-19) pandemic, 145, 148
"Crush Malaysia" campaign (1963), 27
cyber defence and intelligence gathering, 144
cyber security, 143–4

decision-making process, 11–12
"declaratory" grand strategy, 11
Decolonisation, period of, 52, 61
defence capabilities, acquisition of, 76, 80
Defence Cooperation Agreement (DCA), 116, 132, 135, 141
defence policies, of Singapore, 11
   against aggression and the maintenance of internal security, 77
   arms race, 79–80
   of attaining air supremacy, 78
   against attrition of manpower, 78
   British reports pertaining to, 76
   on defence build-up, 80
   defence expenditure, 80–1
   emphasis on importance of technology, 78
   key findings of, 76–7
   military build-up, 78
   military presence of friendly countries, 82
   optimistic and the pessimistic, 77
   over-spending on defence, 81
   "poisonous shrimp" deterrence strategy, 125
   and response to the Vietnamese invasion of Cambodia, 76
   "Total Defence" strategy, 76, 82, 126
defence research and development organisation, 79
Defending the Lion City: The Armed Forces of Singapore (Huxley, 2000), 125
Deng Xiaoping, 92, 118, 131
   visit to Singapore, 71
Desker, Barry, 88, 97, 142

Dhanabalan, S., 86, 92–3
diplomatic and military history, of Singapore, 11
diplomatic community, quality of, 88
Djilas, Milovan, 60
Douglas-Home, Alec, 37
DSO (Defence Science Organisation) National Laboratories, 79
Dudley Agreement (1968), 44

economic growth rate, in Singapore, 51
economic manipulation, 64
electronic warfare, 79
Ellazari, Jack, 35
esprit de corps, 88
European Free Trade Area (EFTA), 110

Falle, Sam, 41
Farrell, Norm, 45–6
financial centre, Singapore's beginnings as, 106
financial services, in Singapore, 106
First Industrial Revolution, 79
Five Power Defence Arrangements (FPDA), 49
   establishment of, 38
   formation of, 50
   Goh's view about, 40
   negotiations, 39
   Notes and Annexes of, 49
   as second-oldest military partnership in the world (after NATO), 50
   views on and attitude towards
      Malaysia, 39
      Singapore, 39
foreign defence assistance, 19–20
foreign policies, of Singapore, 11, 90, 95
   pattern of, 22
   post-Cold War, 13
   vulnerability in, 13
Forum for East Asia–Latin America Cooperation (FEALAC), 112

Forum of Small States (FOSS), 113
"fourth generation" leaders, 147–8
Freedom of Information Act, 15
free trade agreements, 110–12, 116, 119
free trade area, 103
French AMX-13 light tank, purchase of, 79
Funabashi, Yoichi, 146

Gandhi, Rajiv, 115
geography of the archipelago, 78
global cities, 105–6, 148
global economic system, 105
Goh Chok Tong
    administration of, 110
    as architect of Singapore's FTA policy, 110
    bilateral relations with Narasimha Rao, 115
    CHOGM (Commonwealth Heads of Government Meeting) speech (1989), 108
    economic policies and initiatives, 108
    foreign policy towards Malaysia, 120
    golf diplomacy, 111
    good-neighbour policy, 102
    interpretation of the 1990 Agreement, 121
    meeting with President Clinton, 111
    as Minister of Defence, 125
    premiership from 1990 to 2004, 101, 103
    as Prime Minister of Singapore, 100, 128
    proposal of a Singapore–Johor–Riau Growth Triangle, 109
    Singapore's Grand Strategy under, 100
    tenure as prime minister, 110, 119
Goh Keng Swee, 17, 20, 31, 37, 64, 72, 154
    concern about "ill-disposed" regime in Indonesia and Malaysia, 45
    development of the SAF, 77
    Five-Power concept, 46–8
    interest in technology, 78
    issue of military training, 44–6
    meeting with
        Nicholas Parkinson, 46–7
        Norm Farrell, 46
        Tim Francis, 40
        William Bundy, 56
    position of Minister of Finance, 81
    on possibility of Australia providing training space for SAF, 42
    retirement of, 22
    on Singapore's military preparations, 80
    top-secret team to conduct research on electronic warfare, 79
    view about the FPDA, 40
    "What Kind of War?" speech (1971), 97, 125
Goldstein, Avery, 152
golf diplomacy, 111
Gorton, John, 47
government-to-government cooperation, 139
Grand Strategy
    American, 4
    concept of, 1, 8, 10
    definition of, 5–7
    pattern of state behaviour and, 8
    purpose of, 4
    role of, 6
    Russian, 7–8
    of Singapore, 1, 10, 21, 38, 55, 86, 150–1
great power, policy of, 87
great states, 3
Greenvale (Qld.) Training Area, 136
gross domestic product (GDP), 143
    economic growth rate, in Singapore, 51
gross national product (GNP), 81

Habibie, B.J., 124, 140
Han Eng Juan, 125

Han Fook Kwang, 146
Harun, Ben, 103
Hawke, Bob, 109
Hawkins, David, 26–7, 38
Heath, Edward, 39
Hendropriyono, 140
Herzog, Chaim, 96
He Ying, 66
Heyzer, Noeleen, 113
Hindustan Times, 74
Hitam, Musa, 96
Ho Khai Leong, 100
Holdridge, John, 92
Holyoake, Keith, 44–5
Hong Kong Port Authority, 134
Hoo Tiang Boon, 134–5
Ho, Peter, 114, 125, 126
Ho Shu Huang, 14, 82, 99
Hsieh, Pasha L., 71
Huxley, Tim, 15, 125–6
hybrid warfare, concept of, 144

independence of Singapore, 16, 106
India
    economic reforms, 136
    engagement with ASEAN countries, 115–16
    Look East Policy, 115
    position towards the Cambodian issue, 115
    relations with Singapore, 115
        Defence Cooperation Agreement (DCA), 116
        economic partnership, 116
        free trade agreement (FTA), 116
        India–Singapore Comprehensive Economic Cooperation Agreement (CECA), 116
    support for the Soviet Union, 115
Indian Ocean earthquake-cum-tsunami (2004), 140
Indonesia
    end of Confrontation policy in, 29
    Lee Kuan Yew first official visit to, 31
    during the Megawati presidency (2001–04), 124
    military coup of 1965, 29
    military goodwill mission, 30, 73
    recognition of Singapore as a sovereign country, 29
    two-track policy towards Vietnam, 89
Indonesia–Malaysia Confrontation, 60
Indonesia–Malaysia relations, 16
    "Crush Malaysia" campaign (1963), 27
    diplomatic relations, 29–30
    normalisation of, 57
    policy of Confrontation against Malaysia, 27
    rapprochement in, 72–3
Indonesia–Malaysia–Singapore Growth Triangle (IMS-GT), 108
Indonesian Embassy, in Singapore, 97
Indonesian Parliament, 141
Indonesia–Singapore relations, 16
    during 2004 Indian Ocean earthquake-cum-tsunami, 140
    on airspace management and military training, 142
    Bilateral Investment Treaty (2018), 142
    bilateral relations, 31
    on bombing of MacDonald House, 27, 31
    deterioration of, 140
    establishment of diplomatic relations, 18
    under Habibie and Wahib presidencies, 140
    impact of
        Asian Financial Crisis, 140
        Singapore's abstention in the 1975 UN vote on Indonesia and East Timor, 94–5
    Lee Kuan Yew's views on, 27–8
    under President Joko Widodo, 142
    public opinion on, 31

settlement of the western sea boundary, 141
Information Handling Services (IHS), 144
Institute of Southeast Asian Studies (ISEAS), 12
interdependency of nations, 105
International Court of Justice (ICJ), 121, 139
international politics, 19
  of Southeast Asia, 86
International Tribunal for the Law of the Sea (ITLOS), 138
intra-ASEAN free trade, 103
Ishak, Yang Di-Pertuan Negara Yusof, 10, 18, 20, 32, 36, 158
Ishikawa, Koichi, 103
Iskandar Development Region, Johor, 139
Iskandar Malaysia Project, 139
Islamic fundamentalism, Singapore's approach towards, 129
Islamic Party of Malaysia (PAS), 25
Israel, 34–5, 46, 48, 50

Jacob, Paul, 140
Japanese Occupation of Singapore, 11
Jayakumar, Shashi, 113, 138, 144, 156, 158
Jemaah Islamiyah network, 126, 128
Johnson administration, US, 63
Johnson, Lyndon, 75
Johor[e], 24–6, 28, 108–9
Johore Jungle Warfare School, 59
  training of South Vietnamese officers, 59
Joint Counter-Terrorism Centre (JCTC), Singapore, 126
joint war drills, 133
Jungle Warfare Centre, Malaysia, 41
jungle warfare training, 41–2

Kausikan, Bilahari, 85, 90
Keegan, John, 82

Kesavapany, K., 121, 123, 137, 139
Khmer Rouge, 91–2
Koh, Tommy, 88, 110, 127–8, 140
Koo Chen-fu, 118
Ko Tek Kin, 66
Kriangsak Chomanan, 88
Kwa Chong Guan, 108–9

Lee, Edwin, 12
Lee Hsien Loong, 50, 96, 98, 106, 111, 113, 116, 119, 140–2
  Beijing speech (2005), 133
  Chinese reaction to his visit to Taiwan, 134
  "Choice and Conviction" speech (2015), 149, 153
  IISS Asia Security Conference (Shangri-La Dialogue) speech (2005), 129
  on importance of the US presence in the region, 146
  new strategic landscape, 136
  Singapore–Malaysia relations under, 140
  Singapore's Grand Strategy under the premiership of, 127
  "Singapore's Tomorrow, Tomorrow's Singapore" speech (2002), 128
  Tokyo speech (2013), 130
  updation of the 1990 MOU with US, 132
  views on Sino–US relations, 130–1
Lee Kuan Yew, 11, 38, 85, 101, 108, 114, 122, 132, 153–4
  31 August press conference, 58
  administration (1959–90), 76
  Americans' lack of direct communication with, 58
  anti-American views, 58
  attitude towards the US, 58
  "Big and Small Fishes in Asian Waters" speech (1966), 60, 63, 73, 78, 85, 97–8

concept of Afro-Asian solidarity, 55
concern about training facilities for the Singapore Armed Forces, 41
on dangers of US intervention on the side of Malaysia, 57
death of, 145, 147
diatribe against the US (31 August 1965), 58
on jungle warfare training, 41
letter to the New Zealand High Commissioner, 44
Malaysian hostility towards, 17
meeting with James D. Bello, 59
multilateral security arrangement, 74
National Day Rally speech (1986), 120
notion of "right to survive", 20
reaching out to Rajiv Gandhi, 115
reading of the nature of international relations, 60–1
on regional cooperation within Asia, 75
relationship with Chiang Ching-kuo, 71
on relationship with the Afro-Asian countries, 53
"Security Options for Small States" speech, 98
on Singapore as "the hub of Southeast Asia", 52
on Singapore's policy towards Communist China, 66
speech at Victoria University in Wellington, New Zealand (1965), 71
stepping down as Prime Minister, 96, 100
title of Minister Mentor, 127, 134
on using Brunei for air defence training, 41
views concerning multilateral security arrangements, 74
views on Singapore relations with
India, 74
Indonesia, 27–8
Malaysia, 23–5
visit to
Indonesia, 31
New Zealand, 50
Taiwan, 71
US, 61
Lee–Rajaratnam foreign policy Team, 112
Leifer, Michael, 13, 22, 88
Liberal Party, 40
Liddell Hart, Basil, 6
Lim Kim San, 20, 57, 80
Liu, Philip Hsiaopong, 66
Lodhi, Maleeha, 145
Long, Joey, 122
Loo, Bernard, 128
Lui Pao Chuen, 79
Lye Liang Fook, 133

MacDonald House, bombing of (1965), 27, 31
Magcamit, Michael Intal, 109, 112
Mahbubani, Kishore, 21, 88, 89, 91, 116
Mahizhnan, Arun, 109
Malay nationalism, 64
Malaysia
attitude towards FPDA negotiations, 39
attractions of having British forces stationed in, 42
communal antagonisms towards Singapore, 26
Confrontation hostilities with Singapore, 18
"Crush Malaysia" campaign (1963), 27
economic cooperation with Singapore, 24
formation of, 16
Indonesians opposition to formation of, 27
Goh's foreign policy towards, 120
hostility towards Lee Kuan Yew, 17
idea of ZOPFAN (Zone of Peace, Freedom and Neutrality), 62

legacy of separation, 109
normalisation of relations with Indonesia, 57
"one race, one religion" atmosphere, 73
political leadership in, 17
relations with Singapore, 16
   after separation, 18
   agreement on economic cooperation, 30
   deterioration of, 40
   disagreement over land reclamation, 138
   establishment of diplomatic relations, 29
   importance of, 25
   issue of the railway land, 120–1
   Lee views on, 23–5
   ownership of Pedra Branca island, 120
   Points of Agreement (1990), 140
   problem of, 26
   rental dispute over the Royal Malaysian naval base at Woodlands, Singapore, 121
   territorial dispute over Pedra Branca island, 139
   on use of Jungle Warfare Centre, 41
   Water Agreement (1961), 138
   water supply, 25–6
riots of 1969, 79
separation of Singapore from, 16–17
Malaysian Armed Forces, 40–1
presence in Singapore, 33
Malaysia–Singapore Airlines (MSA), splitting up of, 41
Maphilindo concept, 72–3
maritime delimitation, 142
Ma Ying-jeou, 118, 134
McMahon, William, 49
Memorandum of Understanding, 120
Menon, Viji, 90
Michael Fay caning incident (1994), 111, 118
military capability, of Singapore, 15

Ministry of Defence (Singapore), 83, 98, 125, 132
modern industrial countries, 80
Mohamad, Mahathir, 24, 95, 120, 139, 140
Mohammed Ali, Tan Sri Hashim, 25
Monetary Authority of Singapore (MAS), 106
Morgan-Owen, David Gethin, 1, 7, 9
multi-racial society, creation of, 18, 36, 156
Murdani, Benny, 97

Nair, Devan, 56
Nathan, S.R., 31, 79, 87, 88, 91, 119
   on value of the Five Power arrangements, 49
National Archives of Singapore, 10
national consciousness and identity, sense of, 77
National Coordination Centre (NSCC), Singapore, 126
national security, 7
National Security Secretariat (NSS), 126
National Security Strategy (Singapore), 10
National Service (Amendment) Bill (1967), 32, 35
nation building, 12, 36, 77
naval blockade, imposition of, 50
New Zealand Government, 40
Ng Eng Hen, 132, 137, 144, 159
   Total Defence Day speech (2019), 143
Nixon, Richard, 69
Non-Aligned Movement, 55, 88
Non-Aligned Movement Summit (1992), 115
non-alignment, policy of, 19
non-communist resistance (NCR), 93
non-conventional warfare, 145
Noor, Samad, 38, 43
nuclear superpowers, 36

Obama administration (2009–17), 131
   "pivot to Asia" strategy, 116, 132

Omar, Rusdi, 123
Ong Pang Boon, 66
Ong Ye Kung, 148
Onn, Hussein, 95
overseas Chinese, 57, 65, 90

P-9 Poseidon surveillance aircraft, deployment of, 135
Pan-Malayan regional cooperation, 57
Panyarachun, Anand, 103
Parkinson, Nicholas, 46–7
Parliament of Singapore, 10, 16, 18
Pawanchee, Abu Bakar bin, 67
Pedra Branca island, 120, 139
Peh Shing Huei, 111, 112
People's Action Party (PAP), 56–7, 66
People's Republic of China (PRC). *See* Communist China
people's volunteer force, 20
Permanent Court of Arbitration, tribunal regarding Chinese claims in the South China Sea, 134
Philippine Congress, 117
Pillai, Gopinath, 116
Point of Agreement (POA), 96, 120
"poisonous shrimp" deterrence strategy, 99, 125
political leadership, 17, 26, 80, 118
Pol Pot regime, horrors of, 86
Port Swettenham (now Port Klang), 41
power-bloc conflicts, 53
power conflict, between East and West, 52
power politics, 113
Privy Council, 31
Project Starlight, 70

Qi Feng, 66
Quayle, Dan, 117

racial conflict, in Malaysia, 57
racial harmony, 85

Rahman, Tunku Abdul, 17, 27
Rajaratnam, S., 19, 21–2, 33, 66, 79, 87, 88, 94, 100, 130, 148, 154
  foreign policy speech (1965), 23, 54, 63
  foreign policy speech (1968), 61–2
  issue of the admission of China to the UN, 68
  Lecture in 2008 (S.R. Nathan), 87
  Lecture in 2009 (Lee Kuan Yew), 134
  National Day message, 104
  retirement of, 22
  "Singapore: Global City" speech (1972), 105
  as Singapore's first Foreign Minister, 52
  on Singapore's objectives of creating ASEAN common market, 75
Rao, Narasimha, 115
Razak, Najib, 139–40
Razak, Tun Abdul, 27
Reagan Administration, 92
Reagan, President, 92
Realpolitik, 15
regional conflicts, 109
regional cooperation, benefits of, 51
regional defence cooperation, 74
regional economic cooperation, 107
regionalism, sense of, 72
Riau Islands, 108
rifleman's war, 78
Russia
  annexation of Crimea, 94, 158
  invasion of Ukraine, 87, 94, 155

SAF Terrex infantry carrier vehicles (ICVs), 134
Saw Swee Hock, 137
Sayle, Timothy Andrews, 1
Schultz, George, 93
sea transport, 78
security
  of Singapore, 20–1
  state's theory of, 5

Security and Intelligence Division (SID), 79
Security-Trade Linking Strategy, 112
September 11, 2001 (9/11) terrorist attacks, 128
Shafie, Ghazali bin, 24
Shanmugam, K., 142
Sheridan, Greg, 131
Shoalwater Bay Training Area, Queensland, 136
Siddique, Tony, 88
Singapore
  abstention in the 1975 UN vote on Indonesia and East Timor, 94
  admission as the 117th member of the United Nations, 53
  admission to the Afro-Asian Conference, 68
  air force and navy, 31
  attitude towards
    China, 90
    multilateralism, 71
    United States, 55
  British withdrawal from, 20, 61
    economic effect of, 37
  capacity to defend itself against external threats, 21
  capacity to resist big power pressure, 53
  China policy, 67
  counter-terrorism strategy, 129
  Defence Cooperation Agreement with US, 135
  defence expenditure, 37
  economics–security strategy post-1990, 101
  engagement with the US, 61
  establishment of diplomatic relations with China, 65
  foreign and defence policy, 53
  as gateway harbour to the Johor River, 109
  goal for creation of ASEAN "Common Market", 75
  grand strategy, 1, 10, 21, 38
    under Goh Chok Tong, 100
    under Lee Hsien Loong, 127
    US role in, 62
  independence of, 66
  involvement in the Vietnam–Cambodia conflict, 93
  lobbying for increased American assistance, 92
  as Major Security Cooperation Partner of the US, 132
  as 'neo-colonialist' state, 54
  as "New York" of Malaysia, 17, 153
  response to
    Indonesia's invasion of East Timor, 94
    Russia annexation of Crimea and Ukraine invasion, 94
    Vietnamese invasion of Cambodia, 93
  separation from Malaysia, 27
  on strategic importance of the PRC, 64
  strategy with regards to non-alignment, 54
  support for the ruling of the Permanent Court of Arbitration tribunal regarding Chinese claims in the South China Sea, 134
  "Total Defence" strategy, 76
  transformation of, 106
  visits by American air force and navy units to, 131
  voting against US resolution in the UN, 66
  voting for the Albanian Resolution in the UN, 70
Singapore Armed Forces (SAF), 15, 33, 125
  agreement with People's Liberation Army (PLA), 133
  air defence facilities required by, 42
  air defence training in Brunei, 42
  British position on, 42–3

Air Force, 78, 125
Australian offer of training facilities to, 47
bilateral defence activities, 133
composition and capabilities of, 76
as credible fighting force, 82
cyber defence and intelligence gathering, 144
Digital and Intelligence Service, 144
"fatalism" of the "poisonous shrimp" deterrence strategy, 99
formation of, 82
improvement of, 99
issue of rent and training facilities, 43–6
jungle warfare training for, 41
loyalty and patriotism of Malays in, 96
National Servicemen, 81
Navy, 78
orthodox military capability, 77
Project Starlight, 70
provision for Australian training space for, 42
Reserve Battalion, 81
strategy of deterrence, 126
training facilities for, 41
  in US and Australia, 136
training in Taiwan, 70
transformation of, 128
Singapore Army Bill (1965), 20
Singapore Infantry Regiment, 1st Battalion (1 SIR), 33
Singapore Institute of International Affairs (SIIA), 98
Singapore–Johor–Riau (SIJORI) Growth Triangle, 108, 119
Singapore Naval Training Ship, 41
Singh, Bilveer, 120
Singh, Surenda, 59
"six blind men" analogy, 4–5
Snyder, Jack L., 156
South China Sea dispute, 134, 158
Southeast Asian identity, 65
Soviet Union, 53, 115

dissolution of, 114
New Delhi's support for, 115
Straits Times, The, 132 and *passim*
Strategic Framework Agreement, 132
strategic planning, long-term, 4
Suharto, President, 29, 74, 93
  fall of, 140
Sukarno, President, 18, 30
  declaration of Confrontation, 27
  removal of, 29
survive, right to, 20, 28
Suzhou Industrial Park, 118, 133

Taiwan
  Chinese reaction to Lee Hsien Loong visit to, 134
  defence cooperation with Singapore, 70
  Lee Kuan Yew visit to, 71
  military exercises in, 134
  Project Starlight, 70
  relations with China, 134
  right of self-determination, 67
Taiwan Straits Exchange Foundation, 118
Tan Boon Seng, 94
Tan Seng Chye, 88
Technological Society, 79
Temasek Society, 97
Teo Chee Hean, 83, 147
Terrex incident (2016), 134–5
territorial security, issue of, 16
Thayer, Henry, 56
Third China, 57, 65
"third generation" leaders (Singapore), 147
Thomson, George (G.G.), 56
Tianjin Eco-City, 133
Time (US newsmagazine), 111
Toh Chin Chye, 29, 33, 34, 53, 66
"Top Secret" British report (1967), 51
"Total Defence" strategy, 76, 82–3, 86, 126
transnational terrorism, 145

Trans-Pacific Partnership (TPP)
    Agreement (2016), 111
Trump, Donald, 1, 111, 132
Turnbull, Mary, 12
two-China policy, 67

Ukraine crisis, 87, 94, 155
United Nations (UN)
    Albanian Resolution, 67, 69–70
    China's admission to, 66
    Forum of Small States (FOSS), 113
    General Assembly, 66–7, 88
    Question Resolution, 70
    Security Council, 25
    Singapore's admission in, 53
United States (US)
    "anti-Chinese" agenda, 57
    challenge to the rising influence of China, 131
    Consulate General of, in Singapore, 54, 56, 57, 58, 59 and *passim*
    Defence Cooperation Agreement with Singapore, 135
    Department of State, 57
    Embassy in Singapore, 26, 31, 57, 59 and *passim*
    involvement in Vietnam, 63
    Lee's attitude towards, 58
    maintenance of international law and order in East Asia, 117
    policy towards Cambodia, 93
    relations with
        China, 92
        Singapore, 57–8, 71
    role in Singapore's grand strategy, 62
    September 11, 2001 (9/11) terrorist attacks, 128
    Seventh fleet, 131
    Singapore as a Major Security Cooperation Partner of, 132
    Singapore's abstention in the 1975 UN vote on Indonesia and East Timor, 94
    Singapore's attitude towards, 131–2
    strategic interest in Singapore, 58
    support for the ruling of the Permanent Court of Arbitration tribunal regarding Chinese claims in the South China Sea, 134
    training facilities for SAF, 136
    Vietnam syndrome, 92
    views on Singapore as 'Third China', 57
    withdrawal from Southeast Asia, 59
United States–Singapore Free Trade Agreement (2003), 111
unmanned aerial vehicles (UAVs), 143
US–UK anti-China line, 68

Vietnam
    Bangkok's dependence on the Chinese for its security against, 92
    Chinese attack on, 91
    end of Vietnam War, 115, 117
    invasion of Kampuchea, 88, 91
    military occupation of Cambodia, 88, 91
    Singapore's relations with, 93
Vietnam Rest and Recreation (R&R) programme, 60
Vietnam War, 62, 79, 86, 115

Wahid, Abdurrahman, 124
Walt, Stephen, 155
Wang Daohan, 118
Wang–Koo talks (1993), 118
Wang Yutien, 66
war against terrorism, 129, 140
Warring States, in Japan, 108
water supply, 25
Whitlam, Gough, 40
Wilairat, Kawin, 27, 32, 54, 55, 65
Wilson, Harold, 37
Wong, John, 118
Wong Kan Seng, 93

Wong, Lawrence, 148
Woo, J.J., 106
World Trade Organisation (WTO), 110
    Doha Talks, 110
World War II, 11
    Fall of Singapore (1942), 86
    Total Defence Day, 86

Xi Jinping, 118, 134
Xu Liping, 135

Yaacob, Abdul Rahman, 24
Yeo, George, 119
Yusof Ishak, Yang Di-Pertuan Negara, 10, 18, 20, 32, 36, 158
Yuen Foong Khong, 118

Zaiton (Tan Sri Zaiton Ibrahim Bin Ahmad), 38
Zone of Peace, Freedom and Neutrality (ZOPFAN), 62